KT-404-121

ONE CHANCE

SURVIVING LONDON'S GANGS

ONE CHANCE

SURVIVING LONDON'S GANGS

TERROLL LEWIS

First published in 2021 by Ad Lib Publishers Ltd
15 Church Road
London, SW13 9HE
www.adlibpublishers.com

Text © 2021 Terroll Lewis

ISBN 978-1-913543-84-6
eBook ISBN 978-1-913543-76-1

All rights reserved. No part of this publication may be
reproduced in any form or by any means — electronic,
mechanical, photocopying, recording, or otherwise — or stored
in any retrieval system of any nature without prior written
permission from the copyright holders. Terroll Lewis has asserted
his moral right to be identified as the author of this work in
accordance with the Copyright, Designs and Patents Act of
1988.

A CIP catalogue record for this book is
available from the British Library.
Every reasonable effort has been made to trace copyright-holders
of material reproduced in this book, but if any have been
inadvertently overlooked the publishers would be glad to hear
from them.

Printed in Great Britain

10 9 8 7 6 5 4 3 2 1

I dedicate this book to my late granddad Mick Doherty. You were the backbone of our family, my ultimate hero. The man I called Dad. I miss you dearly, but I know you live on through me. Thank you for everything, Dad.

GLOSSARY

Active – on the streets/gang member
B – *see* 'brown'
Bally – balaclava
Beat (them, or after them) – shoot
Bread – money
Brooklyn – Old Kent Road area
Brikki – Brixton
Brown – heroin
Bun – shoot
Bust your gun – 'go on then, shoot' (the most disrespectful thing you can say to a shooter)
Burner – gun
Deleted/cancelled – to drop someone as a friend, sack them or say, 'I don't want you in this world no more'.
Dots – crack rocks
Ends – neighbourhood
Food – crack or heroin
G-check – to ask someone to prove they are a gang member
Hammer – gun
Hood girls – girls who hold weapons and money for gang members
Hot – police activity
Jakes – police

Jezzies – girls who are friendly to, sympathetic with, and often sleep with gang members

Lick you down – knock someone down, to hit someone

Machine – gun

Madness – fighting

Naked – without a weapon

Nank – knife

Nitties – crackheads

Older – older gang member

On smash – to be in control

Pagan – enemy

Pecknarm (or 'Narm) – Peckham

Pop – as in, 'Pop your chain' – to rip/rob

Pulled – stopped by police/arrested

Riding out – hunting down and exacting revenge on an enemy

Ringing – glory

Shining/glossing – wearing expensive jewellery, a target for robbery

Shoobs – house party

Shot – rock of crack cocaine

Slipping – being in enemy territory

Spinner – revolver

Spud – friendly greeting in which two people bump their closed fists together

Squeeze off – shoot

Swag – clothes/trainers

Teet – bullets

The Fields – Myatts Field estate area

Utes – youths

Violated – being dissed or attacked

Wagwan – 'Hello' in Jamaican English

White – cocaine

Zed – ounce

CONTENTS

CONTENTS

PROLOGUE:

THE HEART OF BAGHDAD

Myatts Field estate, Brixton, South London, 2002
I hear gunfire and drop to the road. A deafening blast followed by several shorter ones. The shots are sharp and clattering, drilling the air. The sound rips through my eardrums, spears my brain and shoots down my skinny, thirteen-year-old arms and legs. My heart shakes to the rhythm of the bullets. The pavement is cold against my knees. Must've ripped my tracksuit when I hit the road. I'm sweating all over. Shivering too. I can't see much, as it's dark and the streetlights don't work and I'm all crunched over with my hands on my head, chin almost touching the ground, like I'm surrendering to armed police. And there's this smell of piss in the air: gunpowder. Somebody close by is firing a sub-machine gun, man. Sounds like a war zone for like four seconds or so, but that's a long time for gunfire, innit? Ain't unusual to hear guns go off around here though. I mean, this is the Myatts Field estate. Its nickname's 'Baghdad' 'cos it's all shot-up. Some call it the Devil's Den, y'know what I'm saying? It's deprived.

I'm ducking in a road close to the Hills, the grass area that's like some Teletubbies' *gangland on the edge of the estate. If you ain't from 'round here, you don't go near the Hills, especially at night – unless you want to get shot, stabbed or mugged. Reason I'm here? I came to see the Olders, to be on the block with them and feel the energy, y'know. I'd seen them ahead, about twenty of them, chilling in front of a wall, but before I could get into their space, this happened.*

The Olders lead the OC [Organised Crime] *gang. They wear expensive chains and clothes and drive flash cars like Porsches and stuff.*

You see them counting fat wads of cash, hear them making rap videos and it's like, Wow, these guys are too cool. *The OC gang protects this estate and its territories. It has enemies, other gangs that the Olders call the 'pagans' or the 'Other Side' or 'opps'. I've just stepped into gang warfare.*

Half-an-hour ago I'd been on the neighbouring Cowley Estate, flirting with my friend Sherise. I just took a small diversion on my way home to my nan and granddad's house on Treherne Court, which is, like, a two-minute run from here.

I lift my head, see the stampede: the Olders, running towards me, away from the wall beyond which the spray of bullets came. Some are wearing ballies. Most are holding their waists as they run, ready to pull their machines. Nike trainers thump past me and I freeze. Nobody's noticed me crouching here. The gunfire has ceased but it's still echoing in my ears, cshh, cshh-cshh-cshh-cshh-cshh-cshh-cshh. *Some are shouting,* 'Run', *others yell,* 'Don't run'. *But they* are *running – and running and running and running, footsteps and voices disappearing deep into the estate.*

It's eerily quiet now. I look at the wall ahead, look all around me, breathing hard. There are no police sirens. Somebody close by has fired a sub-machine gun. Whoever did so could fire that weapon again. Fuck, I need to get outta here, man. A switch flicks inside me and my energy changes. I'm off my blocks and sprinting, sprinting, sprinting, back towards the centre of the estate, the heart of Baghdad. Up the slope of Crawshay Court, cut across, take the path next to the play park and beat up the slope onto Treherne Court, along to number seven. I get my key out of my pocket but I'm shaking so much that it takes me a few goes to stab it in the lock. I turn the key, hurry inside and slam the door, trying to catch my breath. Smell of fried potatoes and cabbage fills my airwaves.

I walk into the kitchen and Nan's in there. Her short hair's got pink streaks through it that match her nightie. Mum's done her hair again, *I'm thinking. Nan takes one look at me and goes:* 'Heavens, what've you been up to, Our Boy? Why are you all sweaty and out of breath?'

'Yeah, I just jogged it home,' I tell her, and boost it outta there. I hear her call, do I want some bubble and squeak? But I'm in the bathroom now, sitting on the lid of the toilet and hearing gunfire in my head again. I

have no idea who fired that gun. OC has beef with lots of different areas. Could've been the Peckham Boys, or pagans from Lewisham, Tulse Hill, or anywhere. Either way, how fucking dare they? How dare they attack our estate? Adrenaline's subsiding now. I'm thinking about what I witnessed and I'm not scared. I'm angry, a deep hatred for the Other Side rising within me. I'm also excited. Those OC boys are holding down the ends – and I want to get out there and help them, man. One hundred per cent.

1

WARMING UP

Violence: I was born into it, man. Far back as I remember, violence was all around me. Violence that I *saw*, violence that I *heard*, violence that I *felt*. Y'know what I mean?

Some of my earliest memories are bleak, man. Soundbites and pictures no boy wants in his head: Mum swearing and crying for help above sounds of a violent struggle. Watching cartoons on a pay-as-you-go telly while my parents' Yardie mates chill in the same room, getting fucked on crack and weed. Cockroaches skittering up and down the walls. Guns and drugs on the coffee table, and shit like that. Listen, growing up on south London estates like Myatts Field, you ain't at your window waiting for the trill of the ice-cream van. Nah, you're hearing gunshots, barking pitbulls, the distant screams of someone getting robbed on the block. This was SW9, Brixton – and violence grew me, man.

I was exposed to violence before I was born. Yeah, my mum, Jakki, was twenty-one and seven months pregnant with me when a Jamaican guy punched her in the face and threw her off a balcony on the Myatts Field South estate. Mum had been scrapping with a girl called Sharon on the outdoor communal landing at a gathering in one of the flats in a block on Church Green. Her attacker, let's call him Ashley, struck. My dad, Terence Lewis, wasn't there when all this shit went down, but he was the reason for Mum's beef with Sharon.

'He'd been cheating on me with her while I was pregnant with you,' Mum tells me. 'Wouldn't be the first time, or the last. He couldn't stop himself. Girls loved him, he had the patter *and* the good Jamaican looks. He used to wear his hair like Jazzie B from Soul II Soul – shaved back and sides with locks on top. Oh yeah, he could charm 'em, all right.'

Anyway, on that afternoon in October 1989, Mum remembers holding the sides of her bump as she confronted Sharon, giving it, 'I know he's been cheating on me with you, you fucking whore. Cheating on me when I'm pregnant.' An' all that. Mum also recalls the thrum of techno music bouncing off concrete and the familiar smell of burning plastic mixed with herbs: crack and cannabis. Next, sting, sting, sting in her shins, as Sharon started booting her in her brogues. Mum says I started kicking and thrashing inside her as she went to kick Sharon back, but her foot had barely left the ground when Ashley steamed in.

What happened next happened fast, man. Mum saw a flash of gold incisor just before Ashley's fist crashed into the side of her face 'like a mallet'. She remembers being forced backwards, her back slamming against the balcony wall, choking for breath and hugging her pregnant belly – just as Ashley's fist smashed into her face once more. Bang. She fell to the ground.

Voices, techno, techno, voices, all wheeling up. Burning plastic, a taste of rising bile, then boom, blackness.

Mum didn't hear the frantic cries of the downstairs neighbours who came running out of their flats after seeing Mum drop headfirst like a crash dummy. Nor did she hear the screams and shouting from the balcony towering some sixteen feet over where she lay on the grass courtyard. She didn't hear the sirens or see the blue flashing lights, just as she has no recollection of being stretchered into the ambulance. Yeah, she was out cold, man.

When Mum came to, she was in King's College Hospital, Denmark Hill, her friend Mandy at her bedside. Mum's face was all mashed up and she couldn't move her legs. First thing she asked Mandy through busted lips was, 'Why am I in hospital?' Then, feeling for her bump, added: 'Is the baby OK? Please don't say I lost my baby.'

Miraculously, both Mum and I survived and Mandy told her what had happened on the balcony as she'd gone over. There'd been a proper commotion, folk getting involved, shouting, screaming, cussing. Some people tried to pull Ashley off Mum as some of his mates cheered him on.

'Happened in seconds, Jak,' said Mandy. 'He literally picked you up and hurled you over that balcony.' Mandy said a neighbour must've done a 999 call as police were on it fast. 'Don't worry, Jak,' she added, 'he'll go down for a fucking long stretch for this. Seriously, the cunt's lucky you ain't dead.'

The doctors, in less colourful language, agreed. They said her unborn baby, AKA me, would've died if Mum had landed on concrete instead of grass. Mum might have died or suffered severe brain damage. Yeah, no doubt about it, man, that grass saved us.

Of course, Mum had to speak to the police, and she told them all she could remember. As for Ashley, well, she'd seen him around on the estate before, heard stuff about him. Like, she knew he was a bit of a face who knew people, dodgy people. Not a character you'd want to cross, y'get me? She'd also heard a rumour he'd done a good stretch in jail. She also now knew that he was Sharon's cousin. But all that aside, Mum didn't know Ashley.

After a scan showed I was doing fine, Mum was discharged. And although she'd spent less than twenty-four hours in hospital, her injuries were out there, man. She was on crutches for at least two weeks because her legs were so badly bruised and sprained. She'd also twisted her right ankle. A map of bruises covered her face. She had a busted cheekbone, black eye and had to wear shades whenever she left the house, hobbling on crutches with all her extra baby weight, about to pop. 'My face was so swollen I looked like the bloody Elephant Man,' were her words.

Mum went to recover at her parents' house on the Myatts Field estate, until my dad rocked up, giving it the concerned loyal partner and dad-to-be act and persuading Mum to go back to 16 Newark House, her council flat on the nearby Loughborough Estate. Terence said he'd stand by her and protect her. Just days later, he fucked off back to his mum's place in Gipsy Hill, leaving Mum alone in the flat, heavily pregnant with his kid and barely able to walk.

Then she got a call from the police: Ashley had been nicked and charged with attempted murder. He was being held on remand in jail until the case went to court. Initially, Mum was relieved: at least he couldn't harm her again – right? But the reverse was true; things got worse, as Mum found herself in the eye of a shit-storm of terror and intimidation. Yardies banged on her door, day and night, shooting their mouths off, 'Open up, we know you're in there. You put our bro in the jail, now you's gonna pay …' When she did answer the door one time, a guy threatened to put a bullet in her head. There were moody phone calls, some made to her parents' house. Mum was stressed. I mean, off-the-scale stressed. Bread-knife under the pillow stuff, expecting the front door and windows to be put in at any moment. Scared to stay in, scared to go out. The threats continued, getting more sinister by the day, until it broke her, man.

Around mid-November she called the police. 'I want to drop the charges,' she said. 'Ashley didn't throw me off the balcony, I fell. It was an accident.'

But the police were like, 'No can do, you gotta go court', so Mum – now nine months pregnant – went to court and refused to testify against Ashley. The case got thrown out and the judge threatened to do Mum for contempt of court. How fucked up is that? She would've sprinted to that witness box faster than Sally Gunnell, given the chance, but she had no choice. This was about survival and Mum had two lives to protect. Talking of that other life, few days later, she was back in King's College hospital.

I still laugh when Mum tells me about the moment I was born. I shot into this world at 3.20 p.m. on 14 December 1989 – a Thursday. It rained all day, but the vibe was chilled and festive on the maternity ward, with tinsel everywhere and Christmas music playing. Staff wore reindeer antlers and Santa hats and all that crazy stuff. My dad wasn't there and Mum's friend Joy went along instead. This Joy woman had dreads down to her waist, loved her weed and always kept two forks in the back pockets of her jeans. 'Called 'em her weapons,' Mum says, 'and she wouldn't hesitate to use them, either.'

Respect to Joy: seems she got into the spirit of things, sticking by Mum's side throughout her thirty-six-hour labour, holding her hand in the delivery room and chatting away as the contractions hit. Though when the gas and air got wheeled in, Joy abused her position of birthing partner. 'She kept nicking me mask,' Mum explained, 'She had more of the stuff than me. She was gasping it down.' Joy watched the entire delivery through heavy eyelids, swaying as she peered between Mum's legs. As the midwife cut the umbilical cord and I let out my first piercing cries, Joy staggered backwards, hit the wall, and slowly slumped to the floor, saying, 'Wow, that was one the most beautiful things I've ever experienced, man'.

That evening, brimming with emotion, Mum called my dad's mum's house. There had been bad vibes between her and Terence, but he she had just delivered their child, her first-born. He had a *son* now and Mum wanted to be the one to tell him so. She shambled out of the ward to the nearest payphone. A woman answered, but Mum didn't recognise the voice. It definitely wasn't the Jamaican accent of Terence's mother, Big Mama June. Nah, this girl sounded young and cockney. Rude 'n' all.

'Who are you? What d'ya want Terence for?' she snapped.

Mum went, 'I'm Jakki and I've just given birth to Terence's first child. It's a boy. I just wanted to let him know, in case he wants to see his son … or something?' The line fell silent for a few seconds, then the girl exhaled loudly.

'What d'ya mean? What baby? I'm Alison and *I've* got Terence's baby: I had our girl Sasha in October. Is this a wind-up or what?'

Mum almost dropped the receiver. She was gutted. She suspected my dad had been cheating on her with Sharon, but she hadn't imagined he'd have another girl on the go at the same time, let alone have a kid with her.

'Just tell Terence I've had the baby,' she said and hung up.

I was sound asleep in one of those plastic cot things when my dad arrived at the hospital. Mum had drifted off but was woken by the sound of shouting and swearing on the ward. A bloke was going off, audibly pissed, his voice instantly recognisable to Mum. A nurse hurried over.

'Ms Doherty, I'm sorry but there's a black man in reception who says he's the father of your …'

'I wanna see my fucking son. I'm the father, I'm his fucking father.'

Boom, there he was, staggering towards us, beating his fist into his palm. Eyes blazing, rain-soaked locks bouncing about his head, reeking of booze: my dad. He was there less than a minute before security guards told him to leave. Mum says he was so drunk she couldn't even have a simple conversation with him, let alone confront him over Alison and the 'other baby' drama.

'He stormed out of there, hollering, "I'm gonna wet the baby's head,"' Mum says.

According to my birth certificate, I'm Terence Kersean Lewis. My unusual middle name is a nod towards my Irish roots on

Mum's side of the family and, while I share my dad's first name, my mum called me Terroll from the get-go, so that's who I am: Terroll Kersean Lewis. I think Mum's motive for changing my name was to piss off my dad, although she's never admitted as much. But, yeah, it's fair to say that my parents' relationship was volatile from the start.

They even argued the first time they met at a party in Mum's flat, around November 1988. Her flatmate, Susi, had got the party started when she invited friends over from the Loughborough and Myatts Fields estates. Mum came home that evening to encounter Terence for the very first time, blocking her own door to her, his lips clamped around a fat joint. 'Yo, wagwan,' he went, filling the entrance with his six-foot frame. 'W'cha doin'? You ain't getting in here.'

Mum laughed. 'I live here,' she said. 'It's my flat. Get out my way.'

'I *said* you *ain't getting in*. How do I know who you is; where's your ID?'

'What the fuck? I told you, I live here, I don't need no fucking ID … ' And so the row continued, insults flying until Susi appeared and confirmed Mum's identity. Terence muttered an apology. Mum gave him a dirty look as she barged past. 'Skin up then,' she shot. They got drunk and stoned together and had a laugh. Terence admitted he'd mistaken Mum for a jake because she was the only white girl there. They smoked more weed and realised they fancied one another. And that's how my mum and dad got it on. Romantic, innit?

Mum and Terence had grown up just a few miles apart, my dad on an estate in Gipsy Hill and Mum, from the age of about thirteen, at 7 Treherne Court, where she lived with her parents and her sister, Christine, who's thirteen years younger. I know few details about my dad's childhood, other than he was born in Jamaica, around 1966, and came to the UK with his parents and siblings when he was about three. He has two brothers,

Lloyd and Colonel, and the three of them used to stick together 'like a team', I'm told. I believe he had a couple of sisters, too. Their mother, Big Mama June, looked after all the kids in their small, social-housing flat.

June was quite a name on the Jamaican music scene in south London, running raves and club nights in the area. She was in the mix, big time. Kids at school, people in the street even, would come up to me to talk about my grandma, man. They'd be like, 'Yo, your gran's Big Mama June, 'n't she? She rents out ghettos for raves an' stuff.' And I'd be, like, 'Yeah, that's my gran,' though I barely knew her. Her husband – Terence's dad – passed away when I was about one. I only know he was Jamaican and Indian – nobody even told me what his name was.

I know a lot more about my mum's side. It was very different. My grandparents, Mick (Michael Patrick) and Rose Doherty, were the backbone of our family. Both came from Ireland and they were good people: Catholic, loyal and proper working class. To me, Mick wasn't Granddad, he was Dad. Always, man. I lived with my grandparents for many years – from when I was a young kid right through to my crazy, teenage, street years. Each Christmas, every birthday and all the happy family occasions I can remember happened at 7 Treherne Court. My grandparents did a lot for me. I mean, a *lot*. They grew me and when they both died in 2016 – within five months of each other – a big part of me died with them. Yeah, you'll be reading much more about those two.

In the weeks following my birth, Terence wormed his way back into Mum's life. She says he practically begged her to take him back. 'Like an idiot, I agreed,' Mum says, "cos I was young, I had a baby and he seemed genuine this time, like he really wanted to make a go of things.'

Terence moved back into 16 Newark House, but soon started disappearing again, leaving Mum alone with me for days on end. She didn't know whether he was with 'that Alison woman' and his other kid, seeing other women, or what. He didn't work and, on the occasions when he did stay in the flat, he and Mum would drink and smoke and have massive rows. Terence also knew some shady characters, I'm told; boys who were involved with guns and drugs and knives and shit. Boys who were into the kind of dangerous stuff I would later get into. These guys would occasionally show up at the flat for a chat and a smoke or whatever. 'I don't really remember there being gangs as such back then,' Mum says, 'it was more about having lots of friends – knowing you've got people who've got your back, if you know what I mean.'

There came a point when Mum didn't feel safe with all these other people around, particularly with a baby in the home. The rows with Terence became more frequent and violent. Things were thrown and smashed. Neighbours would hear screaming and shouting and banging, late at night and, sometimes, in the afternoon or morning. Often, police would turn up, responding to reports of another disturbance. But Mum knew how to get rid of them fast.

'I'd run out into the street and catch them before they could hit the door. I'd apologise and say something like, "Nothing to worry about, just a small domestic."'

This toxic routine continued until I was about seven months old and Mum decided it was time for her and me to flee Newark House. She went to the council and we were placed in an emergency B&B in Brixton. They moved us to another estate in the area before finally, a couple of months after my first birthday, we went to live in a women's refuge in Kilburn, where we would stay for the next eighteen months or so.

I remember that place; I thought it was cool, man. It was kinda like a college campus, with lots of rooms and corridors with noticeboards covered in leaflets and posters. There was also a big recreation room that had a kitchen area for the mums and a play area for us kids, with toys and computers and a TV we could watch shows like *Rugrats* on. And we had a good-sized bedroom that doubled as a kitchen, with a cooker, sink and fridge. The curtains were sunshine yellow.

Mum got me into a nursery after a key worker at the refuge put in a good word for us. 'Other parents had to pay to get their kids in,' Mum tells me, 'but because I was on income support and living in a refuge, you got in for free.' I remember my first day – sitting in the sandpit, playing with a toy dumper truck and making *vroom, vroom* noises, looking all cute with my curly hair and gold hoop earring. Almost three and I'm the new kid in school, right? I'm the new baby in town and, rah, man, I'm happy, until I look up and I can't see my mum. She ain't there. I start thinking, She's gone away. *My mum's gone and she ain't never coming back*. And I'm surrounded by all these kids I don't know, plus a grown-up who ain't my mum, 'cos my mum has gone. She's done one, she's outta there. Mum's *gone*.

The room goes all *Alice in Wonderland* fucking crazy on me and I'm like this tiny person surrounded by big alien things. Even the tables and chairs that are actually meant for little people like me become monstrous objects. So now I'm thinking, *I've gotta get out*. Then I'm on my feet and I'm charging out of the pit, sand flying. I see the doorway on the other side of the room, blocked by one of those baby gates, but that ain't gonna stop me 'cos I've grabbed this big bucket, right, and I'm torpedoing across the room with it now, smashing into things as I go, kicking chairs over and screaming, 'Where's my fucking mum? Get me my mum!'

This is it, it's prison-break, man. No time to waste, and I'm looking at the gate thinking, 'Cool, if I can just get over that, I'm outta here'. Commotion behind me. The woman who ain't my mum is shouting something as she gets nearer, but I'm too quick for her. I've already turned the bucket upside down and placed it next to the gate. And now I'm climbing onto that bucket and grabbing the top bar of the gate with both hands before – *vroom, vroom* – I'm over it and on the other side, steaming down the corridor, panting and crying as I run faster and faster – into my mum's arms.

Mum had been having a cuppa with some of the other women in the kitchen downstairs. She'd heard all the chaos above, heard me screaming and had immediately shot upstairs. I'll never forget the relief that washed over me when she picked me up and she says it took a while for me to calm down. The teacher who'd witnessed my escape bid said, 'We've had some moments in here before, but never has a child given us a run for our money like your Terroll did.'

Rah, looking back, I think I was just warming up.

2

CREATURES OF HABIT AND OTHER CRAZY STUFF

Terence came back into the picture when I was about four or five, just before I was due to start primary school. He tracked us down to our temporary accommodation in Finchley, showing up one evening, Mum says, looking smart in a Gabicci shirt and Burberry tweed trousers. He told her he was sorry and wanted another stab at things. He wanted to be a part of his son's life and all that bullshit.

Mum hadn't seen Terence in three years or so and there was too much bad history between them for her to forget just like that, man. I mean *bad* history. Yet she noticed something different about him. 'He seemed calmer,' she says, 'sober too.' He told her she looked 'mad cool' in her stonewash jeans and vest top – handouts from her cousin Matina, who worked in a denim factory. There'd be no more cheating or lies, he promised. Basically, Terence said all the things he knew Mum wanted to hear and, in turn, she thought, 'Fuck it, why not?' Besides, he was the father of her kid, right? She thought, 'Be a shame for the boy to grow up not knowing his dad, wouldn't it?'

They got back together – on-and-off – at the same time as we moved back to south London. Lambeth council had offered Mum a flat on the Kennington Park Estate near Oval, a newly decorated, two-bedroom gaff which she'd snapped up. I remember the day we moved in, me running excitedly from room to room and setting up battle scenes with my Action Man and wrestling figures and making gun noises as Charlie the Jack Russell, a recent addition to the family, chased me. The place felt huge – I had my own bedroom; an entire room to myself with purple emulsion walls. I was one happy boy, man.

Mum's bedroom was light pink and the lounge had cream walls and a brown stringy carpet that reminded me of mincemeat. In the centre was a fake black-leather couch and a glass-topped coffee table. The flat was on the first floor of one of the many red-brick blocks that made up the estate. Our block was called Key House – and we were to have some of the saddest days ever in there.

The flat ran on pay-as-you-go electric and gas meters, and we would spend spells without one or the other – and sometimes without either – when Mum couldn't afford to top up the key cards. I always knew when the gas had gone as we had to boil the kettle loads of times to fill the bath (when we hadn't also run out of electricity). Even the television was a pre-paid, big box affair, with a slot at the back for coins. Wow, that television was my lifeline, my escape. I would watch cartoons – *Dexter's Laboratory* and *Courage the Cowardly Dog* being my favourites – until the money ran out. I used to get so angry if it stopped in the middle of a programme and came up with a few hacks to cheat the system. If I put a penny in the slot slowly and took it out after a couple of seconds, the box would recognise that coin as a twenty- or fifty-pence piece. By doing this several times over, I could watch as much *Cowardly* and *Dexter* as I liked. Happy days.

Times were tight; one hundred per cent. Like, you could never just go to the fridge and grab a carton of juice and there wasn't much food other than bread and some tinned things. But however hard things got, Mum always made sure I was clothed, washed and fed. She also had personal problems and addictions to deal with – first alcohol and weed, and later, much harder shit – but she would do any bits of work she could, just to get by. I can remember her waitressing at a café while also doing multiple cleaning jobs. In her spare time, she'd go door-to-door on the estate selling baby clothes. I think I inherited my entrepreneurial skills from Mum. I certainly didn't get them from my dad – 'I never knew him to ever do a day's work,' Mum says.

He wasn't around much, Terence, and most of the memories I do have from those days are not good ones. Not really. I do recall him telling me, not long after we moved to Key House, 'I'm your puppa, your pups,' but there was no hugging or anything like that. Nah, it was more, *I'm your puppa … laters, I'm off to the pub,* kinda vibe. But something must've stuck in my head as I would always call him Pups from then on. But never 'Dad', *never*.

Sometimes Terence stayed with us for a few nights, sometimes I might not see him for a few weeks. But when he was there, he wouldn't go unnoticed or unheard. Even as a child I could sense he was a harsh guy; he was always shouting at my mum and kicking off about this or that. There were arguments and fights. At night I'd lie in bed, crying as I pulled the duvet tight over my head, trying to drown out the sounds from the living room of Mum screaming, Pups shouting, crashing and banging. Sometimes, I could feel the physical vibrations of those rows bump through the bed.

One time something else woke me. It wasn't Terence, he wasn't there that night. I could hear some weird noises. Scratching and hissing, coming from the wall side of my bed. Something dropped onto the duvet and the scratching got louder. The wall was alive, man. It was freaking me out. I leapt from the bed like it was on fire and ran to the door, got on my tiptoes to flick the light switch and, holy shit, I thought maybe I was having a strange dream or something. There were all these black, plasticky, beetle-like creatures crawling up and down and across the wall above my bed. Loads of them, tip-tapping about. I called out for my mum, though now I'd seen the cause of the noise I was more curious than scared as I had a thing about bugs and animals. I was that kid who'd go out in the rain and grab all the snails, just so I could race them. I'd collect ants, bees, spiders, frogs and all sorts of creepy-crawlies. Mum's never been keen on critters though and that night she came stumbling into my room in her Winnie-the-Pooh nightshirt, Princess Diana hairdo all over the place, took one look at that teeming wall and screamed the fucking place down. Charlie came bounding in after her, yapping and growling and jumping in all directions. Seriously, that dog thought himself ten times bigger than he was. Next day, Mum said we were going to stay with my nan and granddad for a bit while pest control sorted things in the flat. Turned out we had a massive cockroach infestation that had made its way to us from next door.

It was a miracle I wasn't taken into care during those Key House days. It wasn't just the cockroaches or Terence himself – I mean, there I was, a kid of five, watching strange people come and go from the flat. Men with dreadlocks, smoking foul-smelling stuff out of the window in the front room. And those crackheads would speak to me, man. Yeah, they'd try to speak to me as I sat playing with my toys or watching TV and I remember they could never string a fucking sentence together and their eyes would disappear into their forehead and the room would smell of death. Often, they'd leave things on the coffee table – plastic bottles with holes in them, brown burn marks, bits of blackened tinfoil, white pebbles wrapped in clingfilm – and I knew it wasn't no *Blue Peter* craftwork, y'know what I'm saying? Sometimes, I'd see a handgun on the table too, but I never thought to investigate; I was more interested in rigging the telly so I could watch my cartoons.

In September 1995 I started at Henry Fawcett Primary School, which was just opposite our estate on Bowling Green Street. To a certain degree, school was my sanctuary. I loved being away from the flat and all those weirdos who hung out there. I enjoyed painting and learning my alphabet and how to write and stuff. And story-time at the end of the day, when the teacher would read to us? Oh, man, that was golden. I felt safe inside those blue school gates, so much so that I would dread hearing the bell ring at the end of the day.

On the downside, some of the other kids at Henry Fawcett were evil bastards, ganging up in the playground or barging past me in the corridors, giving it, 'Ha-ha, you ain't got no friends,' and staring at my shoes as we sat on the floor in assembly, sniggering as they asked, 'Why have you got holes in your shoes?' Mum couldn't afford new shoes and I'd repair those I did have, sticking bits of cardboard or scraps of material over the gaps in the soles. Last thing I wanted was to add to Mum's stress and I knew what would happen if I asked for a new pair in front of Terence: fireworks, man, fireworks.

The bullies confirmed my feeling that I didn't enjoy being around other human beings much and that I would need to fight my corner to survive in this fucked-up world. They had spotted a truth, as bullies often do, that I didn't have any proper friends. Outside of school I didn't get to play with other kids. I had no brothers or sisters and Mum wasn't the type to be doing things like joining a parents' association, running an after-school club or swapping recipes with other mums at the school gates. I didn't go to funfairs and I wasn't invited to birthday parties. There was no face-painting, bouncy castles or being in the Cubs for me but, y'know what? I was quite happy in my own space; I was creative, good at playing by myself and I was lucky enough to have a big collection of toys, most of which came from my grandparents.

Nearly every toy my granddad bought was military-themed, from Action Man figures to army Lego sets. He had been a soldier himself, serving for the British in Ireland, although he ended up going to jail for refusing to fight in Northern Ireland during The Troubles, according to Mum. But I knew nothing about my granddad's army days when I was playing battlefields around the flat in Key House. I'd create full-on wars for myself, using every army and wrestling figure toy I owned. I'd have an army on the right, another on the left, and they'd fight everywhere – on top of the TV, on the floors, the tables and the kitchen worktops. They even fought in the bath. It didn't matter where because I was the happiest boy wherever I was when I was playing. With all the chaos going on around me, being able to play with toys, away from the noise, away from the drugs, away from the violence … that type of peace, without distortion … that place in my head? Yeah, it was sacred, man. Back then, it was a breath of fresh air just to take a breath of fresh air, y'know what I mean?

To be fair, not all the people who came to our flat were crackheads. Mum also got to know some nice neighbours, one being this guy who called himself Snake. I took a real shine to him. He lived a couple of doors down from us and would always stop to chat, be it on the landing or in the street. Snake fascinated me because he was unlike any other grown-up I knew. He had a shaved head, apart from a thin mohican, at least ten inches high, running from his forehead to his neck. Some days the brush was bright pink, other times neon-green. Occasionally purple or yellow. He was pierced by metal bolts, studs and hoops through his nose, ears and lips and had chains hanging from his face and he wore skin-tight, ripped jeans, more chains about his hips and legs and lots of leather gear. When I asked mum why Snake had a brush on his head, she laughed and said, ''Cos he's a punk.' And I thought, Wow, that's cool, even though I had no idea what a punk was.

Snake had a pet rat, one of those albino ones with white fur and red eyes. Once, when I was playing on the communal landing with my toys, Snake came thumping up the stairs in his big boots, whistling, the rat perched on his shoulder. Mum was nearby, smoking one of her funny-smelling cigarettes. 'All right, Jak,' he said, stopping next to us. Mum flinched.

'Urgh! How can you let that fucking thing crawl all over you?' she said and Snake laughed, crouched down and I was eye-to-eye with his pet.

Snake was like, 'How you doing, T?'

I remember thinking his face looked like it'd been put together by a motorbike mechanic or something. The rat hunched its shoulders and twitched its nose at me and that made me laugh and feel all warm inside.

'Has it got a name?' I asked, as Snake lifted the rat off his shoulder, its long pink tail dangling.

'Here, take him,' said Snake and suddenly the rat was on me, its tiny pink claws clinging to my tracksuit top and I thought it was the cutest thing ever. Clean, delicate, white-and-pink like coconut ice. I could feel his tiny bones moving beneath its fur as I stroked him, his little shaky heartbeat. 'I've just been calling him Rat, but why don't you give him a name?' Snake got up, chiming and creaking. 'Have him, he's yours, if you want him.' And, shit, man, it was as though the real Santa Claus had just rocked up on his sleigh going, 'Ho, ho, ho, climb aboard, son.' Yeah, I couldn't speak for a moment there. Even Mum fell silent. I gave her a massive smile.

'We can keep him, can't we?' I said.

She blew out some smelly smoke and gave Snake a hard look. 'I s'pose so,' she said.

I called the rat 'Jake'. Seemed appropriate, as one of my favourite WWF stars was Jake 'The Snake' Roberts, which brought the whole thing full circle. Our Snake helped me make a home for Jake using a red, plastic toy-box. We cut holes in the lid, attached a water bottle and piled up wood shavings inside the box to give Jake somewhere comfy to sleep. All was good. Jake and I became real tight over the next week or so. I'm talking proper bromance. Terence wasn't around and Mum was more chilled too, even with a rodent in the flat, at least until the morning I woke to find Jake's box empty.

I heard cries from the kitchen, 'Fucking rat, fucking, *bastard* rat,' and my whole world crumbled around me. Jake had escaped during the night, found his way into the kitchen, gnawed his way into the cupboards and gobbled what little food that we had, leaving behind a load of holes and rat shit. A scuttling noise from behind one of the cupboards confirmed my rodent friend had not left the building. Later that day, pest control took Jake away. I ran into the bathroom and stayed there for ages, crying my fucking eyes out. How could they do such a thing? They'd killed my little friend. Broke my heart, man. Broke my heart.

Jake had been gone less than twenty-four hours when Pups returned. I remember Mum was taking me to the shop to buy consolation sweets when I saw him in the courtyard, coming towards us in his long, leather coat. He had a bounce in his step and a smile on his face and gave Mum a kiss on the cheek before ruffling my hair. He said something like, 'How you doing, son?' Mum told me to go and play for a bit.

I ran off looking for worms among piles of autumn leaves while they chatted and I came across a pile of rubble, spilling out from under a hedge. Crumbling bricks, broken tiles and stones, debris left behind by workies, perhaps. I started picking up fragments and lobbing them in all directions, seeing how far I could throw them. Which was great until a pigeon came strutting across the lawn, directly into my line of fire and one of my missiles hit its wing. The bird's legs buckled and its other wing started flapping like crazy, but it couldn't take off. Instead, it just rolled from side to side and jerked, its feathers clogged with blood, and I started panicking, thinking, The pigeon's dying, I've killed the pigeon. They killed Jake and now I've killed the pigeon.

I started breathing really fast, damp air hitting my throat, waiting for the inevitable. The pigeon was still fighting, its good wing going mental now and I called for back-up, screaming, 'Help, help, the pigeon can't fly,' and Pups was on it in seconds, man. Crunch, crunch, crunch through the leaves. Swift as a ninja, he lunged at the rubble, grabbed a brick, dropped to one knee beside the pigeon, lifted the brick high into the air and smashed it down, one, two, three times on the bird. He tossed the brick aside and calmly scooped the corpse into his leather-gloved hands. Poor thing didn't look like a pigeon no more; it was a mush of grey fluff and red gunk.

'At least it's out of its misery now,' Pups said, and that made me feel better about the situation, for a fleeting moment. He chucked the remains in the wheelie bin and the day carried on, but I couldn't stop thinking about that pigeon, and how Pups had killed it.

I was pleased that Pups was home, to begin with, anyway. I remember there being a couple of chilled days when he and Mum weren't arguing. They spent a lot of time in Mum's bedroom while I played with my toys and fed the telly pennies. I even heard some laughter, but then the fighting started up again. Shouting, swearing, banging, smashing, screaming, crying. Night after night after night. The only time it was quiet-ish was when Mum and Pups' strange friends came round to smoke from plastic bottles out of the window. Early mornings could be peaceful, too – when they were sleeping.

Pups must've stayed with us for about two months; I remember the Christmas tree was still up when he went away. I didn't see him leave but the events leading up to his departure will stay in my head for ever. I was watching *Live & Kicking* one Saturday morning and I was still in my Hulk Hogan pyjamas. My Action Man and wrestling figures were scattered around me on the mincemeat carpet, where I was setting up another battle scene. Mum was in her fluffy, spearmint dressing gown, chilling on the sofa. There was a plate of dry toast on the floor. Pups had made it for me, but I didn't want it because it looked and tasted like cardboard. On the coffee table was a silver box that my grandparents had bought for us. Mum said it was a special machine that played cartoons and stuff, but I'd been looking at it, thinking, Yeah, right, it's just a box with a plug. So, I was playing away on the floor, the untouched toast still sitting there, when Pups came thudding into the room.

'Oi, Terroll, eat the toast,' he said, nudging the plate with his bare toes.

'I don't want it,' I said.

'Eat your fucking toast, now,' he shouted. I told him I didn't *like* the toast, I didn't *want* the toast. 'Eat the *fucking* toast now – or else.' I looked at the plate, the toast beginning to blur. His voice sounded much scarier up close than it did through walls.

Mum told him to calm down. 'If he doesn't want the fucking toast, don't make him eat the fucking toast,' she said and I shrunk into my Hulk Hogan PJs, burying my face in my hands as Pups' voice ripped through me. I felt a whoosh of air past my ear and, with a crack, his foot slammed into the side of my head. The room started spinning, my head throbbing and heavy, like someone had drilled a hole in my skull and poured in cement. Mum started yelling and Pups powered out of the room in his string vest and tracksuit bottoms. The front door slammed and Mum rushed over and wrapped me in her arms. 'It's OK, darlin', Mummy's here,' she said as I cried.

I was in bed when Pups returned later that evening. Mum says he was drunk and seemingly remorseful, telling her he hadn't meant to hurt me. When we got up the next morning, Pups was gone. The silver box had also vanished. It would be several years before I'd see him again.

3

NORMAL LIFE?

'Now, tell me what you're going to say to the nice man, darlin'?' said Mum, pressing a grubby, five-pound note into my hand. I grinned, buzzing with excitement. I knew exactly what to say; I'd heard Mum ask boys the same question countless times.

'Can I get a blue? Five-pound-draw-weed?' Man, I was so proud, like I'd just spelled a really long word correctly.

'*Please,*' Mum added, pulling the hood of my winter coat over my head. I immediately pushed it back.

'Please,' I chanted, peering over the landing wall (I was just about tall enough to do that now). I spotted the dealer Mum had pointed out. Jay was his name, and he was near the small playpark. Lanky figure in a hoodie, moving shiftily in the drizzle, muscly dog on a lead next to him. Mum tried to pull my hood up again.

'Off you go then. And be quick; don't hang about.'

I shook off the hood again. 'OK, Mum,' I said and off I strutted, playing the big boy. I was the man of the house now, out there on the Kennington Park Estate, a face in the ends, buying weed for my mum. I was proud, I felt important. I had just turned seven.

Mum didn't force me to buy drugs for her, but I'd seen her do it so many times and I wanted in on the action. I was curious, see. At first, I'd ask simple things like, 'What's five pounds?', and, 'What's a blue?' I knew that weed was the stuff she liked to smoke every day 'to relax' and I was fascinated by the transactional element. You could go up to someone in the street, hand them money and they'd give you a product in return. My interest in the subject grew quite naturally and that was how we got to the point where I'd said, 'I wanna go buy a five-pound weed bag.'

Jay, a mixed-race guy in his late teens, jutted his chin and looped the dog chain round his hand a couple of times. 'Yo, bro, wassup?' he said, and I'm like, 'Wow, I'm a bro, I'm connected, I'm affiliated. Affiliated on the streets.' I looked up at him, trying to keep cool.

'My mum wants a five-pound-draw-weed bag, a blue,' I said. Rolled off the tongue. Jay looked this way and that, so I did the same, and slipped him my screwed-up fiver. Palm to palm, swift and covert. Jay was like a magician; in a flash the note disappeared in his pocket and a small bag of weed was in my hand. That would have been a gram, enough for two good-sized joints, three teeny ones, but in my small hand it felt like a lot. I thanked Jay and he said, 'No worries,' called me 'bro' again and I walked back to Key House, casual, like – until I reached the stairs. I powered up, unable to contain my excitement. Worthy, that's how I felt, like I'd done a really good deed by helping Mum. I'd seen and heard drug deals happening, but now I was involved and I wanted to dabble some more. I thought what I'd done was normal.

Truth was, life for me in Key House wasn't normal: it wasn't only weed Mum was smoking. Even though Pups was long gone, the weirdo crackheads were still loitering; some days you never knew who you might meet in the living room, slumped on the sofa or blowing smoke out the window. Mum seemed stressed all the time, she was not quite with it, if you know what I mean? I remember having to boil the kettle by myself and fill the bath, stuff like that. I'd go to school and pretend everything was OK and I ignored the smell in the living room, but it will stay with me for life and, whenever I come across it now, I'm immediately transported back to Key House. It makes me feel sick; sick in my stomach, sick in my mind. A dank smell, as if off-food was being burned. Strong in my nose, it consumed me, made me feel dehydrated. This is the smell of my childhood, the smell of death: crack cocaine.

Mum did try to protect me from all the chaos, I know that now, and she still told me that she loved me every day. She made sure that there was food to eat, even if it was just a loaf of bread – and she'd go without herself if she had to. She would also send me to stay at her parents a lot, especially on weekends and during school holidays. God, I loved spending time there.

Nan and Granddad Doherty's house on Treherne Court was split over three levels. On the bottom floor there was a living room that led into a back garden through glass doors and through another door into the spare bedroom. Up the stairs was the kitchen, toilet and front door and their bedroom was on the top floor, as too was my aunty Christine's and the main bathroom. I'd sleep in the downstairs bedroom, as would Granddad on the occasions when he was up late watching telly and wanted to avoid waking my nan. We'd be side-by-side, him on the single bed, me on a makeshift bed on the floor. He'd sing me a bedtime song – always the same one: 'Too-Ra-Loo-Ra-Loo-Ral (That's an Irish Lullaby)', and I'd feel safe, man. Safe.

My grandparents didn't have loads, but they spoiled me. And I'm not just talking about toys or clothes, but in terms of the love they gave to me. The time they spent with me. I can still hear my nan, pinching my cheek and saying, 'Come on, Our Boy, we're off to bingo,' in her cheery Irish accent. And I'd watch as she pottered in the kitchen, throwing things into her handbag – purse, keys, cigarettes and a pack of tissues – and I'd race into the hallway to get my trainers on, all excited because I thought bingo was fascinating. Nan used to go at least twice a week, usually later in the afternoon, after she'd finished her shift at the Sacred Heart of Mary Catholic School, where she worked as a dinner lady.

Compared to the life I knew at Key House, going to bingo with Nan was like stepping into another world. The hall intrigued me, man – a vast room filled with people at tables, heads down, looking for numbers on a grid and winning prizes. And I was, like, 'Wow, is this really happening?' I was too young to play for myself and Nan would let me cross off her numbers with a felt-tip pen. I don't recall her ever winning, but that never seemed to bother her. She just enjoyed the social side and her friends would make a huge fuss of me, saying I was cute and all that.

Granddad was a big softie. He'd give me sweets on the sly and say, 'Shh, don't tell your nan.' A Man United fan, he loved his football and never missed *Match of the Day* on Saturdays, when that unmistakable theme music would fill the house. He'd shout and cheer at the telly a lot.

Treherne Court was an oasis of normality for me. I felt comforted by the sense of routine and permanence, right down to Nan's collection of china dolls from around the world who'd give me eyeballs from their cabinet in the lounge. But beyond the walls of my grandparents' house, out on the blocks of Myatts Field and on its neighbouring estates – Angell Town, Loughborough and Stockwell Park – violence raged. At that time, around the mid-1990s, Brixton had a reputation for being one of the most dangerous areas in the UK. Gang-related shootings, stabbings, muggings, robberies and drug wars were rife. Yeah, street life was out there waiting for me, man. I just didn't know it then.

Going back to Mum's after being at Nan and Granddad's was bittersweet. I'd miss Mum while I was away, but I would dread going back to life at Key House. Mum was spending increasing amounts of time in the living room with her 'friends'.

She wasn't the person she had been; one moment she'd be loud and erratic, on a massive high, next she'd be spaced-out and moody. Often, she would send me to stay with our neighbours who lived on the floor above us, a couple called Mandy and Mo. Mo was Jamaican and Irish, with a beard and a gap between his front teeth. This I remember because he smiled a lot. Mandy was a white lady with short, blonde hair. She called me 'sweetheart' and 'darling' and would give me cheese-and-onion sandwiches and glass upon glass of fresh orange juice. Rah, I remember thinking cheese with raw onion was a weird combo, but those sandwiches tasted the best. Mandy and Mo were cool people and there was a real cosy vibe in their flat. It was so nice and warm in there, with radiators that actually gave off heat, unlike the stone-cold lumps of metal in our flat below. I never got fresh orange juice downstairs, either. Their living room was lined with shelves full of books and loads and loads of VHS tapes. I'd never seen so many videos, it was like Blockbusters in there.

Mandy and Mo didn't have kids of their own, but they acted like parents. They looked after me, big time. We'd watch telly or one of their many movies, play video games and chill and, more often than not, I'd stay overnight as there was always a bed made up for me. Looking back, I guess that Mum probably sent me to Mandy and Mo's when she had her drug mates over – to keep me away from all the trouble and stuff. Sometimes Mum would say to me: 'Mandy and Mo are your real parents, you know,' and I would start crying. That fucked with my head; I'd be looking at Mum, thinking, 'You're my mum. Pups is my dad, but he got angry and went away. Granddad is my dad now. Mandy and Mo are the nice people upstairs, but that doesn't mean they're my mum and dad, does it?'

One afternoon, I was watching telly in the living room when the doorbell rang – and rang and rang and rang and rang, until I heard Mum thudding along the hall, going, 'For fuck's sake, I'm coming.' I carried on watching TV, glad to have the room to myself for a change, blanking out the sound of slurred voices in the hallway, until the living room door flew open and this Staffordshire bull terrier came charging at me, an angry thing with brindle fur and a wide mouth packed with slimy teeth. As it galloped towards me, baring its teeth and growling, it looked as though it could've had me whole and I made a run for it.

The dog chased me into the hall, then into Mum's bedroom. I dived onto her bed and tumbled off the other side, the beast now a heavy lump on top of me. I felt its claws pierce my T-shirt and scratch my skin. Its coarse fur, like a broom-head, scraped the back of my neck. I felt a deep, stinging sensation in my shoulder as I curled into a ball on the floor and yelled, 'Help! The dog's biting me, the dog's biting me.'

Mum's voice filled the room.

'Oi! You fucking animal, get off my baby. Get off my baby boy!'

Which must've scared the shit out of the dog as it was quick to obey Mum's orders, pounding out of the room as fast as it had chased me into it. Mum charged after it, shouting, 'Your fucking dog's bitten my boy, you cunt.'

I got up, amazed that all my limbs were still intact. Lifting the sleeve of my T-shirt, I saw a couple of scratches but there were no chunks of flesh missing, as I'd imagined. Not even a bite mark. I called out to my mum, 'It didn't bite me,' but she didn't hear me. She was in the kitchen, slamming doors and drawers, still shouting, dissing the dog over the sound of metal things hitting the floor. Then I caught a flash of green dressing-gown as she streaked past the doorway and into the living room, her voice like machine-gun fire through glass: 'You fucker. Your fucking dog just bit my boy. You fucking …'

A man shouted, 'Calm the fuck down!' and a long, demonic scream filled the flat.

I bolted into the living room, screaming, 'Don't hurt my mum, get off my mum,' but I was in a scene from a different slasher movie. Fireworks exploded in my chest. I choked on my breath. A skinny lad in a baseball cap was slumped on the sofa, clutching his shoulder, his grey tracksuit saturated in blood, top and bottoms. He was wailing now.

'You stabbed me, you fucking stabbed me,' he cried and Mum dropped the knife.

Mum's hand looked as though it'd been dunked in red paint. I let out a scream so fucking loud it didn't belong to me and bolted into my bedroom. The staffie whimpered from somewhere.

John, a drug dealer, was supposed to be making a delivery to Mum but was instead rushed to hospital. It was she who called the ambulance. John took it well. It was an 'accident', he told the medics who stitched him up. He was lucky the blade hadn't hit a major artery. 'We laughed about it afterwards,' Mum says. 'At the time, I thought I was looking out for you, son.' I do get that; even back then I understood Mum had been trying to protect me, but I also knew that having my mum stabbing some random in the home, over a dog, was not a normal part of family life. By then, I knew that Mum's other visitors were crackheads. I *knew* they were taking drugs, and I had begun to understand that this, too, was definitely not normal. I knew I had to take action before something really bad happened. That was always my biggest fear: that something would happen to Mum or me – or us both.

Nan was cooking dinner when I eventually spilled my guts. Man, I can still clearly see myself, aimlessly pushing my toy car around the table in the kitchen at 7 Treherne Court, the waft of chicken pie, usually a welcome smell, making me nauseous. My stomach was in turmoil. What would I say? I didn't want to betray my mum, but I had to say something. I looked at

Granddad, sitting opposite me, then Nan called over from the sink, 'C'mon, you going to help me set the table, Our Boy?' I nodded, but my eyes flooded with tears. I was still pushing my car but I couldn't see it. Granddad saw that something was wrong.

'Hey, what is it, what's up, son?' he said. Nan came over and gave me a cuddle.

And I was, like, 'Please don't tell Mum I told you, please don't tell her?'

'Tell her what? Tell us what's upsetting you, Terroll,' said Nan. And from that point there was no going back.

I told them there were 'drugs at home' and strange people in the living room 'smoking stuff'. I said I was worried about Mum, worried about how she would react if she knew I'd snitched on her and, once I'd got that lot off my chest, I burst out crying. Like sobbing, flooding the place. 'I'm frightened, I'm so frightened, please don't tell Mum,' I cried into Nan's jumper. I sensed that she and Granddad were exchanging looks, like, *What the fuck?* Nan kissed my head. Granddad was the first to speak.

'Don't you worry, son,' he said softly, 'Everything's going to be grand. We won't say a word. We'll look after you – you're safe here, Our Boy.'

4

THE GOOD FIGHT

I never returned to Key House after dropping that bombshell about what was happening at home and my mum's drug use.

'Why don't you stay here with us for a bit?' Nan had said, 'You'd like that, won't you?'

I nodded and Granddad said everything would be cool from now on. He mentioned something about talking to Mum and how she would be 'better soon'. Then Nan set the table and got the chicken pie out of the oven and, from that moment on, the room off the lounge was my bedroom and the Myatts Field Estate would be my playground.

It wasn't that easy, of course. There was an almighty row, which kicked off the next day when Mum expected to pick me up. I stayed in my new bedroom as the voices boomed upstairs. I could hear Mum shouting, 'He's my fucking son, my baby.' Her tone was deranged. I'd never heard her sound so pissed off before and all I could think was, 'This is my fault. All of this is my fault.' I had no idea just how crazy things had become at Key House. Police officers had raided the flat and the crackheads were robbing from each other, as well as from Mum. It was fucking messy, man, and my moving to Nan and Granddad was a wake-up call for Mum.

A social worker later visited Mum and, pointing her ballpoint, basically said, 'If you don't sort your life out, you're going to lose your son.'

It was around the same time that Mum discovered she was two months' pregnant. Terence had only been gone a month or so and she hadn't been with any other men, which meant the writing was on the wall: the baby was his. Mum had not had any contact with Terence since he'd kicked me in the head and she had no desire to make the first move, y'get me? But in a way, Terence had done her a huge favour; she was pregnant, and she faced the prospect of losing me. This was the kick up the arse she needed to finally get her shit together.

And she did. She came off the crack and left the Kennington Park Estate. She moved to a flat off Brixton Road, a top-floor, two-bedroom gaff in a Victorian red-brick house – 51 Crewdson Road, a fifteen-minute walk from Nan and Granddad. Mum split her time between the two addresses, often spending weeks in a row at Myatts Field with me, Christine, Nan and Granddad and our two dogs, Dalinger, an Alsatian-Rottweiler cross and Jet, half-Alsatian, half-staffie. In August 1997, my sister Jazz arrived. She seemed to pop out of nowhere, man, but it was cool having a little sister.

Life was more stable at Myatts Field. Nan and Granddad would give me pocket money (five pound coins a week) and in return I'd do little chores around the house or help Granddad in the garden. I started at Christ Church Primary, a Christian school where we sang hymns and gospel songs and went to assembly every morning. I went in with the attitude, *If anyone gives me beef, I'm gonna inflict some pain. I'm gonna fight my corner, stand up for myself.* But it was actually a pretty decent school and I began to mix with other kids who were friendlier than the dickheads who had picked on me at Henry Fawcett.

We got to do lots of sport at Christ Church, which I loved as an active kid with lots of energy. We'd play football every day and I became shit-hot at it. I was fast and athletic and good at step-overs and kick-ups. A cool acrobat called the Mighty Wanderer would come in as a guest PE teacher from time to time. He ran a local acrobatic troupe called the Whippersnappers which performed at carnivals, jumping through hoops and turning somersaults in the street and all that shit. The Mighty Wanderer had a massive influence on me, man. He was a powerhouse. Like, he'd come into the room, pick up one of the long PE benches and balance it on his head. He taught us how to do handstands and backflips and got us doing some crazy stuff during his workshops. He made a human pyramid with me and my friend Rochelle; the idea was that we ran and jumped onto his knees. In one fluid movement, he'd grab us by a hand each and fling us onto his shoulders as he stood up. I would end up standing on one shoulder and Rochelle would be on the other, balancing at the sides of the Mighty Wanderer's head, his dreadlocks tickling our legs. The skills I learned from him, like balancing and how to lift my bodyweight, were more helpful than any qualification I ever gained.

At home, being able to play outside was a novelty. I got bang into my football, and Granddad (or Dad as I was now calling him) was thrilled I was taking such an interest in the beautiful game, whizzing me to Frank Johnson sports shop on Ferndale Road to buy me my first strip. His face practically flood-lit the store. 'C'mon Our Boy,' he said, squeezing my shoulder as he steered me towards the stand holding the kids' Man U kit, 'Which team do you want to support? You gotta have a team.' So there I was, right, looking at this rack of red shirts, thinking, I don't have a team. I'm a bit weird because, while I enjoy playing football and studying famous players' techniques, I've always found it boring to watch a whole game. Anyway, as Granddad's rifling through the Man U sizes, I've seen this yellow shirt I like. Seemed perfect as yellow is my favourite colour and this shirt has an emblem with a gun on it. I'm like, This image is sick, man. Next thing, I'm going home with an Arsenal away shirt and shorts. Granddad took it pretty well.

On the estate I became that kid in the Arsenal shirt who was always on the square outside the house playing football, either alone and practising my skills or with other kids from the estate, including Zavon Hines – Zav or Keno – a Jamaican kid who lived twenty doors down on Treherne Court. A year older than me, he was a brilliant player, man. You've probably heard of him. He went on to play for England's under-twenty-ones squad and is now a coach for West Ham United's under-fourteens team. Michael Adeusi, an angry looking kid who lived at 13, also played but wasn't allowed out as often as the rest of us, what with his parents being a bit strict and religious and that. Michael's mum, Mimi Asher, a pastor, had a heart of gold and, as I would learn over the years, unwavering patience when it came to us boys. The exception was when our football smacked her windows and she'd fly out of the house yelling, 'You boys trying to smash my windows in? Keep that ball away from this house.'

'Sorry, Pastor Mimi,' we'd shout across the court. A few minutes later our ball would smash another house, usually the front door of Mimi's neighbours at 15, where a Portuguese couple called Mary and Tony lived. Mary would come out, screaming at us in Portuguese. Her husband, who looked like Humpty Dumpty, would be waddling behind her, huffing and puffing.

Yeah, we pissed off the neighbours, but we played like professionals, one hundred per cent. The square, only half the size of a tennis court, was our pitch. We grew up scoring goals there – and that square made professional footballers of kids like Zav.

We kids would play for hours on the estate, in the square, on the field behind Nan and Granddad's, tearing up and down the slope of Treherne Court, chasing each other in and out of the blocks, up and down stairwells, along the walkways and alleyways. Football matches were interspersed with games of forty-forty, British bulldog and run-outs. We'd all stay as long as possible, but at last our parents would us in, well before it got dark. Mimi was always first off the mark, calling from her doorstep, 'Michael, come in now, please. It's dinner time.' So polite.

When Nan called me in from her kitchen window, she'd be like, 'Terroll, in you come now,' in a voice that warned, 'Don't make me do this twice'. Granddad's shout-out would be jovial, singsong, with a promise of a bacon sandwich thrown in on weekends.

Less often I'd hear, 'Terroll! Get your fucking arse in here, you little cunt. I told you not to go out of the square.' That would be my mum, and the other boys would rip the piss out of me when they heard her. Those were the innocent days, man

I became the best athlete at Christ Church and that kept me focused, at least until I started bunking off and getting into fights, especially during my final year there. Some days I couldn't be arsed with classes and I'd escape by jumping over the back gate during the mid-morning break, a manoeuvre that involved trying to dodge a forest of stinging nettles and thorn bushes before I even reached the gate. Once I had reached the other side, on Offenham Road, I'd go to the shop and buy sweets and chill for a while before heading home for lunch, when my granddad would be like, 'Why you not at school?'

''Cos they let us go for lunch early, innit,' I'd say, and he'd go make sandwiches and think no more of it. After lunch I'd sneak back into school, vaulting over the back gate again.

My first fight happened when this boy Jamie tried to rob me during art class. I would've been around nine or ten at the time. Jamie thought he was a smooth gangsta or something, rifling through my pencil case while I was over at the craft cupboard getting paints. I watched as he pulled out my ruler and calmly walked back to his desk with it and I felt this overwhelming heat rising inside me, blood gushing like molten lava through every artery, capillary and vein. Whooshing in my ears. I couldn't believe what I was seeing. This was fucking daylight robbery.

You don't touch another man's pencil case. That's street, that's beef, know what I mean? Jamie was getting it.

I dumped the pots of poster paint I'd picked and boosted over to his desk. He'd nicked my property and now he was gonna pay. I wanted to do a 'Cold Stone stunner' on him, a move my favourite wrestler, Cold Stone Steve Austin, popularised. It involved kicking your opponent in the stomach or balls, then getting them in a three-quarter face lock and sitting down fast so that they drop with you. But that didn't happen. Instead, I banged my fist into his shoulder, yelling, 'You nicked my fucking ruler,' and as I did that, he shot out of his chair and started fighting back. For a few seconds we were smacking each other about the head, as I also tried to kick him in the balls. The teacher waded in and called time, we both got detention and we were sent to separate classrooms to stop us from fighting again. I made sure I got my fucking ruler back.

That's the thing about classroom fights, they're over in no time. It's like bam, bang, bells, know what I mean? They became routine for me, though. I had a certain mentality going on. I didn't want to be that crying kid no more, fearing the next kick in the head. I was rolling with – *If you diss me you are gonna feel my wrath* – that kinda vibe.

A couple of weeks after Jamie tried to nick my ruler, this group of four brothers started on me in the toilets. 'Right, look at your hair,' one of them spat, 'You look like a girl, innit.'

'Yeah,' another bro went, 'You're in the wrong toilet.' They all started laughing then, pointing at my head, 'It's a girl, it's a girl.' They were taking the piss out of my cornrows, and that bubbling blood thing rose in me again. I thought, 'Right, we need a fight now', but I was in a confined space, outnumbered and I had to suck it up. I elbowed my way out and waited for them in the corridor.

I spotted one of the younger brothers heading into a classroom and I put one in him. I followed him into the classroom and caned him. Yeah, I just punched him one and pushed him over a table, and that was as far as I got before a teacher rocked up. Man, word travelled fast at Christ Church.

I got into a lot of fights back then, too many to remember. That said, there's one fight that will never leave my mind, but not for the blows struck or who dissed who or anything. Nah, this fight was all about its outcome. The realisation. It was about respect, and it happened at home on the Myatts Field Estate.

Michael Adeusi and I were in the square outside our houses, having a kickabout. Just Michael, me and a few other boys from the estate. It had been pissing it down for most of the day so we were skidding and slipping about a lot and the ball – a fake leather one with rips and patches – was drinking water, getting heavier. Cut to the chase, Michael, strong, even at ten years old, took a running kick at that ball, aiming straight for my head. I tried to dodge it but the ball thwacked the side of my face and I stumbled back a few steps. Regaining balance, I walked slowly towards Michael, eyeballing him, my face stinging like fuck. 'What the fuck was that?' I went, 'You wanna fight? You want a fucking fight? C'mon then.'

I could hear air pumping in and out of his nostrils, faster, faster. If he were a cartoon character, steam would be jetting from his ears. I was expecting him to swing for me, but instead he turned, sprinted back to his place, went inside and came charging out again, coming right for me, going, 'Ahh!' and waving a fucking milk carton in the air.

Chasing him was Pastor Mimi, shouting, 'Michael, get back here, Michael, stop,' her flowery dress bunched in one hand as she ran in her slippers and, as I assimilated that image, my gaze on Mimi for a split second, Michael smashed the milk carton over my head. The carton was full and exploded on impact.

Milk ran into my eyes as I shoved Michael. He shoved me back and started grabbing at me and I pushed the heel of my hand against his face, using the rest of my body weight to force him backwards, into a garden, where we fell to the ground and continued fighting. I pushed Michael into a flower bed, he pushed me out and by now we had an audience, including my mum, who grabbed the back of my T-shirt and pulled me off Michael. Mimi did the same to Michael, but we were still trying to fight. I was like a pitbull straining on its leash, drooling and trying to lash out at Michael as Mum held me back. Michael growled at me, mirroring my moves and, at that point, I just wanted to bite his fucking head. Mimi tried her best. 'Please, boys, calm down. Let's all calm down,' she said, but it was obvious neither of us were going to back down.

'Oh, fuck it, if they're gonna fight, they're gonna fight,' went Mum, 'I say we leave 'em to it.'

'OK, if you think that's the right thing to do,' Mimi said, her voice laced with apprehension. 'May the Lord have mercy on you boys.'

So, our mums let go and left us to fight. It was crazy; we fought for about two minutes, had each other in headlocks, wrestling on the grass, punching and kicking each other until our mums intervened again.

After our fight, the energy between Michael and me shifted. Before, we hadn't really clicked, even though we were the same age and both loved football. But now there was an unspoken, mutual respect. We started chilling together, playing football and computer games, going to one another's houses and doing geeky things like headstands and the Worm dance. We became best friends, brothers. I called him Mikes, he called me T. Later, we would become partners in crime.

5

ATTITUDE DETERMINES ALTITUDE

Welcome to Myatts Field, which we called Baghdad. The estate doesn't exist today – it was flattened in 2014 as part of a regeneration scheme. Yeah, head over that way now and you'll find the Oval Quarter, the posh name for a set of trendy, new-build flats that many people who lived on the old estate could never afford. But forget about that. Let me tell you about Baghdad.

The Myatts Field Estate, a mile north of Brixton town centre, was built in the 1970s. Not many pictures survive – probably because people wouldn't go near the place to take them. Looking down from above, the estate formed an irregular pentagon, the five sides made up of Mostyn Road, Akerman Road, Cowley Road, Cancell Road and Patmos Road. On the ground, it was a maze of yellow-brick maisonettes built on courts connected by concrete slopes, narrow alleys and exterior, block-style stairwells. Beneath the buildings were underground carparks (deemed too unsafe to use).

The Metropolitan Police had marked the area 'red' on its gang matrix, yet you'd rarely see a uniformed bobby on the beat there, y'get me? I once saw two uniformed officers chased off the estate by gang members, who then torched the bobbies' abandoned marked car. Yeah, uniformed police from the Territorial Support Group (TSG) would approach the estate in numbers. They routinely prowled Myatts Field, about seven officers in one van, looking for lone boys to ambush and perform brutal stop and search routines on.

Some Myatts Field residents had barred windows and doors. Thinking of it now, it looked like something from *Call of Duty*. Man, that estate was built for war. In Treherne Court, one of the stairwells even led to nowhere: seriously, at the top floor, you hit a brick wall.

We were surrounded by violence. We'd see it, hear it and we could even smell it. Ripped remnants of crime-scene tape hung off walls and dangled from lampposts with their lights that didn't work. Flowers and notes reading 'R.I.P.' were left at the spot where some victim had been shot, knifed or beaten to death. Whenever undercover police drove through the estate in their Mondeos, they were often too scared to pull over or get out. (We knew by heart all the registration plates for the undercover cars.) I'd hear gunshots, people getting mugged. Seeing someone get stabbed was the norm. Residents would only call the police to get a crime number to get their window or door fixed. The air smelled of gunpowder.

I was aware of what was going on when I was very young although, along with the other boys my age, I would do normal things like play football and video games and go to school and all that stuff. When we all started to hit the ages of eleven or twelve, however, we began to be more inspired by the older boys on the estate, the ones who had a permanent presence. Predominately black, there were dozens of them. I'd see them chilling by the wall at the end of Treherne Court and they had all the things we younger estate boys could only dream of. They wore designer clothes – Iceberg jeans and Cavalli shirts – and their thick necks were wreathed with heavy gold chains. They flaunted Jacob & Co watches and the latest trainers, drove Range Rovers and Porsches and rode fat motorbikes. You'd see them smoking weed and making rap videos. Just getting close to that energy was intoxicating. They wore New Era baseball caps and ballies, and they ruled Baghdad. They held down our ends. Those boys, aged around sixteen to twenty-two, were members of the OC gang, and we looked up to them. They were our Olders.

In time, Myatts Field would make me think of the favelas of Brazil and I was to become a product of that environment. I was soon hearing about all kinds of shit happening on the estate and I quickly got to understand that to live there, I had to be vigilant, y'know. People would be out and they'd hear a car door open and they wouldn't know if that was someone who'd come to kill them, an undercover cop come to nick them or just a regular person getting out of their car. Likewise, that knock on the door could be a police raid or it could be a pagan coming to rob, shoot or kill you for whatever reason. It might just be the postman but – wait – is it really the postman? I mean, you can buy a postman's outfit on eBay, then knock on someone's door and shoot them in the head. Myatts Field was the stuff of movies. It was a shame as, looking back, the place had so much potential. But there was so much destruction brought down on the area by people who were lost, broken, struggling.

Crime rates soared in our area. Between 2000 and 2012, Lambeth had the highest crime rate and more murders than any other London borough. One murder in particular resonated with me. It happened on rival turf, in Peckham, Southwark, and the victim would become a famous name – Damilola Taylor. I remember that death as if it happened yesterday: I was the same age as Damilola when the whole wave of knife crime started. It was a shock, like, 'Oh, shit, people are dying from knives.' We were young and impressionable and it made me sad to hear that a young boy like me had lost his life. It also made me realise that I had to protect myself, y'know? It was like a wake-up call: not everything was daffodils and roses out there.

I first got stabbed just after I'd turned eleven. Ironically, it happened at a youth club during an arts and crafts workshop. The club was just off Crewdson Road, where I would often go to play football and hang out with other kids when I stayed at Mum's. The club was one of the more positive places in the area and the art classes were run by a tall, white woman called Jane, who wore yoga pants and big scarves and rode a bike everywhere. Jane had good energy about her; she was a community hero around Brixton. Being a creative type, I enjoyed her workshops as she'd always get us making things – papier mâché models, clay animals or collages with autumn leaves. On the day I got slashed, we were learning how to make a box from a flat piece of cardboard. Jane had talked us through the process, showing us how to draw out the six sides, where the flaps should go, and how to use the Stanley knife and ruler to gently score the edges to make the box fold easily.

There was this kid called Ian sitting opposite me and, as I was scoring my lines, he said something about my materials and grabbed at a piece of card in my workspace that I had set aside to make my next box. I pushed his hand away. 'Oi, bro, get your own materials.'

'Fuck you,' he said, cartwheeled his chair across the room and powered round to me. He pushed back the sleeves of his hoodie to reveal a face of fat freckles. 'Fuck you,' he repeated, and his spit hit my lip as I jumped up and crashed my fist into his ribcage.

Although shorter than me, Ian had more weight and he was solid with it, too. We were doing that fighting thing where you just grab at one another and shuffle and spin about the place. I was trying to put him down to give him a kicking and, as we struggled, I stumbled, giving Ian the chance to shove me, forcing me backwards over the table. I felt an intense heat burning in my leg.

My first thought was, 'He's set fire to my leg. I'm on fire', as I felt the pain in my left inner thigh below my groin. But there's no smoke. 'He must be punching me. Why the fuck is this brother punching my inner thigh?'

Ian let go of me, stepping backwards to join the ring of kids who'd gathered, as Jane bustled into the frame. I felt a sogginess in my tracksuit, and, for a second I was thinking, 'Fuck, I've pissed myself.' Then I saw blood pooling on the floor around me, a Stanley knife drowning in it and I went a bit weak, y'know.

My friend Stefan and his dad Alan came with me in the ambulance. Alan kindly put himself forward as my guardian, knowing I didn't want my mum hearing that I'd been stabbed – she'd met this cool man called Dwight, who had recently moved into 51 Crewdson Road with her and Jazz, and she was in a good place. There was no way I wanted my grandparents to find out either and so Alan came with me to get butterfly stitches and I kept my mouth shut. All I was interested in doing was getting Ian back, but he got banned from the youth club and I never saw him again. I remember Jane saying I should make a statement, but I didn't want the police involved. Even at that age, I didn't trust the jakes, man. I did learn one lesson from that incident though. Yeah, I was like, 'From now on, you ain't going nowhere without a blade, Terroll.'

I had a nank hidden in my shoe on my first day at Stockwell Park School, which I nicked from my nan and granddad's kitchen drawer. In my inside blazer pocket I also had a screwdriver with a chip in its flat end that made it as dangerous as a knife. Protection, innit? In my bag was a Motorola flip-phone, a hand-me-down from Mum.

Starting secondary school was exciting and daunting at once. I liked getting done up in my new uniform of navy blazer, white shirt and a grey jumper with a green V-neck and blue-and-purple striped tie. I felt clean, smart, equipped, like I was about to do business – until I stepped into the playground and thought, 'Oh, my God, there are so many humans.' The only other person I knew was Mikes, but he'd been put in a different class. I didn't know who to speak to.

A boy asked me which 'house' I was in, and I was like, 'What the fuck?' Then some other kid pointed at my tie and said, 'You Tagus?' And I just thought, 'OK, this must be a gang thing, that's cool.'

'I guess so,' I said. Turned out Tagus wasn't a gang but the name of one of the four houses of the school, the others being Amazon, Indus and Nile, each named after great rivers of the world. Each house had its own colour – green for Tagus, Nile was blue, Amazon got yellow and red for Indus. It was crazy, like some Harry Potter thing. We even had a school motto: 'Attitude determines altitude'.

Despite getting into a few fights here and there, I settled into Stockwell Park pretty well. I joined the school football team as left-back and got involved in athletics. PE was definitely my favourite subject, thanks to our teacher, Miss Robson. I had a lot of respect for her. She was involved, she was active. An older lady, no taller than five feet, her presence made her seem huge, y'know. She reminded me of some kind of military figure. She was so strict, a little white lady who had no trouble keeping a bunch of Brixton boys in line. Anybody who remembers Miss Robson will tell you she never took no shit off no one. She'd push you, tell you to shut up and kick you out of class if you were being a dick. But Miss Robson had a good heart, man. When she wasn't giving you the storm she would properly sit down and chat to you. She'd make time for you, she'd listen. Wow, Miss Robson … I'd love to see her again.

Ms Tapper was gaffer of the school. She was one angry, angry head teacher who served punishments just for the sake of it. I couldn't get my head around that. She'd stand in assembly every morning, barking, 'Attitude determines altitude,' and I couldn't understand why she looked so pissed off, like she was fed up with life. She'd trawl through the school's CCTV footage for evidence of kids getting up to naughtiness – smoking behind the bike sheds, fighting, bullying, stuff like that – and would play the clips on a big screen during assembly. She would single out the offenders and bollock them in front of the whole school, man. One time I made it onto the big screen, only her plan to humiliate me blew up in her world-weary face. She had, she announced during assembly, discovered video evidence of me doing step-overs down the corridor.

'This is first-year pupil Terroll Lewis,' Ms Tapper said, pausing the footage and nodding at the screen, 'and not only is he breaking school rules by playing with a football – a *football* – inside the school building, but he did so during lesson time.' She said it as if I'd been caught with a MAC-10 instead of a football. 'Totally irresponsible. Another pupil could've been injured,' Tappers went on, while I sat there with my head down. 'Don't. You. Ever. Do. That. Again.'

Mikes was sitting next to me, rattling and snorting. I looked up, clocked myself on the screen, and other kids were looking at me as if to say, 'Yeah, that shit's really cool,' and I had to admit, I did look pretty good up there. Yeah, Tappers had done me proud. By showing the clip she'd boosted my credit, boosted my ratings in the school. From then on, I was known as the football guy, the cool guy. On the way out of the assembly hall, Mikes spudded me. 'Rah, that was sick, bro,' he said.

I jutted my chin. 'Rah, attitude determines altitude, innit.'

To look at us there, you wouldn't think that Mikes and me were the same two boys who'd been fighting in the flower bed just over a year ago. Nah, we were tight now, man, inseparable. We'd walk to school together, walk home together, talking about *Mortal Kombat* or *Grand Theft Auto* or football. Sometimes we'd talk about girls we fancied at school, but, one hundred per cent, our favourite topic was gang stuff. We were obsessed with anything OC: who was who among the Olders, who'd been stabbed or shot, who'd gone to prison and what was this beef all about with the Peckham Boys?

Pastor Mimi's house became my second home. I was always at Mike's, playing video games with him and his two younger brothers, Josh and Peter. Through Mikes, I met Karl Lokko, who was also our age and gangster-mad. Karl lived on the Mandela Estate on the outskirts of Myatts Field, but it seemed he spent more time on our estate. Karl, naturally intelligent, was into his rapping, and, at six feet tall and powerfully built, looked like one of the Olders already. His parents were originally from Ghana and had known Mimi for years. As is customary between close African households, they called each other family. Karl and Mikes were 'cousins' and Mimi was 'Aunty Mimi'. I called her Aunty too, as that was only polite.

Mikes' dad, also a Michael, wasn't home much, which was a good thing as he was a stern motherfucker: we'd be chilling at Mimi's, playing a video game, and Michael would march in, 'Michael, come here now. I hear you've been bad at school. You will be punished.' He'd glance at me next, 'Terroll, it's time for you to go. Pack your stuff,' and I'd be thinking, 'Why's this guy so rude?' Sometimes, he'd make Mikes, Josh and Peter stand on their tiptoes or squat in an uncomfortable position for a long time. I'd jump out the back window at that stage, thinking, 'I can't be doing with that energy'.

Pastor Mimi was firm but she was happy, if that makes sense. Ah, that woman; I could have ten thousand pounds in my hands and still not be as happy as Mimi. Sometimes, she would have no gas or electric left, with no money to feed the meter and still she'd be smiling. And, man, could she cook. Bare magic happened in her kitchen. At home, Nan cooked basic meat and veg meals like toad-in-the-hole and stuff, but Mimi introduced me to African food. She'd make everything from scratch, too, from Ga kenkey, garri and moin moin, to her celebrated 'egusi stew'. First time Aunty Mimi gave me a bowl of jollof rice, I was like, 'Wow, what is this stuff?' I'd never seen orange rice before. Then I tasted it and I was, 'Rah, this is my favourite rice now.' It smelt like a restaurant in that house. Mimi always had a pot or two of something on the stove and she would make enough to feed me and Karl and any of our friends who'd often chill at hers. You could tell she took great pleasure in cooking for us, and she treated all of Mikes' friends as though they were her own kids. She even called us her babies. Mimi would become a community hero in Brixton, helping young people to leave gangs by introducing them to projects run by the Word of Grace Ministries, the evangelical church that she founded.

I was happy living on the estate. It seems contradictory, but a place that was dangerous also felt secure and homely. I felt safe indoors with my grandparents – eating that toad-in-the-hole or that bubble-and-squeak, watching *Match of the Day* with Granddad and doing chores around the home to earn my pocket money. Out of the home I would be going to Mikes' place, feeling the love from Mimi and playing video games with my friends ... all good stuff, man.

I wasn't the only boy to come from a broken home. There were other kids like me who had to move in with their grandparents on the estate. Some had come from violent backgrounds and had parents with drug problems or parents who were in prison, that kinda stuff. Actually, compared to the shit some of my friends went through, I was one of the luckier kids. Not only did I have loving grandparents, but my mum was beginning to be around for me more by that time. She was also with Dwight, who had become a stepdad figure to me. He was chilled, a polite guy who always made an effort to talk whenever I visited. Respect to that brother for accepting me. Nevertheless, as I grew older, I began to think about Pups.

It used to be that whenever Pups would creep into my thoughts I'd pull down the shutters, y'know. Now I felt a strong urge to see him, to have a conversation. I wondered whether he'd been thinking about me too. Mum had only ever told me bad things about him, but what if he'd changed? What if he was desperate to rebuild a relationship with his son? I began to believe that I had to see him. Mum didn't agree.

'I don't think it'll help you, T,' she said, but agreed to contact Terence on my behalf. 'I don't want you getting your hopes up, though.'

A few weeks later, I went with Mum to meet Pups in Villa Park. We didn't tell Nan and Granddad as they would only have worried. They had no time for Terence.

Our reunion happened in nearby Max Roach Park, Villa Road. It was April 2002. Pups was waiting for us by the spider climbing-frame. He looked different, smaller. Or was that because I'd grown? His locks were gone, his hair now in a fade-cut and, when he saw me, his face broke into this massive smile. It was a smile I'd never seen on him before, man. Still loud as ever though. 'Hey, son, wagwan, good to see you,' he said, arms outstretched.

'Yo, Pups,' I said, then he hugged me. His hoodie smelt of weed. We played on the monkey bars and he chased me over the spider frame, laughing. You could probably hear him from Brixton. After half-an-hour or so, he kissed me goodbye and told me he loved me.

'You gonna come and stay with me some time?' he asked.

I nodded. 'Yes, please.'

I would go to stay with him from time to time over the coming years but my more immediate father figures were Granddad – and the Olders.

Mikes and me studied the Olders closely and got to know their street names. Some of them we knew already from playing football. Many of them knew my mum and my grandparents.

Three of them – Tuffy, Albz and Hulk – lived in Treherne Court and would play football with us younger ones from time to time. Albz was sick at football and encouraged me a lot. 'Oi, Arsenal top, looking good, man,' he'd shout across the court and hearing that would make my day. Hulk was only five-feet-two but built like a tank, hence his nickname.

Dread (real name Aaron Simpson), Sabz and Stinks were also faces we knew well. Dread was tough, a really good fighter, adept in martial arts. He would challenge other Olders to attack him, just so he could practice his fighting skills. He could take on up to six Olders a time and still be the last man standing. We'd see the Olders out on the block, night and day, and me and Mikes, in our New Era caps and dusty Brixton-boy tracksuits, knives tucked in our trainers, would loiter in their space. Watching, learning, admiring, trying to get our faces on camera when they filmed music videos on the estate. We were thirteen and dying to be recognised by these cool guys. We soaked up their energy, listened to the way they spoke. How they emphasised the 'O' when they chanted '*OC*'. Once, during a shoot on the block, I heard Stinks say, 'Buss your gun and run when you see me,' meaning, 'Take a shot at me, then run.' And, swear down, hearing that, it was like God speaking to me. About a week later, I got caught up in that shootout near the Hills.

6

THE OLDERS

I was hungry, man. Seeing the Olders in action, hearing the gunfire, *surviving* the gunfire, made me respect those guys even more. As far as I knew, the OC guys also survived the shootout, although any one of them could easily have been killed or injured.

But in my mind it was like this: Those guys risked their lives out there. They did that for me, for my family, for our neighbours, for our estate. They put themselves in the firing line to protect Myatts Field, to fight for our Baghdad and hold down the block, 'cos that's all that we have: our estate and each other. Those guys are soldiers and I wanna be one of them. I wanna represent my ends. I *wanna* be OC.

I started playing football with the Olders; Albz even invited me to their weekly games at the floodlit pitch near the Hills and soon they knew me for my skills with the ball. I had no fear; I didn't care that the Olders were all bigger. I'd steam right in and tackle. I'd go against them, know what I mean? I was *proving* myself. The Olders respected me and encouraged me to keep training.

Whenever I passed Albz or Sabz on Treherne Court, they'd say, 'Yo, T, how's the football going, man? You're playing well, bro.' Then they'd ask, 'How're Mick and Rose doing? How's your mum?' I'd play it cool, y'know, pull down my New Era cap and shrug a bit.

'Yeah, tings are good, man,' I'd say, then once they'd turned the corner my face would explode into a massive smile. Like I said, I was hungry. I wanted to get involved. If something happened again on the block, I wanted to be in the mix. One hundred per cent.

Tuffy was a huge inspiration, for his biking skills alone. You'd see him riding down the block stairs on his pedal bike and he would rip through the estate on his orange Kawasaki Ninja motorbike, doing wheelies and jumps. We'd all get excited when we heard the roar of Tuffy's Ninja. Once, Tuffy let me take a photo of that motorbike. I've still got it somewhere.

After school, Mikes and me could never wait to go find the Olders. It wasn't difficult; we knew we'd just need to follow the road-rap pumping from their car speakers, and the smell of weed. We would boost home, change into our tracksuits and Nike trainers, put on our New Era caps, grab our armour (usually a knife from the kitchen drawer) and go to the railings to find estate bikes. These bikes, as their name suggests, could belong to anyone – you'd just be borrowing them. On Myatts Field, you could always leave your bike outside, unlocked. You ain't gonna get your bike nicked 'cos outsiders and pagans ain't welcome on this estate, y'get me? Bikes were essential for us to do shop runs for the Olders. Holding down the block took energy and smoking weed gave them the munchies and that meant the guys would want cans of juice and crisps and sweets, which was where we utes came in.

When the Olders spotted us on our bikes, they'd call out, 'Yo, who wants to go shop?'

And we'd all be like, 'I'll go shop.' It gave us a buzz, made us feel useful. There was money in it too. I could triple my pocket money in one week.

'Yo, go shop, T,' one of the Olders would say, peeling a tenner from a wad of notes, 'Give man ten pounds. Get man Doritos and Ribena. Yo, keep change.'

I'd slam the pedals over to Saji's shop on Foxley Square, on the edge of the estate. Saji's Budget Food and Wine was a store you'd expect to find in the Bronx, man. Everything, including chewing gum, was kept behind bars. You had to tell Saji what you wanted and he'd pass the items through one of those counter drawers you get in the post office. It was crazy but, then again, running a shop on the Myatts Field Estate was a wild thing to do. Saji was cool.

Mikes, Karl and me would pretend we were OC already – when we were safely outside Myatts Field itself. It wouldn't have been cool for the Olders to find out. But, yeah, we'd be in Brixton or Stockwell or wherever and in the street we were like, '*OC, OC*', and 'We're from Baghdad, Myatts Field. Fuck Peckham,' stuff like that. It was all about the attitude. We knew people were looking at us thinking, 'Those guys are from Myatts Field, they're gang members', and we played on that. We came up with street names. Mikes and Karl suggested Don Boost or just Boost for me – because I was the athletic one who could run fast. Mikes – who had a reputation for instigating fights – became Mad Mikes. And Karl's street name would be Lox, an abbreviation of his surname.

We had affiliates, too, other kids our age who shared our OC ambition. They included Troopz, who lived on the estate with his nan, Alex Mulumba, otherwise known as Tiny Alien or just Tiny A, Shellz, Syikes, Abz and Ratty (real name Nicholas Clarke).

One Saturday, I went into Frank Johnson with Lox and Mikes and we spotted this navy-and-light-blue striped hat and we all agreed, 'Yo, this is the OC hat.' Again, we didn't tell the Olders, though they must've noticed we were all going about the estate in the same bobble hat. It would have been an innocuous item of clothing for most people but, to us, it was one step closer to a green bandanna and balaclava.

The Olders drummed their mantra into us, 'Don't forget where you're from. You're Myatts Field, Bagdhad.' OC was all about protecting its territory. It was a postcode thing. By now we knew that OC's biggest rivals, the pagans, the Other Side, were the Peckham Boys. It was a rivalry that had existed for generations, one that I'd encountered even away from gang life. I noticed it playing football. There would nearly always be a fight after a match. We were known as Baghdad and Peckham's nickname was Peck-narm, or '*Narm,* as they'd say on the road.

One Saturday morning, Mikes and me were walking past the playground in the centre of the estate when we saw some yardie running along Crawshay Court ahead of us. He looked as though he was running from the police, heading towards the Hills. You could hear and see his breath in the cold January air and, as he raced by, he dropped a package that slapped the ground. Mike got to it first, picked it up. It was a black polythene bag, knotted.

'Smells like weed,' I said, as Mike untied the handles.

Inside was another clear, zip-seal bag. Even without opening it you got a waft of the strong odour of green – the woman with a pram a hundred yards or so along the path was probably able to smell it. Mikes slipped the bag under his coat and we sprinted into the nearest block, up the communal stairs to the walkway at the top. We gave it a few seconds, checked the coast was clear – no sign of the jakes or yardie-boy – then had a proper look at our wares. The zip bag was packed with buds, about an ounce of the stuff, possibly more.

'The fuck we gonna do with this lot?' Mikes asked, his brown eyes glowing beneath the brim of his OC bobble hat. I pulled my hat further over my ears, grabbed the zip bag and shoved it firmly down my balls.

'Chill, man, we'll take it to the Olders,' I said.

Calmly, we headed back onto the court and straight into the path of the yardie who'd dropped the package that was currently wedged in my boxers. He was crouched by the overflowing wheelie bin in the recess next to the stairs, rummaging through a pile of litter. He leapt up when he saw us. 'Yo, you seen a bag? I lost a bag, man.'

I pulled a confused face and said I didn't know what he was on about.

'Yeah,' added Mikes, 'Nah, we've been in the house, innit. Not seen no bag, man.' We walked on towards Foxley Square and bumped into an Older called Smoker, known for always smoking weed on the block. He was a clean-hearted brother, about seventeen or eighteen and very chilled. We showed him our bag of weed as, true to his name, he pulled on his spliff, exhaled, and we told him where we found the stash.

'Rah, I'll take that off ya,' he went, his words fogged in a cloud of cannabis. 'Give man fifty for it.'

'Sorted,' said Mikes.

I bopped my head. 'Yeah, fifty's cool,' I added, thinking, Not bad work for fourteen-year-old boys.

Me and Mikes felt like we'd won the fucking lottery and we decided that there was no better time than now to buy a lottery ticket, right? We dissected the events of our lucky accident as we walked to Saji's and reached a unanimous verdict: there was fucking good money to be made in drugs.

Our numbers didn't come in on the lottery, but me and Mikes were deffo on a winning streak. A week later, we were floating on the estate, just chilling in Treherne Court, when Stinks hit the corner, looking cool as ever in his designer swag and chains, white cap worn to the side. A walk that said, 'Touch me 'n' I'll put ten in you.'

'Hey, T, hey, Mikes, you good?' and we were like, yeah, we're good, man, and Stinks just put out his hand and said, 'Y'know, you guys are OC now. Swear down.' He put his index finger to his thumb and made an 'O', curved the rest of his fingers into a 'C' and slapped his hand against mine. He did the same to

Mikes then walked off. We stood there for a moment, staring at our hands, both holding the OC position. Mikes was the first to speak.

'Rah, we're *OC* now,' he said.

I stretched out my words, still gawping at my initiated hand, thinking, I'm never washing this hand again. 'Yeah … we are.'

7

THE YOUNGERS

Me and my friends began to take ourselves seriously, y'know. Calling us 'OC', Stinks had set off a ripple that brought about a change in Mikes and me, one hundred per cent. Like, we began to walk differently, with a bit of a bop and a bit of a bounce. Now we were officially repping and protecting Baghdad.

Lox, Troopz, Syikes, Ratty, Shellz, Abz and Tiny Alien also became certified OC members around the same time. Our group was part of an army of Youngers that included boys from Kennington, Stockwell and Camberwell. The weapons we carried were no longer restricted to kitchen knives but included broken bottles, dog chains, bike D-locks, anything we could lay our hands on. We were part of a team, a family. We'd become OC Youngers and we were prepared to give our lives for the gang and for our estate.

Our OC duties included what we called 'border patrol'. Yeah, we'd literally circle the block, looking for pagans we didn't recognise and say, 'Where's your passport?' It was also known as G-checking. Everybody wanted to be OC and you had to be someone to come through Myatts Field, or you had to know someone who knew someone. Like, you couldn't just pull up in a car. Someone we didn't know could be a set-up chick or a police snitch, y'know. When we saw a car park up on the estate for a smoke break or something, the driver would soon be hearing the tap, tap, tap of metal on their window.

They lower their window and the boy outside will go 'Yo, what you doing round here? Who you on the phone to? You lot gotta cut, you've gotta go.' If they don't leave, they're gonna start seeing knives and hammers. Yeah, that was normal. A gun in the face was the equivalent of us sticking our middle fingers up at someone. Civilians passing through might be OK but they would be stopped, nonetheless. Come in with a camera, and have that camera on show, then the owner might be told to get on their way, but their camera or phone would stay with us.

Mikes was mental. He'd bring his two evil dogs out on border patrol, man, Brooklyn, a red-nosed pitbull and Colonel, an English bull terrier mixed with a pitbull. Colonel had the personality of a serial killer, y'know. I've still got scars on my ankles where that dog bit me. Anyway, Mikes would actually set those two dogs on people he didn't recognise.

We were always on the lookout for Pokémon players to rob and we'd sell the collectable cards on for fifteen quid a pop. We'd go up to people and say, 'Rah, what have you got? Show us your Pokémons.' We'd just hit the cards out of their hands. Phones were a target for robbing too, although that wasn't really my thing. Mikes was a pro: he'd grab a phone, take out the SIM card and hand it back to the owner. Yeah, Myatts Field was a wild place if you didn't live there.

I adapted so well to the OC lifestyle that I didn't even notice the transition. Crazy, now I think about it. I'd go to school as normal, do chores around the home to earn my pocket money, take Jet for walks – sadly, Dalinger had died – and play football on the estate and for the school team. Lox and me would go to Mikes', eat Mimi's food and play video games and have nerdy conversations about space travel and stuff. At all times I would carry the knowledge with me that whatever I was doing – maybe just walking to the shop – there was the chance that somebody might shoot me in the back of the head. It was that real. There were no stages between playing street games and becoming a gangster. None.

It did take me slightly longer to get into carrying guns myself. I was probably about fourteen or fifteen when I began to progress into that business. It's kinda similar to buying a second-hand car. You need to know who to go to, who to trust. A gun needs to be in good working order. You have to know what questions to ask, like, 'Does it come with teet?' In time, I wouldn't go anywhere without my burner in my waistband, y'know what I'm saying? I would feel naked without my gun, unprotected.

I got cautioned for possession of a firearm when I was fourteen. I had found this canister at the back of Mikes' house during the summer holidays and I was unsure what it was, at first. It looked like a big can of deodorant and it had a heavy-duty nozzle. There was some writing on the side of the can but it was too faded to make out. Nonetheless, thinking that it might make a good little weapon, I pocketed it and went about my business. It was a scorcher of a day and, instead of going into Mikes' to play video games with him and Lox, Ratty and Zav, I headed to the playground. Nice day for a walk, y'know. As I was leaving, I saw Troopz coming across the square. I showed him the can.

'Yo, what d'ya reckon this is?'

Troopz grabbed the can, rolled it in his hands and gave it a shake.

'CS gas, man. Pepper spray, innit,' he said.

I snatched the can back before he got any ideas and spudded him.

'Cool, see you later, bro.'

Pepper spray, that was no big deal, right? I mean, women carry the stuff around in their handbags to fend off would-be muggers and rapists. I'd seen CS gas used in the movies. Rah, people can walk around with this stuff, I thought, studying the can again when I reached the park. Yeah, definitely a handy weapon.

Two undercover police cars pulled up out of nowhere, cornering me between the park and the slope leading up to Treherne Court. Two officers jumped out one of the cars while the others kept watch. I was stopped and searched by jobsworth jakes for being in possession of an 'illegal firearm'. Were they shitting me? Initially, I found it funny.

'It's a can of pepper spray,' I said, as they started patting me down, but they kept insisting that the can was a firearm. I'd need to accompany them to the station, they said and I got in the back of one of the Mondeos, laughing to myself.

Sure, I'd go with them. I wasn't scared. I mean, this was pepper spray, for fuck's sake, not a sub-machine gun.

Fear kicked in once I was inside Kennington police station and the situation rapidly became serious. I was taken to a small room in which were a table and chairs bolted to the floor. They said that CS spray is classified as a firearm and I was, like, 'You're joking me.' I'd never been pulled into a police station before. I didn't know what was going on.

They played the good-cop/bad-cop routine as they went through the formalities. They were gonna interview me, but, first, did I want a lawyer?

And I'm sitting there, looking around the room, thinking, I'm going to jail. Pepper spray's gonna put me in jail. I should've gone to Mikes. Did I want a lawyer? What was this, fucking *CSI*? Am I going court or what? I started getting angry, 'Listen, I found that can. I didn't even know what it was. You say it's CS gas, then you're telling me it's a firearm. What is this, some kind of fit-up?'

'We'll arrange for the duty solicitor to see you,' said 'Good Cop'.

'Bad Cop' added, 'In the meantime, you've been found to be in possession of a firearm, so we'll be detaining you here at the station.'

They hauled me down to the cells, man. I found myself in this hot, windowless room that smelled of piss and sewage. The door was locked behind me with a loud, metallic clunk and then 'Good Cop' put his face in the little window in the door and said the duty solicitor was on his way. The window slammed shut and the hours dragged by torturously. There was nothing in that cell aside from a concrete bed, a scratchy blanket and pillow and a toilet behind a brick partition. There was no toilet paper and the overhead lights were dull, one of them flickering, fucking with my head.

I was dehydrated; I couldn't breathe properly; I had a headache. There was a lack of oxygen in that cell, know what I'm saying? On the ceiling was graffiti asking, 'Are you sick and tired of feeling sick and tired?' And I kept reading this over and over again, thinking, 'Yes, I'm sick *and* tired.' It was like death in there.

It was in the early hours of the morning that the duty solicitor finally showed up. He confirmed the jakes' claim that CS gas was indeed classified as a firearm but said, at worst, I'd probably get a caution. I told the interviewing officers that I'd found the canister near the park and thought it was pepper spray and they did only caution me. I was finally released around 7 a.m. and the jakes said they didn't want to see me in the station again. And I'm like, Yeah, you and me both.

Granddad was there to meet me as I was underage and the police had to tell my family. It was he who had taken the call and, fortunately, he told Nan it was me phoning to say that I was staying at Mikes' house. I told Granddad the arrest was a big misunderstanding. 'I just found it in the park,' I claimed.

'Don't get caught again, son,' was Granddad's final words on the matter.

Spending a night in that cell served as a warning: if I was to get more into gang activity, I'd need to be tactical, strategic and think smartly about how I moved. That was the plan but, inevitably, being pulled by the police and going court became normal occurrences for our circle.

I was at Mikes' one day, chilling in his living room, when Colonel started doing his serial killer act, ready to rip someone to fucking ribbons though, thankfully, not me this time. He went for the door and attacked its curtains, clawing and trying to bite the fabric and we heard this banging on the door window, accompanied by muffled shouting. Mikes grabbed Colonel by his collar with one hand, and as the dog thrashed about, whipped aside one of the curtains with his other hand, bringing him face-to-face with our friend Mark, frantically brandishing his hands in police handcuffs. Mikes threw Colonel out, pulled Mark in, locked the door and shut the curtains.

Mark, brown skin slick with sweat, caught his breath, 'Fuck, you gotta get me out of these cuffs, man.' He was yanking his wrists apart, trying to break the chain.

'Yo, keep your voice down, my mum's upstairs, innit,' said Mikes.

'Sorry, man,' said Mark, the cuffs clanking.

'Fuck's sake. Stay there, I'll get tools.'

Seconds later, Mikes was back with a pair of pliers. Fortunately, Mimi was upstairs, hoovering the bedrooms as the chaos started, but, as Mikes pointed out, 'she could come down any second now'. The small toilet next to the kitchen seemed like the safest place to bust Mark's cuffs as he, a fellow OC Younger, described how he managed to escape from Camberwell Green youth court. I sat on the toilet lid, watching, as Mikes crunched and twisted the pliers around the chain connecting the cuffs.

Mark became more and more agitated. 'It ain't working. Man got metal cutters?' he said. I rolled off a length of toilet paper, bunched it over my nose. The smell of stale sweat above the apple Glade was killing me, man.

'Keep still and shut the fuck up,' was Mikes' response and, while I found the whole scenario amusing, I was also a bit panicky, y'know? No more than two weeks had passed since the pepper spray craziness. *Jakes might not be as lenient this time.*

'Yo, Mikes,' I said, 'We're gonna get in trouble y'know.'

'Yeah,' he went, his voice loaded with exertion, 'We'd better start doing press-ups y'know.'

Mark leaned over the sink, grasping its lip, hands wide, keeping the chain taut, with Mikes below him, trying to bust the chain with the pliers. The sink began to wobble with the force, then – chink, thud – the chain snapped and Mikes fell backwards on his arse, still gripping the pliers.

Mark lifted his free hands. 'Yo, result, blud,' and that's when we heard sirens, followed by Mimi, screaming, 'Michael?'

Mimi's house was surrounded by jakes.

Mark had no option other than to go out the front and get arrested. Me and Mikes watched from the door with Mimi, who was, like, 'What in God's name is happening?' All the neighbours had gathered for a look, too. Mark was re-cuffed and bundled into a police van, his prison-break over.

Turned out Mark's escape bid had been caught on CCTV, with cameras clocking him as he ran from the court, through Myatt's Fields park and onto the estate. Police officers came into Mimi's to take statements from me and Mikes and we acted like we didn't know what was going on. 'Our friend just showed up here,' I said, 'We were scared 'cos he was in handcuffs, but we didn't know what was going on until afterwards.'

'Yeah,' agreed Mikes, 'Obviously, if we'd known what was going on, then we probably would've handled the whole thing differently, y'get me?'

'Listen though, *she* had nothing to do with this,' I added, pointing at Mimi.

We got away with that one.

The Olders looked out for us Youngers. We were their siblings, following in their footsteps. Stinks, one of OC's founders and leading figures at that time, would take big groups of us Youngers on shopping sprees to Footlocker and JD Sports and buy us all trainers. The Olders taught us strategies, how to move and they saw our potential as street boys and gave respect and credit where it was due. It could be tough love, though. Like, if the Olders got wind of us fucking up, then they'd give us a proper bollocking. Some of us, myself included, found this out the hard way.

Mikes, Lox, Troopz and me had a madness with a few boys in Stockwell one time. We were on our pedal bikes, cruising about, and we ended up in a street off Stockwell Road. It was lined with posh Victorian townhouses with neat front gardens and shit. About ten white and black lads were chilling and they immediately started on us. 'Oi, where you from, what's your name?' We stopped riding and glared at them. Troopz' hands flew to the dog chain around his neck (Troopz always rolled with a dog chain – that was his thing).

'What the fuck did you say?' he said, lifting the chain over his head. I knew what was coming.

'Yeah, wanna know where we're from?' Mikes chimed in, 'We're from Baghdad, Myatts Field. *OC*.'

'Oh, yeah, where's that then?' one of the other boys said, smirking.

I mean, how dared they fucking ask where we're from?

Troopz steamed in first and licked one of the boys in the face with his chain, blood spurting from his opponent's nose. Lox was next in, taking on about three guys at once, punching, kicking and slamming one in the head with a D-lock. Lox had a longer reach than the rest of us, being so tall. I sprung from my bike, heaved it into the air and threw it at the boy nearest to me, then ran at him and kicked him in the chest. As he hit the ground, I jumped on top of him but while we were punching each other, one of his boys kicked me in the side of the head. Mikes was smashing another boy to bits. The fight spilled into the gardens.

There was a lot of jumping over walls and fences, wheelie bins getting tipped over, everyone a bit bloodied and battered. We were outnumbered and, after about five minutes, we got tired, although we were good, confident fighters.

'Yo, let's get outta here,' I called, ducking a weary fist. The adrenaline had worn off.

We grabbed our bikes and rode back to Myatts Field. It was no big deal. A fight was just part of the day, even though this one had got a bit too much.

Back in the area we bumped into Jaf, an Older. He was coming out of Saji's shop as we were about to go in. He started laughing when he saw us. 'What the fuck happened to you lot?' he said, busting open a bag of pickled onion Monster Munch.

'Had a fight with some boys in Stockwell,' said Lox, bits of garden stuck in his hair, raw graze on his cheekbone.

'Oh, yeah, what happened? Who were they?' went Jaf. He had to tilt his head back to make eye contact with Lox.

'Dunno, but there were loads of 'em, man.' That was Mikes, wiping his bloody nose, while Troopz and I bopped our heads, going, 'Yeah, man.'

I had a few nicks and grazes on my arms and face. Troopz looked pretty much untouched though.

Jaf shoved the bag of crisps into his baggy jeans pocket and gave us a look that was either, 'I'm gonna kill myself laughing here', or 'I'm gonna grab my hammer'. It was hard to tell at that point. He touched the spliff behind his ear, almost as if he was making sure it was still there. 'Hold on,' he said, 'You lot run, then?'

'Fuck, there were like twelve or more of those fuckers, man.' Mikes again.

Jaf did a double-take, then burst out laughing. I'll never forget that laugh, saturated with mockery and menace. Sounded like the Joker in *Batman*. 'Are you lot stupid?' he said, 'Are you fucking stupid?' Silence. Even Mikes was lost for words. 'I mean, do

you lot not know where you're from? You are *OC*. You're from
Myatts Field, Baghdad. You don't run away from fights.' Jaf
released his spliff and sparked up, then walked away, laughing
that laugh again.

We filed into Saji's. Our fucking tails were between our legs,
y'know?

'He fucking took the piss out of us,' said Mikes. 'Took the
fucking piss.'

I nodded. I was stewing. 'Listen, man,' I said, 'From now on
we've gotta deal with our problems ourselves. Fight our own
battles. No running to the Olders for help. Fuck that shit.'

I was serious, man. There was no way I was getting laughed
at again. No way. Y'know what I'm saying?

8

REMEMBER MY NAME

I've always loved being in a team, going against other teams; working together to push through and beat the other side.

In the beginning, when I was around ten or eleven, I wanted to become the best footballer in the world. I'd study Ronaldo's moves and Ronaldinho dribbling down the pitch. Those boys were my inspiration, y'know? Then I got involved in the streets and things changed. Sure, I still wanted to be the best footballer in the world, but I also wanted to be the best gang member in south-west London, right? And suddenly, I'm not studying Ronaldo so much as watching videos of .45 calibres shooting out of pistols.

There are parallels between a football team and a gang. Both have players with positions to play – attackers and defenders. Football is all about energy and tactics; technique and power. It's about scoring while preventing the other side from scoring – protecting your side. Players are put on a pedestal when they score or save a goal. Likewise, when your gang mates hear how you licked over that pagan, your name's gonna be ringing in the ends. One hundred per cent. A team can lose or win, players get injured. The same applies to a gang, right? Score, defend, earn respect and get injured.

All well and good, but the outcome of gang warfare isn't so cut and dry as win or lose. It's live or die, kill or be killed. Sometimes it can mean a lifetime in jail.

Street gangs, like football teams, often have colours, too. Each gang's members would wear bandanas in their colour. The OC colour was green I actually introduced our gang to green bandanas. Yeah, I bought three – one each for Lox, Mikes and me - from a shop on Brixton Road. Lox took the piss at first, but I told him, 'Don't mock man's ideas,' y'know. The trend caught on; even the Olders started wearing green bandanas.

Peckham's colour was black, but there were several other active gangs in the area too. 031 (pronounced 'O-Tray One') operates predominately in Wandsworth, and associates with red. Whenever we'd see them out in their numbers it was like a sea of blood gushing down the street. The 031 gang is an amalgamation of the former blood gangs, G. Street (based in Wandsworth Road) and Corleone Family Riderz (CFR), who operated in the Loughborough and Angell Town areas. SUK, an abbreviation for 'Stick 'Em Up Kids' covered Clapham Junction and Battersea and wore yellow bandanas. I got along well with some of the SUK boys. Stockwell Hot Spot's colour was blue. OC was also tight with members of the Trust No One (TN1) gang in Tulse Hill. They were a good bunch of boys.

Despite occasional standoffs and fights, there was never bad trouble between the SW gangs: we had mutual respect. Once a year, we would all head to Brockwell Park for the Lambeth Country Show. Held over two days in July, it was a massive community festival, attracting a hundred thousand people. There was a music stage, markets selling food from all different cultures, farmers parading their cattle about and doing crazy stuff like sheep-shearing, and a fun-fair with candy floss machines, win-a-goldfish stalls, bumper cars and all the rides and shit. It was about people of all different ages and cultural backgrounds coming together for a fun day out at the park. We wouldn't want to be bumping into any south-east Londoners though. They had their own fun-fair thing in Burgess Park.

Nah, the Lambeth Country Show belonged to SW, man, and if the Other Side dared to slip into Brockwell Park, lives could be lost, y'know what I'm saying?

I went to the 2004 show with my boy Syikes and a few utes we knew from Brixton. They weren't OC members but they were kinda in the mix, dabbled in stuff. We didn't head out looking for trouble that day; I wasn't even armed, a schoolboy gangland error. Nah, we were thinking about getting some girls. I was fourteen and the testosterone was kicking in, innit.

Aside from flirting with Sherise from the Cowley Estate, I'd been in only one relationship. Though, on reflection, my thing with Daniella Baker didn't exactly cut it as a relationship. More of a playground romance; y'know, a bit whirlwind. She was a cute mixed-race girl in my class and I'd fancied her for a while but had been too shy to act on it until Tapper showed that footage of me doing step-overs to the whole school. My new-found fame as a cool-kid footballer gave me a confidence boost. I cornered her mate Sarah in the corridor before registration.

'Yo, listen,' I said, 'tell your friend Daniella I want to go out with her.'

My charm worked. By the end of registration, Daniella and I were 'going out' (which meant we were boyfriend and girlfriend). We spent our lunch hour together, walking to one of those shops with a sign in its window warning, 'Only two school children allowed at one time'. I bought her a packet of Love Hearts and she gave me one of them, reading, 'My Boy', and I thought, Rah, I'm on a promise here. We had a bit of an awkward kiss and cuddle against a wall on Clapham Road and went back to school. That afternoon, I sat next to her in double-English and we played footsie under the desks. After school I offered to walk Daniella home.

'Or we could just chill for a while somewhere?' I suggested as we made our way across the playground to the gates.

I was expecting her to give me another Love Heart or something cute like that but, instead, she stopped and, flicking her long hair over one shoulder, looked at me and said, 'Listen, Terroll, I think you're really cool an' all that, but I don't think this is working out. I don't want us to be girlfriend and boyfriend anymore.'

Bullets, man, bullets. I was a bit stunned, y'know, although I took dem bullets like a man, shrugging my shoulders and telling her everything was cool.

The memory of Daniella popped back into my head as I stood by a burger van in Brockwell Park with Syikes and the boys, our bikes next to us on the ground. I was thinking about how cool it would be to bump into her and for her to see me looking hard with my bunch of boys. Almost two years had passed since our fling but I still carried a torch for her, probably because I saw her every day at school. I was wearing a nice pair of jeans and Nike trainers. My hair was in a neat fade-cut and I was developing a few muscles from all the training I was doing. My green bandana hung out of my back pocket, ready to be whipped out and used as a mask if necessary. Yeah, I was like, 'You should see me now, Daniella'.

My fleeting daydream swiftly dissolved when one of the Brixton utes, Steve, came sprinting over. It had been almost half-an-hour since he'd gone off for a piss. Syikes and the others were stoned. Steve was sweating, out of breath. 'Fuck about,' he said, his head whipping right to left, left to right, 'Just spoke to a brother. He says opps tried to get into Brockwell Park, man. Peckham Boys, like a fucking army of them. Jakes got on it, now opps are on Dulwich Road, heading back to Peckham.'

I felt blood tapping in my temples; I could hear it above the music and the loud voices coming from all directions in the park. How dare they? How fucking dare those Peckham Boys attempt to invade the Lambeth Country Show? This is *our* event, *our* territory. Right, then. I ripped my bandana out my back pocket and grabbed a bike. 'Let's go,' I said, but Steve was saying it wasn't worth it, as the jakes had blocked the main entrance at the lido. 'We'll take the station exit then,' I shouted.

I was already on my bike, tying my bandana round my face with one hand as I pedalled, zig-zagging through the crowds, dodging kids and clowns plodding on stilts, until I reached the exit, where I almost mowed down a couple of stewards in hi-vis bibs. I beat past them, out onto Dulwich Road, then made a sharp left under the railway bridge at Herne Hill station, onto Half Moon Lane. I whipped my head over my shoulder and saw what looked like Syikes and the boys, emerging from beneath the bridge on their bikes. I smashed the pedals harder, accelerating east towards Peckham, thinking, 'They are gonna remember my name.'

I spotted them from afar, a good three hundred metres or so ahead to my right, a knot of hooded figures, all wearing black, moving as one unit along the pavement. I did respect the Peckham lot for always being brave: they moved in numbers. I cut a diagonal across the road, got honked as I swerved between two oncoming cars, half-hopped onto the curb, jumped off my bike and threw it to the ground, shouting, 'Oi,' at the Peckham lot. There was no more than fifty metres between us and, clocking a couple of faces above slipped bandanas, I recognised these boys as being members of DFA ('Don't Fuck Around' or, 'Drugz Fundz Armz'), a subset of the Peckham Boys. Predominately African, this lot were wild; they didn't care what they did. At that moment, I didn't care either. I wanted to hurt those boys. I am Boost, and they are gonna remember my name.

I'm running at them, hand on waist, poised to pull out a non-existent machine, yelling, 'Fucking pricks, Brixton, OC.' I'm getting closer. Boys nearest to me must actually think I'm gonna pull out a gun 'cos someone shouts, 'Run!' and they start to slip, slide and run. I'm chasing. About fifteen of them and only one Boost, but Boost ain't got no weapon, has he? Boost should've brought a fucking blade. Man should never go naked, know what I'm saying? And where is Syikes, where is my team? Man needs his team right now. I'm breathing hard, sucking my bandana, feet going bam, bam, bam, bam. The gap's closing. Few more steps and I can jump on one. Adrenaline's pumping. They are gonna remember my name. But then one of the boys shouts, 'Stop, stop, he ain't got nuffink,' and suddenly my feet ain't working no more. Those boys have stopped running, done the fastest U-turn ever, and now they're forming a wall before me. 'Pussy, Brixton, pussy OC,' spits one, pulling a flick knife from his pocket. He's strong, built like a tank and staring at me with a look that screams, 'I'm gonna stab you, then go and stab your mum.' Things happen fast. I hear my boys ride up behind me. I bend, grab a couple of empty bottles at the kerbside, smash them against the pavement to make stabbing material and I go flying in there.

We fought for about five minutes, which was quite long for a street fight, especially when knives and bottles are involved.

The battle began there on Half Moon Lane and progressed onto a quiet estate made up of 1960s bungalows. I took on the guy with the flick knife, swinging at his face with one of the bottles, hoping to slice him, but he managed to dodge it. In turn, he missed my leg when he went to stab me in the thigh, leaving himself wide open for a kick in the nuts.

Meanwhile, boys from both sides were tipping over wheelie bins, picking glass bottles from the rubbish and throwing them. Syikes had his blade, fighting with a DFA boy brandishing one of those broken bottles. I left my opponent clutching his balls, ran up a driveway and tore down two more bins, releasing more glass missiles. Soon, everyone was lobbing bottles about and all we could hear was the brittle sound of glass smashing. Were residents watching from their windows or calling the police? We didn't know and we didn't care. Such thoughts didn't bug us during battle. When there were no more bottles left to hurl, the Peckham lot kinda jogged off, sneering, 'Peck'nam, Peck'*nam.*'

I turned to Syikes and my boys and went, 'Right, do I have my team with me?'

'Yeah, let's do it man,' said Syikes. I thought about it for a few seconds.

'Nah,' I went, 'Save it for another day.' Random fights like this were two-a-penny between OC and the Peckham Boys. And besides, the opps had fled, meaning we could go home and gloat about our victory to the Olders. Up our rep, y'know. We crunched through the broken glass, back to the road, got back on our bikes and headed west, chanting 'Brikki, *OC.*'

9

ONE CHANCE

'Be an angel and open those curtains won't you, Our Boy?' said Nan, waving a custard cream biscuit at the glass doors out to the garden. 'Need to let the natural light in.'

I got up from the sofa, laughing to myself. Nan was obsessed with 'letting the natural light in'. Every time I was in that room with her she'd ask me to pull back the curtains, day or night. Occasionally, I'd remind her that it was actually dark outside and she'd simply give me a stern look over her teacup. 'Just open the curtains,' she'd say, 'and don't be cheeky.'

I did my curtain duty and plonked back on the sofa. It was a Sunday evening and Nan and I were watching *Antiques Roadshow*. That programme used to inspire and rile me in equal measure. I found it fascinating when old tat turned out to be worth hundreds of thousands of pounds. It'd get me thinking, 'What do I have that could be worth that kinda money?' I'd scan the room. My model cars – a Ferrari and Lamborghini – might be worth a bit in years to come, perhaps? I'd look at Nan's dollies too and then I'd quickly decide, 'Nah, forget it'. I watched the latest episode, with another posh woman feigning shock over the value of some vase and I knew I'd be generating my own cash from a different kind of transaction. All I needed to do was make a visit to a contact in the Vassall Road. This was weed-dealing – and Mikes and I were just getting into it, around the time that I went into year ten at Stockwell Park School.

I was supposed to be meeting Mikes at the end of the court in ten minutes. Our supplier, Carlos, was expecting us. I went to my bedroom, grabbed my Adidas man bag, slipped a nank into my trainer, put on my New Era hat, and walked back into the living room.

'I'm off to Mikes' for a bit,' I said.

Nan took another biscuit from the barrel, dunked it in her tea, 'OK, darling,' she said, 'but don't be too late – you've got school tomorrow, don't forget.'

We had met Carlos through the Olders. An eighteen-year-old Angolan, he wasn't a gang member but he did dip in and out of gang-related activity now and then. Carlos was something like a businessman on the fringes of gangland, in the drug-dealing sector, catering for the needs of the many stoners, crackheads and smackheads in the area. He was all about money, Carlos. Heavy into his designer clothes – Gucci, Hugo Boss, Dolce & Gabbana and the rest of it. Always had the latest trainers; I never saw him in the same pair twice. Man, I'd never known anybody to own so many. He had all the bling, too – chains and rings and he was always wearing a Rolex or Cartier or Jacob & Co watch. Mikes said he would've robbed him if he were a stranger.

Mikes and me would each buy a zed of green for a hundred and twenty pounds. We would meet Carlos in a courtyard outside his flat and the first thing he'd say was, 'Yo, get your money out.' He'd hang around for a smoke and a chat before heading inside for our weed. We'd break it up at home on the scales to make smaller bags and sell them on the estate. I could make two hundred pounds a week off a Z's worth, alongside what I got from Pokémon cards and mobile phones. The weed was easy to shift as there were so many smokers on Myatts Field, including most OC members. Mikes and Lox couldn't get enough of the stuff, but it wasn't for me. Besides, I'd probably passively smoked enough joints as a toddler to last me a lifetime.

Mikes and Lox sold phones through a contact named Sammy, a short Indian guy with a greasy grey comb-over. He smelled of dried tobacco and shuffled around Brixton in a long leather coat that looked like it was five sizes too big for him. When I first met him, I thought he looked dodgy, y'know, but give the man his due, he was good for the money. Mikes produced a Blackberry and two Nokias that he'd robbed hours earlier and, without hesitation, Sammy's hand disappeared into a faraway leather pocket. 'I'll give you £120 for all three,' he said.

I watched him slip Mikes the notes and thought, Rah, I need some of this phone action. I got right on it and began to invest some of my drug-dealing earnings in phones, buying friends' old devices off them for next to nothing. It was almost too easy; Sammy would buy any phone going. We'd meet him on Brixton Road, show him our handsets and he'd be like, 'Yeah, I'll take this one', 'I'll take that one'. He'd give me thirty for an Ericsson flip, fifty for a couple of Nokias. To this day, I haven't a clue what Sammy did with those phones. There was a rumour he was selling them to people in India. Who knew, who cared? I was making a tidy profit, y'know.

My routine was hectic as I turned fifteen; there were not enough hours in the day, man. I'd go to school and think about GCSEs, go to football practice and play in county matches, see Carlos, go weed-dealing, nick and sell Pokémon cards, see Sammy and sell a few phones and I'd hold down the ends with my boys – G-checking, border patrol, all that stuff – chill with the Olders and get involved with their rap videos. I'd drink all that in, *be* that OC gang member, be active, get involved in fights, be Boost. In downtime I'd play video games at Mikes', google stuff like 'How to fire a gun' and meet girls in online chatrooms. There was a lot to think about – things to juggle, y'know what I mean?

At the same time, I was being that family boy, too, my grandparents and mum completely unaware that Boost existed, let alone what he was getting up to on the streets of Baghdad. I wanted them to remain ignorant – my biggest fear at that time was that they would discover my secret. For one, I couldn't bear for them to be disappointed in me or stop me seeing my friends, which they would do if they knew I was in a deadly gang such as the OC. I wouldn't be allowed out. They might even call the jakes.

I also wanted to protect my family; as a gang member I would automatically have enemies and there was no way I'd want them targeting my relatives. Yes, I was interested in guns and knives and drug-dealing, but my family still meant the world. I had a new baby half-brother to think of: Tyrell – Dwight's son – who was just a few months old. Mum and Dwight had got married and, not long after Tyrell came along, they moved to a new flat, 16 Peckford Place, on the Angell Town estate. They were a proper little family – Mum, Dwight, my sister Jazz and now Tyrell. Mum was happy and you know what? I'd never felt prouder of her. It was incredible how she had transformed her life; she'd never once slipped back onto the crack. She was – and still is – an inspiration.

I also valued the sense of belonging I got from being in a gang. As a kid I had really battled with self-confidence. I would walk about with my head down a lot, not out of fear, but more from a feeling of anxiety about being out in public. What I'd witnessed as a toddler – all the drugs and violence – had scarred me. I wanted to feel safe, but I didn't feel there was much protection as a young child. That's what I felt as an OC member, even if it was paradoxically through violence. Violence was protection for the OC and violence bred more violence. That was how we felt safe.

Fighting as a team gave the gang sense of security, deffo. If any one of us were to encounter a mob from the Other Side while out alone, we wouldn't stand a chance. Although some fights were friendly affairs – or so we believed them to be at the time. Take an occasion like bonfire night, when we'd all get together – to have full-blown fireworks wars with neighbouring estates such as Stockwell Park, Loughborough or Angell Town. We'd stock up on loads of explosives, from screamers and rockets to catherine wheels and shooters and strategically plan our invasion. Which estate should we target? What was the best way in? Who would stay behind and guard Myatts Field from rival crews come to blast us in turn? It was 5 November, but we'd still take our knives with us … just in case things got out of hand, y'know. While those guarding Myatts Field would be armed with hammers, on the lookout for pagans.

Bonfire night was our chance to play real-life warfare – and this was something we craved. We would choose an estate, then call a contact who lived there. Both parties would laugh down the phone as the challenge was set. For example, one of our boys would say, 'Yo, we've got a team of 30 and we're coming over there tonight to bomb you lot.'

And the opposition would be like, 'Yeah, come over.'

I had my first fireworks fight in year ten. There were about twenty of us, including Mikes, Lox, Troopz, Ratty, Syikes, Abz, other youngers and a few Olders, all armed with fireworks and lighters hidden in man bags, rucksacks, inside jackets and hoodies or tucked in waistbands and pockets. In the stairwell that led to nowhere at the end of Treherne Court we pulled on gloves, balaclavas and extra hoodies – protection in case we got hit – then set off to bomb the Stockwell Park Estate crew into oblivion. That was our aim, anyway.

We ran over the Hills, did a right onto Mostyn Road and cut through Myatts Field South, mulchy leaves underfoot, fireworks exploding overhead, near and far. A gunshot would've gone unheard amid the blasts.

Stockwell Park Estate reminded me of a prison complex, with its tall concrete blocks joined by walkways and surrounded by rows of maisonettes on confusingly numbered courts that led to dead ends. Our pace quickened as we entered the estate, shouting, 'OC, Baghdad,' into the fizzy night, charging forth into battle, cutting across a couple of courts until we turned a corner, into a space between two of the higher blocks. I pulled a rocket out of my bag as I ran, ready to launch it when, boom-fucking-whizz, we ran straight into a rain of oncoming missiles.

The fuckers had been waiting for us, man.

They were active, they were on it, shooting at us. They were letting off like 100- and 200-shot firework boxes, for sure, as well as bangers, rockets, screamers and red things that came at you like exploding bottles of cherryade. For a few seconds we were laughing, bumping into one another as we tried to dodge the explosives, then we were like, *Oh, shit! This is really happening.* We moved on, splintering into smaller groups as we ran, more fireworks zipping after us. I felt one singe my arm as it burned past. I was running with Mikes, Lox, Ratty and Syikes and, after a few minutes, we got out of their range but still inside their estate, seemingly lost. We stopped on one of the courts to catch our breath.

'Man better get bigger fireworks,' said Ratty.

'That was fucking mental,' said Mikes, lighting a joint.

I was about to suggest boosting when we got ambushed again. About thirty Stockwell boys appeared at the far end of the court, blasting a few screamers our way and we ran in the opposite direction, Stockwell boys chasing us. We fled straight into a dead end.

I stopped, heard one of the Stockwell boys shout, 'Bun 'im, bun 'im,' and, as I turned, I saw this small comet flying towards me. I stepped to the side and it missed me, zoomed past Ratty and Mikes and shot straight into Syikes' hoodie.

We all started shouting, 'Get it out your hoodie! It's in yer hoodie!'

Tick-tock ... bang.

The Stockwell lot fucked off as the screamer flashed and exploded inside Syikes' hood. Oh, my God, they've killed Kenny! But no, miraculously, Syikes was uninjured except for a tiny burn on the side of his neck. The firework had exploded through the back of his hood. Next day, we bought more fireworks, including a 500-shot.

Being a teenager and living on the Myatts Field estate, it was difficult to avoid OC life. As soon as I stepped outside my door, I was immersed in their world. I'd see the Olders and think they were perfection, y'know what I'm saying? They become big brothers, gangland life coaches – father figures even, passing down all that they knew and what they had learned in turn from their elders. It was a generational thing, and I was fast becoming a member of that family.

At the same time, I was beginning to get noticed as a footballer, so there was also that *Maybe I'll become a Premiership player* daydream playing in my head. It seemed like that might really happen in spring 2005, a few months after I turned fifteen, when I got scouted by one of West Ham's then youth coaches, Paul Senior. Alongside Zav I was taken to the West Ham Academy, Chadwell Heath, to train. If we proved ourselves, we'd be offered a place on the academy's youth training scheme. Ultimately, we could end up playing for West Ham. Chance of a lifetime for a teenage boy, right?

My first day was daunting, man. There was me and Zav from the Myatts Field estate next to the best of players from Belgium, Italy, South Africa, Kenya and beyond. Then there were the academy players themselves and, wow, they looked like the Ronaldos, know what I mean? They had everything: the new boots, the whiter-than-white socks, the confidence. They looked well-looked-after; definite stars-in-the-making. All the boys were a year older than me – and a year makes a lot of difference in football.

Paul Senior gave an inspiring dressing-room speech, telling us how we'd been handpicked because we were talented players who showed great potential. 'Give it your all,' he said, 'this is going to be intense – the most intense training you've ever known. Work hard, express yourselves, but relax and enjoy yourselves too.'

The standard of the other players was off-the-scale immense. In the first training session I found myself playing alongside Junior Stanislas, who would go on to play for West Ham and is currently a winger for AFC Bournemouth. Junior was playing left-wing and I was playing left-back, defence to his midfield. He was an inspiring player to watch, very quick, super-talented. He had a cockiness to him and I was like, 'Rah, he knows how to carry himself'.

It was a daunting environment for me, y'know. The academy was tough and it was a big canvas to paint on. I'd gone from being at the top of my game in school and county level to feel like a minor part on that huge pitch. Still a skinny young man, I didn't feel so tough out there beneath the glaring floodlights. Being the new guy, I played it safe, thinking, 'I'll just walk in the shadows for now; learn the basics'.

Zav didn't hold back. When it came to football, he was always the star. A striker, Zav was tackled non-stop, but he didn't care. He'd bash his head off the goalpost, repeatedly got knocked down, but still he powered on, shooting, shooting, shooting, scoring, missing, scoring, missing. Zav was hungry, dedicated.

We had to travel back and forth between Brixton and Chadwell Heath three times a week for training, which involved a two-hour commute to the east of London via tube and train. It was tiring, one hundred per cent, but worth it for the kudos. At school, me and Zav were like the jocks of football, the two cool kids with our trial for West Ham. We were earning respect and we got to leave school early some days for training and matches. Teachers were cool about that. West Ham, innit? The Hammers. If the teaching staff got one or two of their pupils signed by a major club then Stockwell Park School's name was gonna ring, man.

The academy covered our travelling expenses and, with a little jiggery-pokery, me and Zav made a small profit that paid for our chicken and chips after training. They also gave us old West Ham strips to train in, which we were supposed to return at the end of the sessions, but me and Zav were like, 'Bollocks to that, we're keeping this gear.' We nicked the lot – tracksuits, shorts, shirts. I was out on the Myatts Field in that claret-and-blue top with a number on the back and I earned a different level of respect. I played differently when I wore the kit and I wore it everywhere. I wasn't supposed to keep it because I hadn't been signed, but I loved the confidence it gave me. OK, it wasn't yellow and there were no guns on the shirt, but there were hammers and that was good enough for me.

My heavy training schedule meant I had less time for gangsterism, although I had far from given up on that other sphere of my life. I saw football and OC activity as two ticking timebombs and I thought, 'Let's see what blows up first'. Yeah, I wanted to be a footballer, but street-life also glittered a little over there, y'know. Money and excitement motivated me. One hundred per cent. I loved playing football but it is hard work and time-consuming. Even if I did make it into the West Ham Academy, it could be years before I would make a decent wage as a player. Drug dealing, however, provided instant cash. I think I looked for excuses not to become that footballer. At times I would programme my mind to hate it because the lure of the streets was so strong.

Zav, by contrast, wasn't OC. His only bomb was football. He had no interest in the streets whatsoever, although he was in our circle of mates and we would play football and video games together. We'd hang out and go to the West End or whatever – the Trocadero, Piccadilly Circus, was our go-to place on a Saturday evening. The centre had arcade games, a few rides and some shops. From Vassall Road we'd jump on the 159 bus that could take us all the way to Piccadilly Circus. Sometimes we'd leave earlier, getting off at Oxford Circus and heading to Nike Town before walking to the Trocadero via Soho and Chinatown. Every time we saw a no. 12 bus pull up or go by, we'd all be scanning its windows for the enemy – all of us except Zav. We knew that the no. 12 was the route you'd take to the West End if you were travelling from Peckham, y'see. Yeah, Peckham utes were also regulars at the Trocadero. Like us, they probably went there in the hope of meeting girls.

I'd been training with the academy for about three weeks when I went up to the Trocadero for one of the usual Saturday nights, along with Zav, Mikes and Lox. We took the 'rocket escalator' – a normal escalator with Sega-themed decoration – up to Funland amusement arcade. This was where we came face-to-face with the Peckham Boys, about ten of them, standing around arcade machines. As soon as one of them clocked us, he alerted his mates and they all wheeled round. You wouldn't always recognise individual Peckham Boys because there were so many of them, but tonight I could see two familiar faces scowling at me – Diamond Babamuboni and his younger brother Timy. The brothers were notorious figures in Peckham. We'd often bump into them and their crew at the Trocadero, when our encounters would invariably end in a street fight.

Zav headed over to the other side of the room, head down, but me, Mikes and Lox stood our ground, giving the Peckham Boys the hard stare, chests puffed, hands on waist and all that. They glared back, the flashing rainbow of the arcade lighting picking out a smirk or two. If we had been anywhere else, the knives would have been out by now, but security was tight in the Trocadero, with CCTV and security guards covering the whole place. As our fights could get messy, neither side would usually start anything in the Trocadero itself, if it could be avoided. We restricted ourselves to the usual exchange of 'Peck-*narm!*' and 'Baghdad!', before our side stalked off to the other end of the arcade to play a boxing video game. Half-an-hour or so later, the arcade started getting busy. A group of hard-looking Chinese lads, probably around our age, began playing machines next to us. Some had their hair dyed gingery-gold and a few of them had dragon-themed tattoos on their necks. They looked like triad gangsters to me. I kept myself busy sizing them up as a possible threat while I waited my turn on the punchbag machine.

I was startled out of my thoughts as I felt hands on my hips, tapping my pockets. I spun round faster than the Looney Tunes Tasmanian Devil to see Timy next to me.

'Rah, whatcha got? Whatcha got?' he said, reaching for my pockets again.

I pushed him away. 'Fuck you,' I said and he stumbled backwards, bumping into a Chinese woman in a pink tracksuit who was watching cherries and lemons whizz round on a fruit machine, phone in her hand.

My boys were already circling, chanting, 'Rah, what's going on?'

I balled my fists, the veins in my temples bulging. Timy's touch turned me maggoty inside, diseased. There was a funny taste in my mouth. I was ready to fight. Fuck security, I wanted to smash Timy to bits, slash him to ribbons. I had a blade in my shoe.

The woman in the tracksuit gave Timy a dirty look and whacked more coins in the slot. The triad boys were on the aging *Daytona* racing car game when, fast as the spinning wheels of cherries and lemons, Timy snatched the phone out of the woman's hand and ran, barrelling through a knot of people. His victim started shouting in Chinese, waving her hands about, and the triad boys came over to find out what was happening, just as a couple of black guys walked by. The woman pointed at one of them, as if to say, 'It was him' and, fucking hell, it all kicked off. I'd never seen anything like it. The triads jumped on this random, innocent guy, no older than seventeen, and absolutely caned him. I'm talking proper Jackie Chan shit – hitting him off snooker tables, smashing him against machines. They were doing roundhouse kicks on him, he was getting elbowed and punched and it was all a case of mistaken identity.

We didn't want to get caught up in that shit and got out of there as the security stormed the arcade. We discovered the Peckham lot were waiting for us outside, including Timy – who should've been inside getting a doing off the triads instead of the other guy. He started on Zav now, trying to tap his pockets.

Zav gave him a shove. 'Cut it out, man,' he said, paranoia written all over his face, eyes flicking this way and that. It was about 7.30 p.m. and Piccadilly Circus was heaving, people brushing past or weaving between us, making it difficult to manoeuvre as Timy banged Zav in the face. Zav ran, blood trickling from his nose, quick-stepping and slaloming around tourists. The Peckham crowd chased him and Lox, Mikes and I chased them, across the road towards Piccadilly, dodging people and traffic. Lox darted in front of a bus, causing it to screech and skid, missing him by centimetres. The Other Side gave up the chase at the Eros fountain. Zav was long gone.

We arrived seconds later and managed a micro-fight – a few punches, kicks and jumping on each other's backs amid the spray of the fountain and flashing cameras – before the police turned up. Then it was game over unless we wanted to get pulled. The Peckham lot got on the no. 12 and we caught the 159 back to our area, our hatred simmering for the SE15 gang.

Stabbing, shooting and death are common in gangland. A typical phone call between Mikes and me might go like this:

Mikes: Did you hear John got shot on Crawshay Court last night?
Me: Fuck, no. Is he dead?
Mikes: Nah, don't think so
Me: Fancy a game of FIFA?
Mikes: Yeah, man.

But when it's our nearest and dearest, our gang 'family', who are hurt or killed, it's a different matter, y'know what I mean? It makes us more vengeful. We were yet to lose a close friend in the ends, but many were regularly shot or stabbed. Lox was a frequent target. Today, he jokes that he's been stabbed and shot more times than he's had birthday parties. He's thirty-one.

Everyone went for Lox, be it a pagan from another area or someone in-house in Myatts Field or Brixton. He had no fear, though. I was with Lox one time he got slashed. I remember it happened during my West Ham trial period, when I had on the team tracksuit.

We were walking to Saji's shop. It was early evening but still light out. We cut across the grass before Hammelton Green and this boy who lived on one of the courts started talking shit to Lox, who punched him in the stomach. Although his opponent was strong, a big black guy who could handle himself in a fight, I reckoned that Lox could put him down with a couple of blows. I was surprised when Lox let out this loud grunt and doubled over, holding his face, blood pouring from a wound. In the few seconds they'd been fighting, the other guy had pulled a knife on Lox and sliced him, horizontally, along his forehead. Blood gushed out, as if someone had undone a zip on Lox's head and all the blood in his body was spewing out of the hole. I flew in, sweep-kicked the attacker and down he went, as Lox and I fucked him over in the grass. We punched him, kicked him, bashed him up. I jumped about two feet in the air and landed on his head. Lox's face was pouring. He couldn't see for the blood in his eyes and my focus switched to him, allowing his assailant time to get up and limp away.

We walked back to Treherne Court, Lox pressing his rolled-up hoodie to his head to stem the flow. My tracksuit was splattered and we looked like we'd walked off the set of a zombie film. Pastor Mimi shrieked when she answered the door. 'Sweet Jesus! Who's done this to you?' she cried, hurrying us inside. Lox staggered to the bathroom, leaking everywhere. Mimi called for an ambulance and ran into the bathroom with more towels. Lox stuck his head under the tap in the sink, cursing. Mikes appeared and was like, 'What the fuck?' Mimi wanted to call the police. Lox said 'No' to that. No jakes. Mimi went with Lox to the hospital and me and Mikes stayed behind and played FIFA. The next day we all behaved as if nothing had happened: I went to school and on to Chadwell Heath for training with Zav.

Lox was stitched up and came back with a scar that made him look like Mufasa from *Lion King*. As for that other boy? He had to move out of the area, know what I'm saying? Lox was tough. We were all tough, though Lox getting knifed by somebody on our own turf served as another reminder that we weren't invincible. This made us stronger as a gang, as a team. And that's when me, Lox and Mikes came up with another title for OC. Sure, those initials would always stand for Organised Crime, but our gang would also now be known as One Chance: 'One Chance to live'. Our fellow gang members, including the Olders, loved our new title. Soon, we were all chanting, '*OC*, *One* Chance.'

10

THE SEND OUT

A few days before my West Ham trial was due to end, Paul Senior called me into the office where I would usually collect expenses. He got straight to the point.

'Listen, Terroll, I'm sorry, but we're releasing you from the academy,' he said sympathetically. 'You're a talented footballer. I think you could go far. But we feel you didn't really express yourself enough.'

I nodded, feeling dejected.

Senior added that I was on the skinny side and that I should put on some weight which, in time, would make me a better player. 'Keep training,' he urged.

'Yeah, it's cool, I get it,' I said. 'I appreciate the experience, innit.'

I'd be lying if I said I wasn't disappointed. Of course I was but, equally, I understood where Senior was coming from. He'd wanted me to run longer. Take on players. Shoot and miss, shoot and miss, but keep on going. Instead, I'd played it safe, with short passes and runs. To be honest, I'd been too scared to go for it.

On the plus side, I'd learned loads about football and gained a West Ham kit (I was keeping that) and, anyway, I had been getting pretty sick of travelling to Essex three or four times a week (I didn't mention that bit to Senior). Best of all, Zav's hard work had paid off and he earned himself a place at the academy. Man, I was so pleased for him when I heard. I spudded his hand and slapped his back over and over on the journey back to Brixton that evening. Zav played it down, but I knew he was buzzing, man. Couldn't finish his chicken and chips, y'know.

'I'm sorry you didn't get in, bro,' he kept saying. 'Would've been cool if we'd both got through, innit?'

I laughed. 'Listen man,' I went. 'Just enjoy it. When Myatts Field hears about this, your name is gonna ring, bro. You've been signed by the Hammers.'

'Yeah, fucking cool, right?'

I touched my fist to his again.

I was, and still am, so proud of Zav. I mean, he nailed it. He became a footballer while living in Baghdad, despite having us gang members getting into madness around him. West Ham swiftly shipped him out and put him up in digs at the academy. With that, Zav escaped Baghdad and that boy would go on to make a name for himself far beyond the ends. I started to think about what the end of training meant for me. 'Rah, I'm not gonna become a Premiership player overnight,' I thought, 'so maybe that gang timebomb is gonna blow up first'.

We broke up for the summer holidays and that meant I could throw myself into being more active in the gang without school or football training getting in the way. I set to it, robbing more Pokémon cards, selling more phones to Sammy, upping my weed-dealing and getting into more fights. I increased my weekly weed profit to around £120 but it wasn't long before that seemed like fuck-all income. That kinda money bought me new jeans or trainers, but I wanted more. I wanted the chains and the Jacob & Co watch; I imagined myself in that Porsche, with a machine on my waist. Yeah, I needed more money, deffo.

Dealing weed was becoming tiring though. Wasn't singing volumes, y'know. Me and Mikes had to cycle for miles to make deliveries. Then there was all the time spent hanging about in the rain, trying to push weed bags to randoms or waiting for customers to turn up.

I complained to Carlos, 'Rah, this weed business is too slow, man. Doesn't bring much money in.'

Before replying, Carlos lit the twisted Rizla knot of his joint, took a few tokes and passed it to Mike.

'Everybody needs green, man, y'know.' he said at length. 'But, if you wanna make serious money from this shit, man needs to be shifting white and brown, y'know what I'm saying?' He gestured at Mike, 'Yo, 'nuff man, c'mon.' Mike passed the joint, sleepy grin on his face. Carlos gave me a serious look. 'Think about it, man.'

I clocked Carlos' latest Rolex, glinting in the afternoon sun. White and brown: he meant cocaine, crack cocaine and heroin. Yeah, he'd planted a seed there. Trouble was, surely we'd need a lot of money up front to buy the gear? Funds we didn't have right now. 'Yeah,' I went, 'we'll give it some thought.'

The next day I was due to go to Butlins in Bognor Regis with Mum, Dwight, Jazz and Tyrell. The timing wasn't great although, don't get me wrong, I was looking forward to spending time with my family. At the same time, a whole week seemed a long time to be away from the area and my OC family. A lot could happen on the block in one week. I didn't want to miss out. Still, I packed my holdall, threw in a few weed bags to (hopefully) flog to any stoners I might meet at Butlins and told myself the break would do me good.

I actually had a chilled time in Bognor, y'know. Mum and Dwight being busy with the kids meant I was free to do my own thing. I played on the arcade games, went shopping on the high street, bought a pair of earrings and some fridge magnets for Nan (it wasn't only dolls she collected) and I paid a visit to a tattoo parlour. An idea formed as I studied the images displayed in the window: I could get an OC tattoo. That'd be so cool. I wasn't of legal age for a tattoo, but Mum was well up for it and she came to the parlour with me. When the tattooist asked my age, Mum said, 'Yeah, he's nineteen next month.' The guy was cool, man. He didn't even ask for ID. I told him I'd like an O and a C, the letters interconnected, inked on the side of my neck. He showed me some fonts and he got his needle out. The inking didn't even hurt, man.

'What's "OC" mean?' asked Mum, once we were out of the parlour.

'"One Chance", innit?' I said.

Could mean anything, right?

Mum screwed up her face, puzzled. 'Yeah … I don't get it,' she said. 'One chance for what?'

'Oh, one chance to live,' I said, 'a celebration of life and all that stuff.'

Mum was like, 'OK, whatever,' but she had a point. Maybe my tattoo didn't make much sense. I slept on it − then went back to the parlour the next day and got the guy to add '2 live' beneath the O and the C.

OC was a team, working together to protect our area, sharing information about the Other Side, etc., but many Youngers would have other hustles within the gang, running errands for the Olders, for example. Youngers who did this were known as 'send outs'. In one respect, getting hired as a send out was a huge coup. It proved the Olders trusted you. Plus, they'd pay you a wage. On the other hand, no Younger wanted to admit being a dogsbody for the Olders. It's an ego thing, y'know. Send outs were easy to spot. They were the ones who suddenly appeared on the block in new tracksuits and trainers or a chain. Some would show a flash of machine on their waist, like, *I'm moving up now*. I became one of those kids.

Zam took me under his wing in the final week of the summer holidays before I was due to return to Stockwell Park School to start year eleven. 'Zam' is a made-up name, and I'm protecting his identify because the man changed his life around and has since died and it would be disrespectful of me to expose him now. I knew Zam through a friend who used to work with him. He was 25, Albanian and short, but built for war, if you know what I mean. That boy was head-to-toe muscle and he taught me a lot.

I was making a delivery on the Cowley Estate when I bumped into him one afternoon, coming out of Penelope House, and we had a convo in the stairwell. He asked how I was doing and I spilled, man. I was getting sick of selling green and wanted to make serious money. His gaze went right through me and up the stairs behind, like he was expecting somebody to appear, but he nodded at appropriate moments. 'Everything feels so slow right now,' I said. Zam, his thick neck looped with chains, was still staring up the stairs, his facial muscles twitching. 'But, yeah, other than that, I'm good, man. You good?'

I heard a bleeping sound emanating from Zam's Iceberg jeans.

'One second,' he said, pulling his mobile from his pocket, and whatever appeared on the screen must've been good news because tension melted away from his face. 'Yeah,' he went, shoving the phone back in his pocket, 'Listen, I can help you with some food, bro. Let's go chat.'

'Yeah, man,' I said, even though I was already late for my next drop-off. *Fuck it, they'll keep.*

We took a circuitous route to Zam's flat off Brixton Road, Zam continually looking this way and that. 'Never take the same route twice in one day,' he said, hurrying me through the front door. 'Do that and you'll make yourself an easy target for the police, another food vendor or the enemy who wants to shoot you.'

'Deffo, one hundred per cent,' I said.

Now I knew why he'd led us all around the houses. I followed him into his lounge and, wow, his place was smart: a shiny wooden floor with a grey silk rug; L-shaped sofa in black leather – I could smell the leather; a wall-mounted flat screen TV. Zam closed the blinds and switched on an arc desk lamp on a table at one end of the sofa, angling it downwards. 'Have a seat,' he said, indicating the sofa.

I swear that leather swallowed me whole, man. Zam fetched a Sainsbury's carrier bag and a mobile phone. He sat next to me and switched on the phone with a fusillade of bleep-bleep, ping, bleep-bleep, pings as texts and voicemails arrived. Zam handed me the phone.

'This is your contacts book,' he said. 'Guard it with your life; lose it if things get hot, know what I mean?'

I took the phone from him, a Samsung D600 camera phone. Nice. He passed the carrier bag.

'Here's the food, man.'

I peered inside to see crack rocks, each individually wrapped in cling film.

Zam outlined the job description. I was to take orders over the phone, deliver the food, collect the money and take the cash to Zam at the end of the week, who'd then give me a cut.

'Yeah, that's cool, no probs,' I said. 'When can I start?'

I worked my arse off during that first week; every time that phone rang or pinged I'd shoot out on my BMX, selling rocks to nitties in Zam's area. These were small transactions, but they soon mounted up. I'd pedal home, man-bag stuffed with ten- and twenty-pound notes and filled a shoebox with cash that remained hidden under my bed until the end of the week. Although excited about the money I had made for Zam, selling crack did make me think about my mum's addiction to the drug years ago. I was aware that I could be feeding another mother's habit, but I pushed that thought to the back of my mind.

'Good work, bro,' Zam said, as he counted out the cash on the sofa in his flat. He peeled off a load of twenties and pushed them towards me. 'Here's five hundred.'

I held the money in my hand, trying to appear cool but, fuck me, that was a lot of money to earn in a week for a fifteen-year-old schoolboy. I was still selling weed too, increasing my earnings by another hundred.

'Wanna work next week too?'

I stuffed the cash in my bag. 'Yeah, could do.'

I was high as the nitties I'd sold rocks to, only my high was natural. No chemicals, no paranoia, no comedown, just cash in my pocket. *Yo, you're the man, Boost.*

I went shopping in Oxford Street with Kenny, my boy from Clapham Junction. He had just launched his own clothing brand called Playdot, so knew his fashion. He took me to his go-to shops, advising me on the trendiest names and styles. It was like having a personal shopper. I blew five hundred quid on Adidas tracksuits and Nike trainers and went back to Brixton feeling every inch the Premiership footballer. I'd never known money like it; my mum and grandparents could never afford this stuff. I had been that kid who put cardboard in his shoes, remember? I wore my new tracksuits with pride on the block. Nobody said anything. They never would. I noticed a few other Youngers in new gear too. I didn't say a word. At home, Nan would occasionally ask, 'Is that a new jersey, Our Boy?'

I would shrug and say, 'Nah, I borrowed this from Mikes.' And she never argued the point. Granddad wouldn't study my wardrobe or notice I was wearing new swag.

It wasn't long before GCSE mocks came around, with teachers spouting crap about revision and stuff; meanwhile, the money rolled in. Some of the toothless nitties got on my nerves but, all that aside, this was an easy way to earn. How could I not be seduced? Sometimes, if I'd had a particularly good week, Zam would bung me an extra fifty quid or so. He would big me up and, while he gave me another bag of pre-wrapped food, he would dish out advice. He taught me how to hide shots under my tongue.

'Jakes pull you and you can't dispose, you'll just have to swallow,' he said.

OK, so eating and shitting crack didn't appeal. But getting pulled? That was always a hazard in our line of work; man needed to be vigilant.

For a while, Zam had been talking about helping me find more work and money and at length asked me if I could give his team a hand with what he said was some prep. We drove to a posh, terraced residential property on a new-build estate somewhere in Crystal Palace. It didn't look much like a crack house with a well-tended front garden and doormat. I didn't know if this was Zam's own place, but he did have keys to get in. Inside, it looked far from the crack house cliché – the place was spotlessly clean, with white walls and laminated floors. A scented candle burned on a ledge above the hall radiator but, aside from that, the house appeared empty of furniture.

After bolting and deadlocking the door, Zam took me upstairs and into a bedroom at the end of the landing. The floor of the white-walled, empty room was covered in decorator's plastic sheeting. Seated, cross-legged, were a girl and a boy, both around eighteen, who looked as though they were from Zam's part of the world. They were wearing surgical gloves and using razor blades to chop rocks from bigger lumps of crack. A set of scales, rolls of cling film and Lidl-brand plastic bags – some empty, others filled with more crack – lay in the middle of the plastic sheet. The girl looked up from her work.

'Hey, I'm Em,' she said.

The boy said his name was Dan.

'Boost,' I went, thinking that it was best not to give my real name. Zam gave me a nudge.

'Help them bag up, then.'

I sat down, the sheeting giving off a crackle. A smell engulfed me, damp and familiar and I could feel it hit the back of my throat, enter my follicles, invade my bloodstream. I felt myself becoming dizzy, getting a bit high, just from the stink of it. If I were to shut my eyes, I'd be back in Key House. I blanked that thought as Em passed me a pair of gloves and roll of cling film. I'd never bagged up before and I wasn't sure where to start. Zam gave me a quick tutorial. He ripped open one of the Lidl bags and placed a lump of white in the centre. He showed me how to cut, weigh and wrap and I was like a sponge, drinking it all in, thinking, 'Yo, one day I'm gonna have youngers do this for me, so I'd better pay attention'.

The wrapping part was really fiddly. You had to stretch the cling film, place the rock in the middle, then slowly twist the plastic around it, tightening each time it went round. After a few goes I got tired and my fingers ached from all the twisting. 'I can't do this anymore,' I said, sweeping aside my Lidl bag, 'It's giving me cramp, man.'

Zam gave me a sarky look. 'Yo, you wanna make money? You've gotta work. You can't be lazy in this business, bro.'

'Yeah, I s'pose,' I said. He had a point.

I felt I had a good arrangement going with Zam for a while, until it began to be obvious to me that he was taking the piss. He wanted me to get involved in county lines work, supplying to Essex and Kent and beyond, but that seemed like too much hassle and, besides, I'd started playing a lot of football again.

I was taking my playing more seriously and I had county football matches and trials; opportunities to get scouted again. Although I was getting more active on the streets, I still loved my football and travelling to supply would take up too much of my time.

Zam tried to convince me otherwise. 'County lines is where the top money is, Boost,' he said. 'You could earn a fortune, bro.'

I knocked him back, insisting I was happy with the work I was doing, thanks. When I thought about it some more, I was even less enthusiastic about the idea of doing anything else. I realised that even without taking on county lines, it was me that was doing all the running around while Zam made shitloads of money. It was after I had that revelation that another one of Zam's workers gave me an idea of how to remedy the imbalance.

Stewart had recently joined the team. He lived on Cowley and, like me, would cycle around for hours selling food to crackheads. When Zam gave me and Stewart three zeds of crack to split between us over the course of a week, we took the gear to one of our hood girls, Narinda.

Hood girls – would get a buzz from being associated with bad boys. They hid our accessories – drugs, knives, guns, baseball bats, fireworks or whatever – in their bedrooms. They would also hold money for us. The plan this time was to visit Narinda over the course of the week and pick up small amounts to sell as and when we needed them. But Stewart had something else on his mind.

'Y'know, we could just keep this food for ourselves. Sell it and keep all of the money. Burn our bridges with Zam.' Stewart suggested as we left Narinda's.

'What d'ya mean? Rob him?'

'Yeah, fuck it. He's ripping us off, man.'

I let the thought percolate for a few seconds. Dealers robbing other dealers happened all the time. It was a cut-throat business (literally so sometimes) and business was business, right? I turned to Stewart.

'Rah, why not?' I said.

11

CURSE OF THE REBORE

The Olders gave us Youngers power. They put batteries on our backs and taught us how to operate. They taught us about protection, about making sure there were enough weapons on the block – from baseball bats to machetes and from spinners to machine-guns.

Believe me, there were guns hidden in every corner of Myatts Field: in plant pots, buried in flower beds, down manholes, in the disused garages, beneath the dog's bedding or under the bed of a sleeping jezzie.

Guns. Everywhere.

And the Olders would show us those machines and demonstrate how they worked. Their sole reason for doing so was to teach us how to use a firearm. They wanted us to feel protected on the block. I watched those demos in awe. The confident manner in which an Older would slap the clip in, cock the gun and fire it at a wall or a fence. Pure power, man. Once, an Older took me aside and showed me a bullet. 'See this,' he said, motioning at the pellet in his palm, 'If one of these hollows hits you in the chest it's gonna shoot out of your leg. Don't get caught out, bro,' he said, laughing. Seriously, the conversations were that real.

There was no strict Mafia-style hierarchy as such in our gang. Obviously the Older-Younger divide existed. Age was a major factor when it came to leadership. Dread, at twenty-two, was the eldest OC member and therefore classed as a leader. Stinks, a couple of years younger than Dread, held the same rank but was more vocal and acted as the gang's spokesman via rap videos – a role that Lox would later assume.

Members' 'achievements' or 'failures' on the road would affect their position in the gang. Frequent questions asked by the Olders included:

Have you ever been 'violated' in Myatts Field before and, if so, did you handle the situation?
How well can you fight?
Are you a rider? If so, who have you 'rode out' on?
How big is your heart; do you have balls of steel, or are you a coward?

Yeah, you were expected to be a good fighter. 'Take violations from no one,' we were told. The more of the above boxes you ticked, the more respected you became within OC.

The Olders would put us on the drug lines and pay us good money and suddenly we were feeling as though we were sitting on the fattest, fastest, flashiest motorbike on the planet. We had access to shiny guns, like those that we'd seen in the movies. We were excited kids, looking at the weaponry as if they were sweeties in a candy box. We were earning money, buying tasty swag, becoming proper gangsters. Or so we thought. We were still learning.

Robbing Zam could easily have ended with both Stewart and me being stabbed or shot. As it turned out, there was no fallout. Zam disappeared off the radar days after he'd given us the three zeds. Yeah, he got raided and went to jail, man. Got a five, so I heard. I never did see him again, but the word was that when he got out he moved out of the area and became a devout Christian. Sadly, he passed away a few years back after a long-term illness. This I only learned a few months ago when I bumped into a mutual friend on Electric

Avenue. My heart-strings were tugged at the news. Even though I robbed Zam, I still liked him as a person, y'know. He taught me a lot, instilled in me a strong work ethic (albeit the wrong kind of work) and, yeah, I can still hear his voice in that house in Crystal Palace, when I complained that my hands were hurting. 'Yo – you wanna make money? You've gotta work. You can't be lazy, bro.' R.I.P., Zam. You were a good bro. Forgive me for robbing you.

Me and Stewart sold the three zeds and made just over a grand each. I took a note of the numbers in Zam's former Samsung, destroyed the SIM and sold the handset to Sammy. My money went on swag and drugs – weed and cocaine from Carlos. I sold the drugs, made money and bought more drugs. The cycle continued.

Lox, Mikes, Ratty, Troopz and Shellz. There were other Youngers too, but those were my main boys, y'know. We were young. We were *active*. Whenever our paths crossed with the Peckham Boys, it would result in all-out war. Out on the streets we would always be on the lookout for utes in black bandanas. Occasionally, we'd have beef with boys from other local areas such as Kennington, Tulse Hill or Angell Town. Troopz, for example, often had trouble with the Angell Town boys. As much as that might be friendly beef, he'd fight them back and forth. But that was Troopz, he loved a fight. We all did.

Some of the conversations we boys would have were scary, man. Evil. Like, I'd be walking down the street in Myatts Field with Lox, Mikes, Syikes, Shellz and Troopz and one of us would pipe up, 'Oi, Shellz, bet you can't knock out that guy across the street.'

Shellz would be jumping up and down, but Mikes might say, 'I can do it. I'm gonna go across the road and knock that guy out.'

They would challenge each other, saying stuff like, 'Rah, you can't knock out that guy. You ain't got a bang.' The conversation would then escalate into one about who had the hardest punch. And that was our entertainment. It sickens me to think that now.

In addition to fighting with pagans, regular border patrol duties, drug-dealing, robbing, running errands for the Olders and generally holding down the block, being in the OC was also about keeping up with gang branding and marketing, y'know. Getting the OC message out there.

The arrival of camera phones and social media sites such as My Space and Bebo gave us a new PR platform. I remember my Bebo page. The background colour was green to represent 'OC Myatts Field', with 'Don Boost' and 'OC' emblazoned over it. Rapping was part of our lives and we would upload our music videos and freestyle raps in which we'd brag harming our pagans. We'd wear balaclavas, hoods or bandanas over our faces and make shooting gestures as we spat over sixteen-bar tracks infused with gunfire sounds. Many of those early videos can still be found online today on YouTube. In one, you can see Stinks and his boys promoting their mixtape, *Salute Me When I Pass.* The clip shows the Olders freestyling on the Myatts Field Estate as they hold their CD cover up to the camera.

We were making our own type of music, unique to Brixton and Myatts Field. Peckham had its own sound, epitomised by Nathaniel Thompson, better known as Giggs, short for his street name, 'Giggler'. Giggs was sick, I mean really good, but I couldn't praise a Peckham rapper in front of the Olders. If I wanted to listen to Giggs I'd do so on my headphones in the privacy of my own house, y'know what I'm saying? Never be heard endorsing the Other Side, man. Never.

Lox became Brixton's answer to Giggs and became OC's official rapper. He went by his street name as well as being called 'Lox-A-Mill'. When Lox was shooting a music video, we'd get a camera guy to come down. And, if it turned out we didn't like the cameraman, he'd leave without his camera. Mad Mikes would always want to rob the cameramen.

Becoming a rapper wasn't a big ambition for me at the time, but I did enjoy writing lyrics and wanted to make some music, mainly because I was on the streets and thought I was the shit. I loved gang talk. We had our own language that represented us as Brixton. One of my songs was called 'Bullets'. Its recording no longer exists, but the chorus went something like this:

Bullets, bullets, bullets in my gun
I'll pull it, I'll pull it, I'll pull it 'til ya done
I'll put a bullet in your lung
No leg shot, head shots
I'm aiming
I need to aim for your head
Straight upper body, I'm aiming for your head till you're dead

We'd started going to shoobs on the ends and 'Bullets' used to get played a lot at those. Yeah, people would go crazy for it. They'd be like, 'Wow, that's sick, wheel it up.' It's mad when I think about it now. I didn't write those lyrics with an audience in mind; a part of me was taking the piss out of the whole rap scene, to be honest. And yet there was truth in what I rapped as well. I was reflecting my own experience and everyone knew it. OC was ruthless. We hurt a lot of people and in turn a lot of our brothers got hurt too. Protection was always at the forefront of our minds – Lox had been stabbed so many times he'd taken to wearing a stab-proof vest. He even slept in that vest, man.

We had One Chance, right? Man had to be armed and, as I spelled out in that song, it wasn't enough to have a knife, broken bottle or a baseball bat. I needed a gun.

A boy named Tank provided access to my first machine around that time. I knew him through mutual friends and we agreed to meet in Camberwell on a weekend morning. Tank wanted five hundred quid for the weapon, a black Beretta pistol, but that was taking the piss. He'd already told me he was offering a rebore rather than a complete gun. The barrel had been drilled and would only fire homemade bullets. But I also knew better than to communicate via text for a transaction such as this. We had to do it in person. He'd given me an address and said he'd be waiting in the stairwell. I took those stairs two at a time. I was going to rob the boy.

Tank looked to be around my age, almost sixteen or thereabouts, with chin-length dreads and a thin body, all ribs and sharp angles. Looking at him made me wonder how he'd earned his street name, y'know. He was shuffling nervously on the spot on the third floor at the end of the smelly, outdoor concrete landing, hugging a plastic JD Sports drawstring bag.

'You Boost?' he asked, looking all about.

'Yeah,' I went and, nodding at the bag, added, 'Let me see that thing.'

Tank handed me the bag and, instead of looking inside it, I slung it over my shoulder and told him, 'I'm keeping this, it's mine.'

Tank's bony jaw hit the piss-drenched floor. He didn't say a word, didn't move. Like anyone who knew me – or knew of me – back then, he was careful to keep his mouth shut. I walked back to Myatts Field with my bag and a silly grin on my face. Rebore or not, I had a gun.

Nan and Granddad were still at mass when I got home, but still I locked myself in the downstairs bathroom before opening the bag. What was inside didn't disappoint. It didn't look any different to a live gun and you'd only notice that it was light if you were holding it. I turned the weapon over, the casing cold but silky in my hands. Colder still against my waist, but, man, as I stepped out onto Treherne Court, I felt like the man, y'know.

That Beretta was on my waist less than half-an-hour before it almost got me into deep shit.

I headed in the direction of Saji's shop and I was turning into Foxley Square when I clocked an older, black guy in a tracksuit, hood up. Nothing unusual about that, but he was staring right at me. I swear he didn't even blink. I thought, 'Why the fuck is this guy staring at me?' He was standing a few metres in front of Saji's, hands in the pocket of his hoodie. Staring. Anger pulsed through me, faster and faster with every step. As I got closer, the guy put his head on one side and said, 'You good?' Those two words, coupled with his look, sent me over the cliff.

I got right up in his face, lifted my top so he could see my machine and hissed, 'Yeah, I'm good.'

He sort of backed off. 'Rah, I'm not your enemy, y'know,' he said.

At that point, Albz came out of Saji's shop, saw me flashing my rebore at this guy and immediately stomped over, *News of the World* fluttering from under his arm and slapping the pavement, tits-up.

'Oi, Boost, put your toy away, man,' he said. 'Don't you know who this is?'

I took a step back, let my top fall to my waist. I still didn't know who I was looking at.

'It's Ray,' said the stranger. 'How're Rose and Mick doing? Still playing football, man?'

'Rah, it's Ray, man,' Albz repeated, spudding Ray while looking at me. 'He's only been out a couple of weeks, y'know. Man doesn't need that kinda welcome from his brothers.'

Albz flicked his fingers towards my waist and all the blood in my body rushed to my face. Ray – *now* I remembered the name. He was an Older who had watched me play football when I was a kid. He'd been in jail for seven years or so. I barely recognised him. He'd shaved all his Rasta hair off.

I tried to look cool. 'Yo, sorry man. I didn't recognise you.'

Ray just laughed. 'Nah, it's all good man, all good.'

It turned out that Ray knew my mum and grandparents. He called me later that same day and asked if I wanted to go over to his place on Vassall Road. 'Something I'd like to run by you,' he said.

The least I could do after threatening him with my rebore was to show up and see what he had to offer. I still felt a bit stupid over my aggression. I'd been ready to bun him in the leg, if I'm honest. I set off on my bike with my Beretta. I wouldn't be flashing that thing at Ray again, but its presence made me feel safe.

This something that Ray wanted to run by me was more of a pep talk. Before I'd even reached his settee he began, 'Look, Boost, I know you wanna be on the road, man, but you've gotta know how to protect yourself.' He pulled the curtains shut.

I sat down, pulled my jacket around me. Fuck, it was cold in there. Felt like a funeral parlour.

He continued, 'You need to protect yourself, and you need to make money. You also need to be smart, tactical. You don't want …'

'Rah, I know all that,' I said, 'but y'know, I'm still playing football and stuff. I'm still trying to make it with the football thing, but I want to make money too, y'know. I still wanna to be a street boy.'

Ray narrowed his eyes at me, as he'd done outside Saji's, but there was a hint of a smile breaking through his stare this time. He stood by the window, a soft-leather sports bag slouched by his feet. Without speaking, he picked up the bag and dumped it between us on the settee as he sat down. Relaxed as you like, he unzipped the bag and pulled out of it a 9 mm pistol. Yeah, Ray just lifted that machine and cupped it back.

'Yo, hold that,' he said, offering it to me.

I took it, smiling. In fact, I couldn't stop smiling the whole time that machine was in my hands. First thing I noticed was how weighty it was and I was like, 'Yeah, this is some real shit. This is powerful. This is confidence.' Made my rebore seem like a Mickey Mouse prop from a pantomime.

'Listen, what I'm telling you is this,' Ray went on, regaining custody of his gun, 'you can do the football thing or the road thing but you need to make a decision. Look, I've just spent a long time in jail. The roads don't last, y'know, so either get out or get smart.'

'I get ya, man,' I said. Ray put the gun back in the bag. I was sad to see it go.

'But, if you wanna be a gangster, you need to protect yourself. Otherwise, you'll end up dead. Arm yourself with the right weapons. Never stop looking over your shoulder, because the moment you do ...' Ray shaped his hand into a gun, held it to his head and mimicked the sound of gunfire. 'In the meantime,' he said, 'I'll give you some white to sell. Keep all that you make, it'll help bring some bread in.'

'Wow,' I said. 'Thanks man.' I appreciated Ray's raw advice. Reading between the lines, his message was 'kill or be killed'.

He gave me a lump of crack – about a zed's worth – and told me to stay focused. That night, once my grandparents had turned in, I locked myself in the downstairs bathroom again and, armed with a carrier bag, razor blade and cling film, chopped and wrapped the crack and hid the rocks in a bag inside another bag inside the shoebox under my bed.

The October half-term holiday had just started and I had the whole week ahead to make some serious money from my gear. That was the plan – before the rebore took over proceedings.

The next morning I spotted my Uncle Brendan while on my way back from walking Jet, rebore on my waist. Brendan Hamilton was my nan's younger brother and he cracked me up, man. Irish, loud and in his mid-forties, every day was St Patrick's Day to him. I'd never seen him sober. He'd walk up to any one of the Olders and start a conversation, even if he hadn't met them before. Any other stranger would've been chased off the estate, or worse, but the Olders instantly warmed to my uncle. With his Lucozade-coloured hair and red face, he was impossible to miss among the small group of Olders gathered by the wall at the end of Treherne Court. He was swigging from a can of Stella, laughing and joking and giving Stinks a playful punch on the arm. I was pleased to see him, man. I got on well with Uncle Brendan. He had a soft spot for me; every time he visited he'd give me a fiver and say, 'Buy yourself something, T.'

Brendan spotted me and waved his Stella in the air. 'Hey, T., how're you doing, Our Boy?'

I started laughing but was interrupted by a cry of, 'Jakes, run! Jakes, *run!*' This was Smoker, who'd been sitting on the wall and spotted undercover police pulling up and flying out of their cars. I'd never seen Smoker move so fast. He jumped off the wall and started running, the other Olders behind him, I gave Jet's lead to Brendan. 'Look after her for a second,' I said and joined the running pack, jakes chasing us.

After ten seconds or so, we all started running in different directions. I managed to break free and run onto one of the courts and sprinted back towards Treherne, jumping over walls and fences. I looked over my shoulder and, seeing no jakes, pulled my rebore from my waistband and threw it into a bush in our garden. I ran on and on, heart banging, reached the slope – and two of the undercover jakes.

Thank fuck I hadn't packed a nank or drugs. The officers searched me, found nothing and let me go. Walking home, I breathed a sigh of relief. Now all I had to do was retrieve my rebore. I searched all over our tiny garden, under every bush, digging in the flowerbeds until my fingernails were black with soil. I looked inside and outside Jet's kennel, and as I did so, thought, 'Shit, Brendan and Jet.' I'd forgotten about them amid the commotion. Defeated, I went indoors. Granddad was standing in the hall in his winter coat.

'Yo, Dad,' I said casually. 'You going out?' He said nothing, raising his eyebrows and cocking his head. I knew that look. It said, 'Have-you-got-something-you-want-to-tell-me?' 'Brendan's taken Jet for a walk,' I said, but as the words spurted from my mouth, Granddad lifted his coat – and what's he got on his waist?

He'd seen it all. Granddad had been watching from the window when I ran past.

'Sorry Dad,' I said, as we stood there in the hall. 'It's not mine – I was just holding it for somebody and then the police arrived, y'know. And it ain't real or nothing.'

Granddad sighed, but appeared surprisingly calm.

'Well, good job your nan's at bingo,' he said, handing me the gun. 'Listen, you don't need this thing, Terroll. Don't get caught up in the wrong crowd. Get rid of it. Give it back to your friend, whatever, but get it away from here. Your Nan would have a fit if she knew.'

'Yeah, sorry,' I said, and stuffed the gun in my coat pocket.

Granddad's reaction left me confused and paranoid, questions whirling in my head. Why was he so chilled? Had I been framed? Did he know about my involvement with OC? Or maybe, being ex-army, guns didn't faze him? Did men in their fifties get what was going down on the streets? Perhaps he assumed this was a typical teenage thing to do and he was putting it down to my being at a 'difficult age'. In the end I went with the ex-army idea. Kinda made me feel better, y'know. But I would need to be extra careful from now on. The gun was staying though, regardless. That night, I hid the Beretta under Jet's bedding in her kennel. She didn't know it yet, but Jet would get to sleep on many firearms over time.

Half-term didn't get any easier. I began to think that the machine might be cursed: every time I took it out with me, something happened. The day after the police chase, I was with my friend Thomas in his car when he got pulled over near the Loughborough Estate. We were heading towards Myatts Field, back to HQ, when blue lights started flashing behind us. I had the machine on my waist but remained calm as a police officer approached the car. I whipped off my seat belt and leaned towards the officer as he loomed in the rolled-down window, my elbow stabbing Thomas's chest.

'Rah, how're you doing? You all right? We're going to Myatts Field to play football. Is there a problem?'

Thomas's forehead gleamed with sweat. I could feel his heart as it shuddered through my arm. Thomas wasn't a gang member, but dabbled in criminality from time to time. I was chancing it, but I had a plan B: if the officer asked us to step out of the car, I'd kick him and make a run for it. I wasn't worried. I was fast, I was Boost. Luckily, my chat did the trick, although I knew that next time I might not be so lucky, right?

Much as I loved having a machine on my waist, I started to think, 'Rah, this don't feel like the gun for me. There's something not right about it. I can't be rolling with this thing no more.' I gave the Beretta to Bradz, a boy I knew from Kennington who was also OC and a year younger than me. He was well pleased when I asked him to take care of my machine for a bit. To be honest, I still wasn't sure what to do with it; ideally, I'd sell it, but it would take time.

'It ain't live,' I told Bradz. 'Keep it in a safe, but if things get hot and you need to ditch it, do what you have to do, man. Just be careful with it, know what I mean?'

Bradz was, like, 'Yeah, no worries man, I'll look after it.'

I gave the gun to Bradz on Wednesday but still the curse of the Beretta continued. The next day, he called, sounding like he was being tortured. 'Boost, I fucked up, man,' he started. He was making choking sounds interspersed with deep groans. 'Fuck, I bunned myself in the chest, man.' More choking.

'What're you talking about, man?'

'Ambulance's coming. Left the thing in the wheelie bin,' he spluttered. 'Sorry, man.' He hung up. I couldn't get my head around it. How the fuck did he manage to shoot himself?

Bradz ended up OK, aside from a burn and a bit of bruising. He told the ambulance crew he'd been 'hit by something' in the street and that seemed to work. He managed to avoid any police involvement. Another contact retrieved the rebore from Bradz's bin in the middle of Thursday night. On Friday evening, me and Mikes made some inquiries and a man in Norbury agreed to buy the Beretta for six hundred pounds (I wouldn't want to sell it to anyone in Myatts Field) when we convinced him that it was live.

It was mostly Mikes who did the talking; he had the gift of the gab in these situations. He could be loud and aggressive as fuck when he wanted, but he was also the finesser on our team. The guy took his word at face value, the deal went through and, come Sunday night, me and Mikes were both three hundred pounds better off. But that was the only money I made that week, aside from one trip to Brixton Road, where I dished out a few samples to crackheads and told them to 'spread the word'. It was back to school on Monday.

Still, at least I'd got rid of the gun. Like I said, we were still learning.

12

TINY ALIEN

As I look back now, I'm horrified to think of the way we Youngers operated on the streets. We were teenagers, running around with real guns playing real-life *Call of Duty* and that visual alone haunts me to this day. Y'know, I'm ashamed to admit this now, but I would actually get excited at the prospect of either being shot at, or shooting a pagan myself. I can't lie. Such was my mindset back then. In those days the Peckham Boys would often try to circle our estate. They would come in numbers, on foot or on bikes. Now, I say respect to those brothers; they were the only boys who had the balls to come to Myatts Field. Back then, the Peckham Boys were a threat. Sometimes there would be shootouts… I can't watch violent films or video games no more. I only have to hear a gunshot and I'm breaking out in a sweat, y'know what I mean? Whenever I think back to some of the crazy scenarios in which I was involved, I'm surprised I'm here to tell my story. Not everyone I knew was so fortunate.

I was on the 159 bus when I heard the devastating news about Tiny Alien. The driver had just pulled away from the stop on Villa Road. I was visualising the chicken and chips I'd buy when I got off at Brixton, on my way home from training at Tooting and Mitcham FC, where I had started playing for the under-eighteens team. I was starving, man, that's what I remember. Strange how the mind connects insignificant detail with tragedy.

It was a sweltering Friday afternoon in June and the 2006 FIFA World Cup had just started in Germany. My phone rang.

I'll never forget Mikes' voice. Raw and broken. He could barely get his words out. I was, like, 'Yo, bro, what's happening?'

He fell silent, then gasped down the phone. 'It's … Tiny A, bro.'

'What is it, man?' My brain was trying to work out what was going on. The first thought I had was that Tiny A had been pulled or that a court appearance hadn't gone in his favour (I knew he was on bail for a couple of bits). 'Is he all right?' Silence from Mikes, a contrast to the racket on the bus of a wailing toddler. 'Mikes,' I said again, sticking my finger in my free ear as I strained to hear a response from my friend.

'He's dead, man. Tiny A is dead.'

'What the fuck are you talking about?'

'Bro, there was madness. Tiny A got stabbed last night. Lox was with him when it happened, man … ' Mikes' voice fell down a hole.

Chicken and chips … football training … World Cup … crying kid and every person on that sweaty top deck … none of it meant anything to me. My throat began to swell. I pressed my head to the window, squeezing the bridge of my nose as tears trickled down my face. My voice cracked.

'I'm coming back now, bro.'

I got off the bus at Iceland and walked back to Myatts Field. I was finding my way on autopilot, in shock, y'know.

People got stabbed all the time on the streets. It was an occupational hazard of gang life. You got stabbed, go to hospital, get your stitches and get the fuck out before police get involved. But nobody in our circle had died before.

Pastor Mimi answered the door, dabbing her eyes with a tissue. She spread her arms and I fell into them, sobbing as she hugged me. Man, that woman deserves an OBE. She looked after us boys all afternoon – me, Ratty and Mikes and Troopz – as we tried to get our heads around things. At that stage, Mimi was obviously aware of the madness that going on around us, out on the estate, but still she hadn't a clue that Mikes was active in a gang. It would be a while yet before she found out.

Everybody in the area who associated with Tiny A was devastated by his death. I'd known Alex quite well, but Lox had been his close friend for years and the death hit him hard, not least because he was there when it happened on Ethelred Estate, Kennington. He'd witnessed his friend being knifed in the heart by some boy from the Kennington area. Later, Alex's dad posted a picture of his boy during his final moments in hospital, insisting Tiny A wasn't in a gang.

Tiny A, like the rest of us, was just about to finish his GCSE exams. He was due to go on to study electrical engineering at college. His killer was eighteen when he was sentenced to eighteen years in April 2007.

A death always affects a whole community. I went to Tiny A's funeral but left straight after the service. It was too painful, man. He was a good brother, loved by many. Look on YouTube and you'll see the tributes. Yeah, it was a wake-up call but losing a friend on the streets didn't stop us carrying knives or guns and using those weapons to protect ourselves if necessary. If anything, a death in the hood fuelled the rivalry among gangs. It certainly did as far as I was concerned: I surrendered to a new impulse to hate and to hurt. Yes, I'd cry in the downstairs bathroom – but then I'd walk out on the block, knowing I could destroy another person's life.

I left school that summer with five GCSEs – in maths, English, science, PE double award and technology. My highest grade was B, for English, as I was good at being creative and I enjoyed writing stories. I also got a few E grades – for effort, y'know.

I didn't have a clue what to do with my qualifications. There was nothing I wanted to study further and a nine-to-five career didn't appeal. I was a gang member-cum-footballer – normality scared me, y'know. I didn't want to get sucked into a nine-to-five routine. Office work was not for me. However, I had to do something to appear normal, for the sake of my family, at least. The lure of gang life was pulling me deeper and I even came to the warped conclusion that, were I to make it as a footballer and earn loads of money, I could invest more in being a gang member

I signed on to take a health and social care BTEC course at Lambeth College, purely to hang around and meet girls. I wasn't interested in working in the sector at all and I was thrown off the course after a few weeks for not attending any classes. At least the college pass had come in handy for that brief period: whenever the jakes stopped me in the street, I'd just point to the lanyard around my neck and say, 'On my way home from college, innit.' I tried the same trick with the same course at Hammersmith College. Again, I thought I'd meet some nice girls, but relationships were hard to start, let alone hold down, for me as a gang member. I was more devoted to the fearsome team I now made up with Mikes and Lox.

There were no rebores in our camp, only live machines. Yeah, we'd reached a new level of survival in our real-life *Call of Duty*, and it came with an elevated attitude of entitlement and ruthlessness. We would get into fights day or night at any location – outside McDonald's, KFC at a shoobs, anywhere. If we decided that we didn't like you, we would get active. Now. We'd use our fists or our weapons. There were loads of times that I nearly got stabbed – or did get stabbed – or shot at. That was everyday life with OC. Listen, I've experienced bullets coming at me like fireworks so many times. And nine times out of ten, I would never find out who fired them – because the gunman would be wearing a balaclava.

Fortunately, being fast and agile enabled me to dodge many of those bullets.

I'd still nick knives from Nan's kitchen. I can't remember the number of times that I watched her rummage through the drawers, shaking her head, saying, 'Where have all the knives gone?' A lot of the time, I had no more idea than she did. I'd take a knife and would often have to dash it for whatever reason. I'd just go back to the drawer and take another. I'm not proud of that but, without my nank, I didn't feel safe out there. I believed that my sole reason for carrying a knife was for protection and as a deterrent if things got heated.

One Friday night I had a flick knife outside Tennessee Fried Chicken, Kennington, where I was ordering peri-peri chicken, when I bumped into a few girls I knew from the area. I stopped to chat to them, flirt a bit, y'know. It was around 11 p.m. – late for some, early for others – and the girls were talking about going on to a club.

'Come with us, T,' they kept saying and I was tempted, but Mikes and me had deliveries to make. Green and white.

'I can't. Got other commitments, innit. Listen, next time though. One hundred per cent.'

'Oh, come on, T, it's Friday night, man.'

Back and forth that convo went. A group of lads came out of the shop and tried to get between me and the girls. There were about five of them, black utes I didn't recognise, blatantly crowding my space, man. One of them, his mouth full of burger, affecting a limping, wannabe gangster gait, flashed me a snidey look and moved in on the girl I was talking to.

'Yo, what's happening?' he asked her and it made me incandescent with it, right?

Swift as fuck, I kicked my heel to the back of my thigh, reached into my trainer and pulled out my flick knife, keeping it hidden in my palm for now.

'Yo, prick, get out the road,' I yelled and he turned, looked at me, his laugh smelling of ketchup and mayo.

'Who the fuck are you?'

His mates were gathering, muttering insults. They all took a step towards me and the girls walked away. I glared at the cunt with his burger.

'You wanna know who I am?' As I said this, I saw a slice of silver in my peripheral. One of them had a knife. Time to step up. You are gonna remember my name.

I press the button and the blade ejects with a click and a swish. I turn the knife to a stab position, gripping the handle, blade pointing down and lift my hand. I stand still, staring at them. A demon voice takes over my mind: the first person who comes near me, I'm gonna stab them so hard, he's gonna drop and leak in front of his friends and they're all gonna scream and run for their lives. My chest lifts and falls, lifts and falls. Hot breath geysers from my nose, then someone says, 'Leave it, man,' and the boys back off and leave.

Knife culture. That was what the press called the scourge of blades and stabbings on the streets, innit. Same as anything to do with firearms becomes 'gun culture'. It pissed me off to see how they'd write this sanctimonious stuff. 'Knife culture', 'gun culture', 'gang culture'; everything they don't understand is a 'culture' to them. They didn't know *our* culture. I was equally infuriated about the articles that appeared following the death of Tiny A. 'He was part of a gun-toting gang' and all that stuff. I'd read those stories and think, 'Do you know what it's like to grow up on an estate like Myatts Field?'

I became addicted to gang life. Addicted to the power and the confidence it gave me. To be able to walk into a shoobs in a pair of black leather gloves and make everybody think I was carrying a gun when I wasn't? That was power. Like any addiction, mine grew and grew. A college course wasn't going to earn me money, not in the short term. Football wasn't paying, and Mikes and me weren't making a huge profit selling drugs. I'd become a bit lazy with it, if I'm honest. It was so time-consuming. Robbery, however, was invariably a quicker way to make instant cash. I don't mean bank jobs, steaming or anything like that. Nah, we would rob people in the street, usually at night, outside bars and clubs. I never much enjoyed doing this and I'm ashamed to now be owning up to doing it, but it was what it was and sometimes it had to get done. I started going to raves and nightclubs with Mikes and Shellz looking for targets, people wearing expensive bling, y'know.

We did our first robbery at a rave in a yardie club in Croydon. The job took less than an hour from start to finish. Soon after we entered the club, Mikes spotted a yardie wearing an expensive Rolex watch studded with diamonds. Man, even in the manic strobe lights you see the glint off them diamonds. We followed the yardie around the club, keeping our distance without losing him in the crowds of ravers. I was tagging along for this one – it was more Mikes and Shellz's area of expertise than mine – wondering what our next move would be, when the yardie made a beeline for the exit. The strobe lights caught Mikes' expression: pure glee.

Outside, we tail the yardie until he's turned a corner, then, bang, Mikes grabs his shoulder as Shellz punches him on the nose. Mikes sweeps the yardie's feet. He goes down and now I'm fighting with a few randoms who've come to help. The yardie is getting a kicking from Shellz as Mikes grabs the guy's Rolex watch and runs. Shellz boots the yardie one more time and beats it up the road too. Someone shouts, 'Has anybody called an ambulance?' The yardie's spitting blood. People circle him. I hear sirens and run for my life.

To avoid any comeback, we swapped the watch for a sawn-off shotgun rather than trying to sell it. I sorted this via a contact in Bermondsey, one of the lads over there, who went on to become my go-to boys if I wanted to know about robberies or jewellery or selling stuff on.

Not long after that I got into a fight at the Mint bar, Streatham. There were about six of us this time, including Mikes. A boy had started asking me where I was from and, as usual, violence erupted and I ended up fly-kicking him in the chest. While he was down, we popped a chain from his neck, fled and thought no more of it until Mikes, Shellz and me were chilling next to the play park on the estate some days later, chatting to a few girls. A guy named Sting walked past. He wasn't from Myatts Field itself but lived in our area and I knew him to say 'All right?' to. He was hard to miss – at least six-foot-five, with a wide neck and dreads. He did a double-take when he saw me. He glared at me, throwing back his shoulders and pulling up his hood.

'You're the cunt who kicked my brother,' he yelled, 'D'you know what you're dealing with?'

I laughed. 'Yo, he ain't talking to me, is he?' I said to my boys.

'Yeah, I'm talking to you. You kicked my little brother. Outside Mint in Streatham, remember? D'you know what you're doing?' Sting looked down at me, waiting for a reaction. Didn't he want to punch me or something? He looked at the girls, then back at me.

I smiled at him. 'Give me one moment, please,' I said, 'I'll be back in one minute.' I jogged back to Treherne Court, leaving Sting to argue with Mikes and Shellz. They knew I wanted my moment and I hoped that they would refrain from kicking the shit out of Sting. I slipped into Jet's kennel and grabbed a machine I'd recently bought from a contact in the Old Kent Road area, shoved it down my jeans and jogged back, fizzing with adrenaline, but raging too. No boy disses me in front of girls, y'know what I'm saying? No way.

Mikes had managed to keep Sting talking and was on the brink of convincing Sting that he'd accused the wrong brother when I appeared behind him. 'Yo, look at me when I'm speaking to you,' I said calmly, drawing my machine and aiming it at the back of Sting's head. A few of the girls started screaming.

Sting faced me and lifted his hands. 'Take it easy, man,' he said, his voice juddering, 'We can talk about this y'know.'

I sneered at him. I could hear people shouting, voices blending into one:

'No, no, T.'

'You can't do that T.'

'Stop it, T.'

'Put it down.'

'C'mon, T.'

'Oh, my God, oh, my God, oh, my God.'

'Fuck.'

But my mind wasn't programmed for reason just then. I tightened my grip on the handle, finger twitching against the trigger and, in a slow, deranged voice, looked Sting in the eye and said, 'Listen, I could lick your head off right now.' Sting sidestepped to his right, hands in front of him. 'Now, get the fuck out of my area.'

Sting took a few more tentative steps, accelerating into a walk, then a jog, then a run. The girls walked away like mourners as a funeral. I put my hammer away, swearing under my breath. I went a bit floaty, y'know, my arms and legs like straws. It was a weird one because, although I was aware of what I'd just done, it kinda felt like I'd been watching myself in a movie and missing moments when my concentration wandered. Even my recollection of running home for my hammer was becoming sketchy. I'd been on autopilot. I looked at Mikes and Shellz. 'All right?' I said.

'Yo, I'm starving,' went Mikes. 'Let's get a burger, man.'

Say the jakes had swung by the playground that afternoon and seen me aiming my hammer at Sting? They would've had me bang to rights – possession, acquisition and carrying in a public place. That was just for starters. What if I'd squeezed the trigger and put one in Sting? None of those questions were on my radar as we walked to Dallas chicken shop on Vassall Road.

13

ESCAPE FROM MYATTS FIELD

I was kicked out of Hammersmith College shortly before I turned seventeen for the same reasons I had been booted out of Lambeth – not showing up to classes or submitting any coursework. Again, I'd just wanted the badge so I could chat to girls, but that fizzled out once my pass was deactivated. I wasn't too fussed as it meant I could focus my energy into making money on the streets through dealing rather than robberies.

I was immune to the levels of violence around me and I moved up the OC ladder when some of the other Olders were jailed. A few of my fellow Youngers joined me and we began taking on more responsibility, scouting for new Youngers while also still looking up to the Olders who remained on the block. It was still hard to keep OC activities separate from my home life. At one point, Nan discovered a 9-mm bullet while doing the dusting.

It was my fault. I'd left the ammo in my bag, hanging, unzipped, on the handlebars of my bike, in the hallway. She bumped into the bike, the bag slipped and out tumbled the evidence. I got home to find Nan sitting in the kitchen, arms crossed. I'd breezed in and swung open the fridge, at first not noticing the lead cartridge on the table before her.

'Yo, how's it going, Nan? Why ain't you at bingo?'

Nan never missed bingo.

Silence.

I turned to look at her, and there it was, sitting alone, where the teapot would usually be.

'Found this today while I was doing the cleaning,' Nan said, darting her eyes at the bullet. 'Fell out of your bag.'

'Oh, yeah?' I said. My heart started hammering, man. I hadn't been scared of bullets up to that point but, fuck, now I was, y'know.

Nan nodded. 'Looks like a bullet to me, Terroll. What … why … how … what are you doing with a bullet in your bag?'

Think, Boost, *think*.

'Yo, I found that in the street,' I said. 'Was gonna get it put on a chain or something. Seen stuff like that online. What d'ya reckon?'

Nan pulled a face like she was considering the idea. 'Is that a thing? Is it safe?'

And I said, 'Rah, yeah, people do it all the time.'

I had somehow managed to avoid disaster with Nan, but that was close. What if she'd chosen to spring-clean the living room and had opened the drawers and cupboards in the dresser and had found those wraps of crack I'd squirreled? I was on thin ice and I did wonder how long I could keep this act going. I was almost seventeen. Nan and Granddad would surely start asking what I wanted to do with my life and all that crazy stuff. Then an opportunity came my way.

In summer 2007, I got scouted to try for Stevenage Borough FC Youth in Hertfordshire. If picked, I could play for the club and study sports science at North Hertfordshire College. And much as the studying part was off-putting, I had good vibes about this one, y'know? Although I'd been busy on the streets, I'd never taken my eye off the ball, so to speak. I was still training and continued to play for Tooting and Mitcham. Older now, my confidence had grown. I wasn't that scared kid playing it safe at West Ham Academy no more. Nah, I had energy, I had strength, I had attitude,

I was Boost ... off *and* on the pitch. Maybe this was a sign from above that I should escape from Myatts Field, be like Zav, who was still going strong at West Ham. Could this be my One Chance?

The Stevenage gig was a one-day affair with back-to-back games, rather than weeks of training as had been the case with West Ham. This time my form was good, man; first touch of the ball I got I made the best impression ever, thanks to a boy playing for the other side – a Peckham Boy, as well, and a relative of a former Premiership and England player. The goalkeeper threw the ball to me on the left wing and the other boy – I'll call him JT – playing on the right-wing for the opposition, came running at me and, as he reached me, I scooped the ball and booted it into the air, skimming his hair. He continued running towards my team's goalie while I powered ahead. I flicked the ball over his head and ran around him – a perfectly executed manoeuvre. At the end of the game, when we shook hands with the other side, JT gave me a look that said, 'Respect, bro.' It shocked me a bit to think that, despite our warring background, that JT and me were able to put our differences aside that day. We may have been enemies in Lambeth, but in Hertfordshire we were professional footballers. It turned out we'd be seeing a lot more of each other in the future as, at the end of the trial, both of us were signed by the club's manager, Darren Sarll.

Both of my families – blood and street – were pleased for me, man. I was getting out of Myatts Field, moving to Hertfordshire, chasing a footballing career. People were saying I was 'the next Zav'. When I went round to tell Mikes my news, he was like, 'Rah, proud of ya, bro. But Hertfordshire? You really wanna move there? What about the Fields? What about OC, man?' I got a bit choked, man.

'Listen,' I said, 'I ain't going far. I'll be back at weekends and shit. I'm still your brother, still OC, y'know.' I made an

O and a C with my fingers. Mikes did the same and I slapped my OC against his, like Stinks had done to us three years ago.

'Rah, *OC*,' we said in unison. A week later, I moved to Hitchin, Hertfordshire. I didn't pack a machine, but I did take a knife, just in case, like.

I rented a room in a four-bedroom house on an estate near Windmill Hill, Hitchin. My housemates were a Scouser boy, Phil – also a Stevenage Youth FC apprentice – and the landlady, Jane. She was probably in her early forties, which then seemed old to me. Phil – or Philly, as we called him – came from a rough estate in Toxteth, Liverpool. He too had experienced gang life and we had loads in common.

My first few weeks in Hitchin were strange, man. It took me a while to settle. Apart from playing football, every aspect of my life had changed overnight. One thing that hit me was how quiet Hitchin was, compared to Myatts Field. It was all a bit Thermos flasks and wellies and I had some adjusting to do to get with country life in a market town some forty miles north of my home. It was villagey, with old buildings, shops selling pottery and pubs that did ploughman's lunches and quizzes and shit. There was no smell of weed in the air. I couldn't hear gunshots. This was a culture shock, as was the academy, which was hard graft, I'm telling ya.

Philly and me would get up at 6 a.m., have breakfast, walk to college, do training, go to classes, do more training, go home, have dinner, go to bed, then get up and do it all over again. Same routine, Monday to Friday. Was this how it felt to be a 'good boy'? Was this normal life? It was all a bit military for me. After each training session we had to take the nets off the goals, wash the balls and clean our boots. I found the sports science classes to be tedious and they reminded me of being in school. The training side of things kept me focused, especially when I felt homesick. I missed my grandparents and street brothers, but I was also making a new set of friends, among them JT, member of my sworn enemies the Peckham Boys.

Don't get me wrong, it wasn't all daffodils and roses to begin with between me and JT. During our early training sessions, we'd rip the piss out of one another on the pitch. If he missed a shot, I'd laugh and say, 'That's 'cos you're from Peckham.' Whenever I fucked up, he'd be like, 'Brixton boys don't know how to play.' Our banter started out as being pretty spiteful, but it did become funny and friendly after a while. Without saying as much, we recognised we were similar. Both from south London, we'd both left gangland behind in an attempt to make better futures for ourselves as footballers. Away from the battlefield, there was a mutual understanding vibe going on. We were sharing our escape from the road together and that was kinda beautiful, y'know. Though I wouldn't repeat those to thoughts to my OC boys.

One afternoon, as we were scrubbing our boots, JT mentioned he was looking for new digs. 'Fucking housemate's a dickhead,' he said. 'Gotta get outta there, man.'

'Rah, you should move in with me and Philly,' I said. 'Our landlady's got a room going.'

JT spudded me. 'Really? That'll be sweet,' he said. Next day, he moved in and it was happy families from thereon. Wow – an OC boy living under the same roof as a Peckham Boy. Who'd have fucking thought it?

Student life was crazy. I barely had any money. As part of the youth scheme, we got fifty pounds a week – thirty quid in Education Maintenance Allowance, and twenty from the club - to play for Stevenage FC Youth team, which was bollocks for all the sweat involved. I was paying twenty pounds a week towards my digs and the same on food. Every Tuesday after college, Jane would take Philly, JT and me to Asda in her blue Nissan Micra. We'd stock up on mince, tins of beans and anything with a yellow 'reduced' sticker and bundle back into Jane's Micra, bulging carrier bags squashed between us. Jane was cool, man. She was always cooking for us or giving us lifts to places.

Despite being skint, we still managed to lead a social life although, as academy sportsmen, we weren't supposed to party during the week – or on weekends if we had matches. Darren Sarll – nicknamed Sarlly – made that clear from day one. But what he didn't know now wouldn't hurt him, right? We'd go to parties and pick up girls, saying, 'I'm a footballer for Stevenage Borough FC' – without mentioning we were playing for the youth team or that we were only earning fifty quid.

I met one girl, Clara, in a club called Liquid. She was striking, man, mixed race with blueish eyes and a student at Hertfordshire North College doing a business course. But things didn't work out, partly because I got bored after just a few weeks but also because she was really smart. I'd be lying in bed next to her thinking, 'She's too clued-up for me. She is gonna figure me out'. I felt similar vibes with the next girl I went out with, Abi. She was also mixed race and posh. Very posh – I'm talking private-schooling, holidays-on-Daddy's-yacht and ponies-for-your-birthday level posh. I'd be lying in bed next to her thinking, 'She is too posh for me. She is gonna figure me out': street paranoia, it never leaves you. I think I noticed this even more because I was away from Myatts Field. Conversations in Hitchin didn't revolve around machines or drugs or 'jakes on the block'. I was beginning to see how normal people lived, y'know. I was out of my comfort zone. Myatts Field, gangland … that had been my 'normal' until now. Needless to say, things came to an end with Abi. It was like two different worlds colliding, polar opposites. That one would never have worked out.

On Tuesday nights, I'd go to Penthouse nightclub, Sun Street. Some of us were too young to get in, but we got to know the bouncers and they would sneak us in the back door.

After a few vodka-and-Cokes, we'd be flying, busting moves on the dance floor, getting stuck into the drinks promotions and chatting up girls until the early hours, when we'd stagger back to Jane's. Wednesday morning training sessions were a killer after a night at Penthouse and it showed in our playing. Our reaction times were slower, we missed passes and shots and got tired more quickly. Sarlly would bark at us and started asking, 'Why do you lot play so badly on Wednesdays?' Didn't stop us though.

One Tuesday, there were about ten of us academy players in the club. One of our boys, Craig, had just turned eighteen and we were in proper celebration mode. Craig kept buying rounds of shots between the usual drinks, spending what he called his 'birthday money'. There was a different energy among us that night; we all usually enjoyed letting our beards down at Penthouse but, generally, thoughts of having to train on Wednesday would always be niggling away at the back of our minds. Now, no one seemed to give a fuck. Craig boasted that he'd pull a sickie the next day and, as another Aftershock burned my throat, I decided I'd do the same. Soon we were all on the dancefloor, mucking about to some hip-hop track, me and Philly trying to impress a group of girls dancing next to us who clearly weren't interested, when, boom, the music stopped. Everyone looked around, going, 'What the fuck?' Philly was still dancing, oblivious.

The mic cut in: screech, crackle, tap. Someone started what sounded like a shout-out. 'Good evening Hitchin,' he said. Hang on, that voice was familiar ... 'Sorry to interrupt your evening but I have a special announcement to make. This one goes out to all the Stevenage Borough Youth players here tonight: I know you're in here. Get. Out. Now! And don't even think about bunking off tomorrow. I want you all on that pitch first thing.'

Fuck! It was Sarlly, *fuck*.

We sobered up fast, running in different directions, pushing past people. I ducked for cover under a table, almost knocking a woman off her stool. The music returned and the regular crowd went back to clubbing. But Sarlly might be prowling the club! I needed to get out of there fast, man, without being seen. *I don't wanna be doing runs tomorrow*, I thought. I charged from my hiding place and escaped via the back door. JT, Philly and a few of the others were outside. One of the boys was kneeling on the pavement, throwing up.

Oh, my God, the day after. Wednesday.

We all made it to training on time, feeling and looking like shit but trying to pretend everything was cool. It wasn't though. Straight off, Sarlly had us doing timed runs: ten laps of the pitch in ten minutes and whoever went over that time had to do an extra lap. Fail to finish that lap in one minute and do another one. That punishing regime continued for the entire, four hour, session. Imagine that with a hangover from hell. I thought I was gonna die. At the end, as we crashed out on the grass, spluttering, panting and sweating pure alcohol, Sarrly delivered his final party piece.

'Do you lot think I'm stupid?' he shouted, pacing back and forth, giving us daggers from above. 'I know some of you boys were out partying last night. You know who you are. *I* know who you are. You smell like a brewery, the lot of you.' We sat with drooping heads, staring at the grass. 'I told you, *no* partying during the week,' he went on. 'We've got a game this weekend and you'll probably be playing like shit. Now, get out of my sight. Sort yourselves out.' We hobbled back to the changing rooms in silence. I got to the toilet just in time before puking. Never again, y'know.

I was feeling jaded and it was nothing to do with my hangover. After three months at the academy, being short of money all the time was depressing. I missed being on the streets, making proper money. I missed my OC boys, missed my gang, missed

Myatts Field, man. And the boys back home, Mikes, Lox, Abz, Troops, Shellz and the rest seemed to be thriving. They'd call me up, asking how the football was going and talk about how great things were back home. They'd be like, 'Yo, we're making all this money. We're selling drugs. We're driving Range Rovers, riding motorbikes.'

'Rah, what'ya doing up there, man?' Mikes asked one day, after I'd bored him with a rundown of my week: training, classes, going to Asda in Jane's Micra, playing a match, getting elbowed while going for a header and snapping a bone in my nose (my nose is still broken today), going to Liquid but leaving early. Skint, man. 'You should come back, Boost. Things are good, y'know. I'm talking serious money.'

I got off the phone thinking, Nissan Micra and Asda versus Range Rover and bundles of cash? I'm deffo missing out here.

My perspective on Hitchin and the academy began to shift. It no longer felt like my One Chance; it had become a trap. The only part I was enjoying was football, but I could play anywhere, for any team. In truth, I was on my way to leaving the academy and my decision was fuelled by terrible disruption and tragedy in my personal life.

I got the news that my Uncle Brendan had been murdered at his ex-girlfriend's flat in Peckham. He was forty-eight. Mum gave me the news when I was home for a break. I burst into tears. 'What do you mean, murdered?' I didn't understand. How could a life be taken like that? Who'd kill Brendan? He wasn't in a gang and if he was involved in criminality, he'd kept it well-hidden. Poor Nan; Brendan was her little brother. She thought the world of him, as did we all. I cried all the way back to Hertfordshire, still not knowing who'd killed my uncle. Whoever was responsible, I wanted them to suffer. Like, really suffer. They never did though. All I knew was that Uncle was kicked to death. They said in the papers that the place was left looking like an abattoir. Two men were later tried for murder, but they got cleared, man.

I spent my eighteenth birthday in Hitchin. It fell on a Friday, meaning I could at least go out for a few drinks with the boys. My heart wasn't really in it though; I was grieving, y'know. Christmas in Myatts Field was a sad one, too. We were all in shock over Uncle Brendan's death.

When 2008 began, I was thoroughly bored with my routine – living in Jane's house with JT and Philly. Same routine, day in, day out. All three of us were getting bored. We also began noticing a few faces on the estate, country boys who didn't have a clue where we were from, looking at us as if to say, 'How dare you walk through our estate like you own it?' Philly eventually had a run-in with them. They asked him where he was from one time, so he was like, 'I'm from Toxteth. I ain't from this stupid area.'

We were laughing about the incident again as we walked home from training a few days later. 'Rah, would like to see that lot try it on in Peckham,' JT said.

'Fuck you, and fuck Peck-narm,' I went.

JT laughed. 'Fuck you, Brixton.'

Philly piped up in his Scouse accent, 'Fuck Brixton and Peckham, I'll see 'em in Toxteth.' At that point, a car pulled up beside us and this boy leapt out and smashed Philly round the head with a golf club.

'You not in your town now,' he sneered and jumped back in the car and sped off.

I chased them down the road, shouting, 'Come back here, you fucking utes.' I sprinted till the car disappeared, raging at myself for not being vigilant. I would've licked those spineless utes down in seconds had I known they were going to attack Philly. None of us were expecting that to happen. Not in Hitchin.

Philly didn't want to go to hospital. 'It's fine. I'll stick a plaster on it,' he said, blood gushing down his neck. His ear was split in two, bottom half of it hanging.

'Yo, bro, you need to go hospital,' said JT.

I agreed; his ear was flapping. It looked like one of those gory props you buy to go trick-or-treating with as a kid. We went with Philly to the hospital and he got his ear sewn up.

JT and me went out looking for those utes (in between college and football training) over the next few days while Philly recovered. It was probably a good thing we didn't find them. I can't lie, I had a hammer in my bag…

Not long after the golf-clubbing incident, Philly packed up college and moved back to Toxteth. 'This isn't for me,' he told us. We understood. In fact, Philly started a trend.

JT went next, said he missed London. 'It's too slow out here, bro.' Then it was just me and Jane left in that house. Asda on a Tuesday wasn't the same no more. I missed having JT and Philly around and, in turn, that made me more homesick for Myatts Field. I called Mikes on my way to training one Friday morning. It was mid-January, pissing it down and I went off on one, ranting about how I was sick of college, sick of training, sick of Hitchin, sick of having no money, sick of people dying, sick of life, sick and tired of feeling sick and tired. Mikes yawned down the phone. I'd woken him up.

'Come home, then, Boost,' he said. 'Come back to the hood, bro. We miss you.'

'Miss you too, bro.'

By that same dinner time, I was walking up the slope of Treherne Court, a bounce in my step. I stopped for a moment, inhaled deeply through my busted nose. Mm, gunpowder, weed, a waft of jollof rice from no. 13. Man, it was good to be home.

14

RETURN TO MYATTS FIELD

I'd been away from Myatts Field for five months, but as soon as I stepped back out on the block it was as though I'd never left. Hitchin was a distant memory, like a long, crazy dream.

The only part I hadn't enjoyed about leaving Hertfordshire behind me was breaking the news to Sarlly. Thinking that he'd try to talk me round or insist I serve a notice period or something, I came up with a lie to fast-track me out of there. I thought I needed to say something that he couldn't possibly question. I tried to catch him in his office before training, planning to leave town as soon as we finished talking. I didn't even sit down. I stood in front of him as he looked up at me from his swivel chair. He was eating a banana, his feet up on the desk.

I said, 'Listen, Darren. My mum's not well. She needs me. I need to move back to London.'

Sarlly bit into his banana, staring at me as he munched slowly. He didn't say a word until he'd thrown the skin in the bin. Calm as you like, he finally said, 'Yeah. You know what, Lewis? I know you're lying right now, but here's the thing … ' He drummed his fingers on the desk for a few seconds, thinking. 'I ain't going to force you to do anything you don't want to do. I want you to make the right choices for yourself. This is *your* life, not mine, Lewis.'

'Yeah, I know,' I muttered, staring at my trainers.

'OK,' he went, 'you can go. If that's what you want? Yeah, if you wanna leave, then leave, go … but before you do, I'm going to tell you one thing.' I looked up, caught his eye. His face was so serious, man. 'You will never, *ever* forget this.'

I nodded and said, 'Cool, thanks, Darren,' and walked out of the academy, away from college, away from Hitchin. I haven't seen Sarrly since, but he was right: I haven't forgotten.

Nan and Granddad were cool about my decision. I told them that I'd been really homesick. I'd missed them and my friends and Brixton so much, I said. We were all still grieving for Uncle Brendan, too, Nan especially so, and that seemed as good a reason for us to be together as a family, I added. 'I've not given up on football,' I explained. 'I'll just play in a team in London, like I was doing before. And I want to get a job, too.'

'Well, it's your life, son,' said Granddad, 'If this is what you want then we're right behind you.' That was my Granddad's attitude, man: make your own decisions in life – and learn from those choices. Go against the grain if necessary. He and Nan were from working-class backgrounds. Their careers advice to me was, 'Work on your CV and take it around all the shops on Oxford Street,' y'know.

I'd meant what I said about football. I did still want to play for a team, and Tooting and Mitcham FC were pleased to have me back. Life was returning to normal. Now all I had to do was get out there and make my money. It was from this point that Boost really began to express himself and blossom.

I was in the mix, back on the block, surrounded by people who got me. My boys looked proper swagged-up in their Roberto Cavalli, Iceberg, True Religion, latest trainers and Y3 tracksuits. And their iced out chains blinged, man. Yeah, they were making serious money and now Boost was gonna have some of that.

Most of our Olders had gone to jail or left the streets altogether. Unfortunately, Stinks was one of those serving time at Her Majesty's pleasure and was almost a third of the way into a ten-year stretch. But steel bars and razor fences didn't deter him when it came to his gang. Stinks lived and breathed OC; once he knew I was back on the block, he began calling me from prison. 'Yo, hold down the ends. Make sure you hold down the ends for me bro,' he'd say.

Albz, Dread, Jaf, Smoker, Tuffy and Sabz were among the remaining Olders, but they seemed less energetic since Stinks' departure. However, we still looked up to them. Stinks and his boys had built solid foundations. OC was a force to be reckoned with. We Youngers had worshipped Stinks like a god at one point. Now we would put into action everything he'd taught us. We would enforce our power as the next wave of Olders. We had big shoes to fill. And we did fill those shoes. We filled them and filled them some more.

As we grew into Olders, the next generation of OC youngsters emerged and it was our job to teach them, mould them and look after them. We would also bollock them, when necessary, for their own good, understand? Now it was our team – me, Lox, Mikes, Troopz, Abz, Shellz, Syikes, Ratty, and many more – sending the utes on pedal bikes to Saji's shop.

Those kids, aged around twelve to fourteen, were known as the OC Tinies, our own protégés, who'd grow up to be even more violent than our generation. I would scout for newbies, turn them into mini-versions of myself, give them street names. When I was their age I'd been a sponge, absorbing all that my Olders said and did. Now, I was a filter, passing on everything I'd learned. Mikes used to bully those youngsters something rotten.

I employed two of my Tinies, Devon and Sai, when I was at Mikes' place one Saturday afternoon. Both around fourteen and black, they were friends of Mikes' younger brother, Josh. I'd noticed them before, earwigging on our conversations in his kitchen, thinking we hadn't spotted them nudging each other, eyes wide with excitement. On this occasion, they were sitting on the stairs in the hall, munching cheese sandwiches, their tracksuits muddy after playing football in the rain in Myatts Field Park. They looked up when me and Mikes came in. 'Yo, how's it going, Boost?' said Devon, the taller of the two.

'Yeah, I'm good, y'know, man,' I said, 'You lot good?'

Their faces lit up.

'Yeah, been football, innit,' said Sai.

'Yeah, man,' added Devon, sandwich disappearing into his mouth. I could see those two had potential. They reminded me of a younger Mikes and me: acting cool but wanting to impress. They were hungry, deffo. Josh was in the kitchen with Mikes' other brother, Pete. Mimi was elsewhere in the house and while the four of us were alone in that hallway, I seized the moment.

'Listen,' I said, pulling what I hoped was a hard-man face. 'You two are bad boys, right. You wanna be bad boys?'

Devon and Sai looked at each other, then at me.

'Yeah,' they went in unison. Mikes started sniggering.

'For fuck's sake, T,' he said.

'Yeah, rah, y'know what?' I went on, nodding slowly at the boys, 'You lot are gonna be my youngers.' I pointed first at Devon, 'You're gonna be Baby Boost,' then at Sai on the stair below, 'And you're Little Boost,' and Mikes burst out laughing.

'Rah, I don't think they're about this life, man,' he said, but I carried on, trying not to laugh myself as I made the OC sign. 'You're OC now,' I said, and tapped my fingers against theirs in the same way Stinks had done in front of us. Devon and Sai sat there beaming, speechless. 'You boys know what this means? Do you know where you're from?' I asked, and they began to nod. 'You're from Myatts Field. Baghdad. You lot have to stay together, look after one another, protect yourselves, y'know what I mean?'

'Ah, c'mon, man, really?' That was Mikes, barely able to get his words out for laughing, which made me laugh, but still I went on.

'Nah, listen, bro, these two have got potential – they're good use.' Straightening my face, I turned back to the boys. 'Who are you? Tell me who you are,' I went.

'Yo, I'm Baby Boost,' said Devon.

'And I'm Little Boost,' went Sai.

'We're OC,' they said together.

'That's right,' I said.

From that day forwards, Devon and Sai became hazards, man. Hazards.

Later, I recruited another Tiny, a white boy called Adam, who I called Younger Boost. Man, he had no fear. Lox and Mikes had their Tinies too. Lox's boy might have been called Younger Lox but he was taller than Lox, for fuck's sake. That used to make me laugh, man. Younger Mikes was Troopz's little cousin. Tough as Troopz with little springy plaits.

We got straight down to business, working with our Olders and our Tinies, three generations together, locking down the ends. As with any job, to do it and to do it well, we needed the right tools and equipment. Firstly, we had to make sure there were enough machines on the block and enough teet for those weapons. I'd go out with a machine on my hip and we'd also have a machine or two hidden under Mikes' bed. There were also 'community' guns that people would buy for the block. Guns would be like footballs on Myatts Field, dotted about the place for the OC to use as they needed. We were all expected to replace bullets if we used them – or stump up the cash equivalent. Manners, innit. As roadmen, a balaclava and leather gloves were must-haves and Lox continued to roll with a bullet-proof vest. Personally, I never went down that road. If I were to go out in a vest, I'd anticipate getting stabbed or shot that day, y'know. It was a psychological thing for me.

I also bought a few pairs of night-vision goggles as the estate was completely blacked-out at night. Someone on the estate, whose day job involved working with street electricity, had gone out one night and burned all the CCTV cameras and streetlights recently installed by the council. I remember seeing the fire engines the next day, thick smoke billowing over the estate. Nobody got pulled for it and the street furniture was never replaced.

Secondly, we needed to assemble the right team. There was no room for nerds who couldn't protect themselves. We needed skilled shooters, people who were good with knives, those who knew how to swing a baseball bat and not miss their target. To compare it to a football team, we needed strikers, defenders, managers and substitutes. Sometimes, we needed physios.

We also used hood girls to hold money, weapons, drugs or whatever. By this I mean we had loyal girls who didn't fuck with other areas, y'get me? Our hood girls knew us. They enjoyed the notoriety and excitement that came with being associated with gang members. We'd look after them, bung them twenty or forty quid here and there, always aware that the second any of them dipped into our cash or fraternised with pagans, they would get cancelled. End of.

As for earning money, returning to drug dealing seemed the obvious solution. I knew the ropes, had contacts in the trade and, if done well, I knew it could earn me a fortune. Remembering my previous attempts, I understood that I hadn't fulfilled my potential as a dealer. Aside from the good run I had with Zam – including the robbery – I'd been lazy, too busy with football and school and other life stuff. This time, I was determined to make a go of it. I would set up my own lines, make new connections, hopefully beyond the Brixton area, and eventually recruit others to do the leg work for me. But a boy has to start somewhere, y'know?

Mikes, Lox and I went out together, selling wraps of crack and heroin, trying to build names for ourselves as dealers. We stood on Brixton Road at night, freezing cold, fingers going numb, tracksuits tucked into our socks, holding wraps in our mouths and down around our balls while going up to junkies saying, 'Rah, I've got good food,' or, 'Rah, I've got white', or 'Rah, I've got B.' Sometimes we'd give a nittie a wrap so he or she could tell their friends we had good food.

We did OK, making enough profit to invest in more drugs while also keeping some cash for ourselves and yet we knew there were dealers in other areas who were making a lot more. It was a challenge for us to make money outside the OC area because we were known to be so violent. We weren't trusted and the addicts themselves wouldn't wander onto Myatts Field looking for a dealer; they wouldn't dare come near the place for fear of being shot.

Somerleyton Estate, home of the gang known as Murder Zone (MZ), was a hotspot for nitties and we tried to muscle in. Me, Mikes and Lox would go to Somerleyton, give it the bad boy routine and try to intimidate their block. We'd stand in front of the dealers and say, 'Rah, we're taking your shots.' But we realised there was no point. The nitties remained loyal to their Somerleyton dealers. The only way we'd get those MZ boys to get us into their thing, we concluded, was if we befriended them. Lox kept going over and eventually got in with the MZ boys, while Mikes and me did our own thing in our usual locations. We couldn't be bothered with the hassle. And besides, I had other shit going on.

In order to appear legitimate – and to keep my word to Nan and Granddad – I got myself a proper job where I had to pay tax and national insurance and show up at specific times. It was a temporary gig, working as a sales assistant in the women's department of a well-known fashion chain on Oxford Street. It had not been an item on my bucket list, I must say, but it made me look good, at least on paper, right? Plus, I could continue dealing around my shop hours. But, man, that job was boring. Eight hours standing on the shop floor, a Kings Of Leon album playing on loop, and too many people in my space. My manager, Brian, was this four-foot-nothing guy with loads of dandruff and breath that smelled like a pet shop. Brian did nothing but order me around, trying to belittle me, y'know. Dickhead. He'd get right up in my face, with his horrible breath and greasy hair, pissed off at me 'cos I wans't putting the clothes in the right place. Every time he had a go at me, I'd smirk at him, thinking, 'One day, Brian, I'm gonna come and see you outside of the work place. And you'd better be prepared. Yeah, I'm gonna say "Hello" to you, Brian. In the meantime, you need to go wash your hair'.

I never did do anything to Brian. At the end of each shift, I traipsed to a little park in Marylebone, where I'd buried my knife beneath a bush before work. I was always praying it would still be there.

Sometimes, I'd rock up to work straight from raving the night before. I'd come out of clubs like Dstrkt, Leicester Square, or Chinawhite, Soho, wander for a bit, then head to Starbucks, have a coffee and change into my work uniform before facing the Brian and the Kings Of Leon for another eight hours with a raging hangover.

I put a positive spin on my shop job, treating it as a springboard from which to leap into bigger and better things: earning regular money meant I could invest in more drugs to sell. During my first month, I actually worked really hard, taking on extra stockroom shifts on weekends and nights, bumping up my first pay cheque to £1,600. Which was fuck-all compared to what I could make in one a day on the streets, but enough to treat myself to a new machine. A nerdy boy from Brixton who I played football with connected the dots for the deal. He had a few old Indian uncles who were doing this thing properly, y'know what I mean? They were getting guns in from different parts of England and my friend put me in touch with them.

I had no bank account back then and to get the money for the gun, I picked up my pay cheque after my shift and cashed it at a Bureau de Change on Oxford Street. After retrieving my nank as usual in Marylebone, I jumped on the tube to Victoria and caught an overhead train to Crystal Palace, where I'd arranged to meet a guy about a .38 spinner in the living room of a semi-detached house. I took one look at that spinner and thought, 'Nice'. It was sleek, silver and capable of holding eight teet. It felt heavy in my hands, powerful, y'know what I mean? It's difficult to describe that feeling; it was sort of getting a new pair of trainers.

I asked the Indian guy, 'Rah, does it come with teet?' I wasn't too fussed about the answer; the gun was worth about two-and-a-half grand and I was getting it for eight hundred because I knew his nephew.

'There are seven,' he confirmed.

'Cool,' I said, looking the thing over.

I did my checks: I made sure it went into full lock-up, looked down the barrel and checked that the pin was clapping as it should do. It was.

'Yeah,' I said, 'I'll take it.'

I loaded the machine, tucked it into the waistband of my jeans and got a cab to a park. I had to test this thing out, make sure it banged OK. I didn't want to be walking around with nothing but a sense false security. I found a quiet corner and a sturdy tree and put on my balaclava and gloves. I lifted my new machine, aimed it at the tree and fired.

Most people I knew would have tested out their weapons in the dead of night and I do realise that banging a gun at a tree some time around midday sounds a bit mental. I just thought that I had less chance of being seen by jakes at this time for exactly that reason – I was hiding in plain sight. Nobody would expect that. I had my balaclava on, I wasn't there to hurt anybody and, if the police did turn up, I was ready to beat after them, make them run, y'know. That was the Myatts Field mentality.

Luckily, it didn't come to that. The thing banged just right and I returned to Myatts Field, where I took the spinner to my hood girl, Chantelle, at the house she lived in with parents and younger sister on Fountain Place. Chantelle was cool, said she'd leave her bedroom window open. 'You can just climb through any time,' she said.

'Sweet,' I said, and walked along to Mikes', unaware I'd be needing that shooter sooner than I expected.

15

PAGANS ON THE BLOCK

Mikes and Lox were in the bedroom playing *ISS Pro Evolution*.

'Yo, Boost, how's work? Sold many dresses, man?' Mikes started, laughing to himself. Lox laughed too.

'Yeah, I did. Got paid, too,' I said through a yawn. 'Bought a spinner. Bangs good, man.' I yawned again. 'Going for a piss.'

I'd packed a lot in to the last twenty-four hours and now the excitement of the morning had worn off, my brain was telling me, 'You need to nap, Boost. Man needs to reset'. I moved in slow motion to the bathroom, had a piss, then sat on the toilet seat and shut my eyes for five. Ah, peace felt good. My head dropped a couple of times. I was drifting – until my phone trembled in my jeans pocket.

It was Abz. 'Yo, pagans in the ends, bro.'

I shot up from the toilet. 'Right, whereabouts? I'm coming!'

The house began to shake – footsteps, people crashing down the stairs. Lox and Mikes must've heard the news, too.

Abz in my ear again, 'Pagans on the block, pagans on the block.'

I thought, I don't have my machine. There were pagans on the block and I was naked. I needed my machine. Now. I flew out of the bathroom and down the stairs. Lox stormed outside, slamming the front door behind him. Mimi came running out of the kitchen, fork in her hand, all confused, asking, 'What's going on? What's going on?'

Mikes reassured her that everything was cool. 'Stay in the kitchen, Mum,' he said, as Josh and Peter ran up the stairs from the living room.

I need my machine. Gotta get my machine.

Outside, Lox started yelling, 'Go on, bosh your thing. Shoot.'

I heard a bang and a crack and a bullet shot clean through the front door. Light shone through the hole it had made.

Mimi rushed to lock the door. 'Everybody stay in the house,' she said.

If I could just get my machine everything will be all right. I can't be feeling naked. My people can't die in front of me. Not on my watch. Then Lox started shouting again. *That's good, means he's alive.*

Mikes and me looked at each other. *I need my machine.* Mikes read my mind.

'Let's go,' he said and we belted downstairs and jumped out of the living room window. Mimi's voice was behind us. 'Michael? Come back, Michael!'

I left Mikes to search while I peeled off to get my machine, hurdling the fence to Chantelle's garden. She was already there, waiting at her bedroom window, spinner hidden in a handbag sitting on the ledge. She jabbed her chin towards the bag. 'In there,' she said and asked no questions. I grabbed my machine, put it on my hip and bolted.

I ran back round to the front of Treherne Court, but there was no one outside Mimi's. No pagans and no sign of Lox either. Where the fuck were those pagans? I had to find them. It was a cold February day but already I was dripping in sweat, man.

Those pagans could've gone in any direction to get out of the estate. They might have headed towards Akerman Road, or gone out to Cowley Road. Maybe they'd left in the direction of Saji's shop, then onto Patmos Road? But experience told me Mostyn Road, via the Hills, was the most likely route.

I pounded on like I was going for gold, phone buzzing in my pocket, heavy metal locked to my pelvic bone. Nice and tight.

Safe, protected. Fired up, not tired now. All I could think as my feet slammed the pavement was, 'Where are those fucking pagans? How dare they?' As I hit the path that ran alongside the Teletubbie mounds, I saw Mikes sprinting towards me.

'Over there,' he said. He cut a diagonal onto the grass, stopping after a few paces.

I joined him, and we both stood there for ten seconds or so, no longer, watching two figures in the distance, probably too far away to hit but close enough to see they were wearing balaclavas. They looked awkward, not walking but not quite running either. They didn't move like they were from Myatts Field, y'get me?

'That's 'em,' I said.

'Bun 'em.'

In one movement, I pulled out my spinner and got down on one knee. I pointed and, *boom-boom*, I let off two, and the two figures ran. Those were just warning shots. The pagans, whoever they were, would've done the same to us if we'd gone after one of their boys.

We never found out who'd fired at Lox. Me and Mikes walked back to Treherne Court and found Lox, Ratty, Abz and a few others chilling on the block. Lox hadn't recognised the two pagans who went for him. They were wearing balaclavas and hadn't spoken. He said one of the boys had lifted the black handle of his machine, aimed it at Lox's head and banged it.

'I stepped to the side and the bullet went straight past me. Then they ran. Cowards. I couldn't be bothered chasing them, so I went for a walk instead.'

'Boost beat after them on the Hills,' Mikes said, which got a round of plaudits, but still we were all raging that our enemies had got into Myatts Field in the first place.

Half-an-hour later, Me, Lox and Mikes were back at Mimi's, back on the *ISS Pro Evolution*. Mikes' brothers had just got home from school and Mimi was back in her kitchen, the warm spicy smell of her cooking filling the house. She'd had a word with Lox when we'd walked in.

'I don't know who you're mixing with, but don't bring that trouble to this door again,' she said.

Mimi considered Lox a bad influence on her sons and she had every right to be pissed off with him right then. Her front door had a bullet hole in it. She'd found the bullet's casing on the front step and pieces of the pellet stuck in a curtain. She could've been killed. Any one of us could've been killed. Why hadn't she called the police, you're probably asking? Well, this was Myatts Field, enough said.

Mimi had turned to me and Mikes next.

'And, sweet Lord, you two shouldn't have gone chasing out like that – look what happened here today,' she went, motioning at the hole in the door. 'There are people running around with guns out there. It's not safe.' I pulled my coat around me as she said that, conscious of my machine showing beneath my jumper. Lox crossed his arms solemnly in front of him.

'Sorry, Mimi,' he said, 'That was clearly a random thing. I'll pay for the damage.'

Mimi sighed, her eyes moving from Lox to Mikes to me. Even when Mimi was angry her face radiated compassion. 'Well, thank our dear Lord you're all alive,' she said.

16

STROKE OF MIDNIGHT

Street life was a non-stop rollercoaster, barrelling along at breakneck speed. I wanted to control it but I couldn't. Not really. It was a bit scary at first, then it got exciting and addictive and I was like, *more, more, again, again.* Street life was a killer ride, y'know.

I'd been back in the hood less than two months and not only had Lox been shot at, but a few other friends had been slashed and OC had swelled its numbers, making us even more fearsome than before. The Tinies, especially, terrorised the streets. Myatts Field had enemies everywhere.

I cut my hours in my retail job, going down to two or three days a week. I had this idea: *I'll get rich fast then leave the hood. How hard can that be?* I wanted to take things to the next level, beyond being just an OC member. I was thinking of becoming involved in full-on, organised crime. I wanted to broaden my horizons on the streets, to make connections outside Myatts Field and Brixton. My aim was to set up big drug lines and muscle in on other dealers' lines, too. I wanted to learn about control and how to manipulate, how to build a business from the ground up. I wanted to meet people who were doing robberies and stuff.

I did not want to be that boy in a dusty tracksuit, standing on the block all day, smoking weed and shouting, 'Gang, gang, gang.' I didn't want to be giving it all the street slang but do nothing. A life spent holding down the ends wasn't going to make me loads of money. The Tinies were doing a pretty good job of that, anyway. Making rap videos wouldn't rake it in and besides, I was more, 'I'll go and see your mum if I've got a problem with you,' y'know what I'm saying? Making threats in rap verses was not my modus operandi; I would seek revenge by hurting your family. Such was my twisted approach to dealing with pagans.

To earn money from the streets, I had to be out there and I needed to educate myself. I started listening to audiobooks such as *The 48 Laws of Power* and *The 33 Strategies of War*, both by American author Robert Greene. Those books, popular in US prisons and with rappers, taught me how to manoeuvre in life. I read about how to overcome challenges and master the power of perception. I learned how to spot enemies and 'smoke them out'. I changed my outlook and conversations and I was beginning to think, I'm a full-on bad boy now. Then along came a recent recruit to the OC ranks, Midnight.

Wow. Midnight was crazy, man. I mean, wild. A friend of Lox's, he was a year or two older than us. He was African, full of angry energy and always wore his balaclava and black leather gloves. He was all about his guns. Midnight's street name came from his habit of sleeping for most of the day and coming awake at night, 'like an owl', as Lox put it. Everybody knew Midnight wasn't one hundred per cent there. Girls loved him.

I first met Midnight on Treherne Court on a Friday night as he was coming out of some girl's flat, pulling on his balaclava. Lox introduced us.

'Yo, Boost, Midnight, Midnight, Boost.'

We touched fists and said, 'All right'. Midnight crouched, reached behind a plant box, and stood up with a MAC-10 gun. He held it in his gloved hands and stared at me, his bally pulled down to his mouth. His eyes were as mean as his weapon.

I nodded my approval. 'Man, you've got a sub-machine gun, nice,' I said. He shrugged.

'It's here. It's local, you can use it,' he said, his words a bit muffled as his balaclava had no mouth-hole. 'We need to get more teet for it though. Get some if you want.'

'Sweet, that's good to know, bro,' I said. I knew I wouldn't be touching that MAC-10. While I appreciated he'd put the gun on the block, I didn't go in for all that sharing stuff. Too many hands, y'know. I made exceptions for Mikes and Lox.

Lox told Midnight that a few of us were heading to Medussa, a club on Coldharbour Lane. 'You should come,' he said.

Midnight, still holding his MAC-10, said, 'Rah, yeah, that'll be good, man.'

Medussa, situated in what used to be the ticket office of East Brixton station, was one of our go-to nightspots in the area. We liked it for its chilled atmosphere; the music was good – from trance to yardie rave vibes. We'd go there, flirt with some girls, get some numbers, keep it moving and have a good night.

Zav was back from West Ham for the weekend and insisted on taking his car, even though Coldharbour Lane was only a fifteen-minute walk from the estate. We all piled into his three-door VW Polo, Midnight – without his mask – in the passenger seat and me, Mikes and Lox in the back. Lox perched, head bent, knees up to his chin, just to fit. Midnight was jabbering in Zav's ear about voodoo, talking about bathing in ground gorilla bones or some crazy shit like that. When we stopped at traffic lights, he put on his balaclava, still chatting to Zav.

'Fuck's sake, Midnight,' Lox said, moving his head fractionally. 'Ditch the bally, man. You'll get us nicked.'

Poor Zav, rising West Ham star: we'd promised him a night without any madness, y'know. It was funny, man.

We had a good couple of hours in Medussa, buying drinks, chatting to girls, dancing a bit, the usual. The energy began to shift when Midnight took to the dancefloor. I was talking to Shelly, a Jamaican girl I knew, when I saw him. He was staying on one spot, bopping his head to the house music, a maniacal grin on his face and what was clearly a machete in his hands. I could see the blade glinting every time the pulsing lights hit it. I looked away, pretending I hadn't seen Midnight or his knife. Bizarrely, nobody else appeared to notice Midnight's unusual dance accessory. I told Shelly I was going to the bar but instead went to find the others. I had a feeling it was all going to kick off, y'know what I mean?

Midnight must've put the machete away not long after I'd seen him with it. By the time I found Mikes, Lox and Zav at the bar, Midnight was no longer even on the dancefloor. I bought another Henny (Henderson) and Coke and laughed it off, thinking, 'That boy's off the scale mental, man'.

On our way out of the club we got into a little argument with another group of boys. One was having a go at Mikes for 'looking at my girlfriend' or something like that. It was quite minor and although a few words were exchanged it didn't seem worth getting into a fight. We didn't even know them and, after a few fuck-yous back and forth, we jumped into Zav's car and drove off, Midnight in the front seat again. We thought no more of it until a few minutes later, when the other group pulled up in two cars next to us, on Midnight's side. They leaned out the windows, shouting abuse at us, 50 Cent blasting.

Midnight flung off his seatbelt and pounded the dashboard, yelling, 'You fucking cunts are dead.'

Mikes, Lox and I started going nuts in the back and Zav's eyes started pinging in the rear-view mirror. Zav said, 'Just ignore 'em, man,' but Midnight had already shot out of the car.

The other lot jumped out of their cars, too.

Doors slammed and Lox threw Midnight's seat forwards. Watching him emerge was like seeing Goliath emerging from a Matchbox toy car. Mikes also jumped out and I scrambled out on Zav's side so fast, I somehow sent him flying into the steering wheel and the horn blared. At the same time, my foot tangled in his seatbelt.

The other boys were shouting, 'Rah, come out the car then, come out the car.'

When I did manage to get myself out, Midnight charged up from nowhere, pulled out a flick knife and stabbed at one of these boys, missing, before we had some thirty seconds of fighting. Bottles flew, punches too. There were knives out on their side as well as ours. All of it was happening in the middle of the road and that meant we had to be quick and both sides had to get out of there if we wanted to avoid getting shifted for that shit. I came out of it with a bruise on my arm from elbowing someone. Mikes and Lox had a few small cuts. Zav, who'd stayed in the car, was a bit shaken by the drama. Midnight wanted to hunt the boys down.

It was a typical occurrence for Midnight. I would never see anybody pull out their machine faster – or more often – than Midnight. He was always poised for trouble, y'know, and would beat after people for no reason. One time, he, Mikes and me were walking along the street, somewhere on the outskirts of Myatts Field, when this guy ahead got off his pedal bike to cross the road. He wasn't a pagan. We didn't even know him. Midnight yanked his gun from his waist and fired it at the guy. The bullet hit the bike frame with a ting and the guy put his hands in the air, petrified. Mikes and me said, 'What the fuck are you doing, man?' at Midnight as the guy's bike clattered to the road. Then Midnight went, 'Yeah, sorry, man,' put his gun away and continued walking.

That was Midnight. He was loose and hot-headed, even more so than me, but he was also very focused, with good connections on the streets. He influenced me and introduced me to his affiliates. Midnight was beginning to play an integral part in my transition from gang member to organised criminal. He became the big brother I never had, know what I mean?

If that makes things sound smooth, the truth was that my life was chaotic. And that's an understatement. Looking back, I don't know how I kept going. When I wasn't on the shop floor, daydreaming about licking off Brian's dandruff-infested head, I'd be at football training or helping Granddad with odd jobs around the house and garden. Once a week, I played in football matches, home and away. I spent the rest of my time dealing drugs and protecting myself.

Being a drug dealer was lucrative, one hundred per cent. On a good day, I could take home over two grand, y'know. Although I still did bits and bobs with Mikes, I'd branched out on my own a bit more too. My gear came from a variety of sources. Sometimes our Olders – those still on the street – would bung me a stash to shift, but I had also built up a good network of suppliers in the Brixton area, many of whom were soon to be robbed by yours truly. Carlos was no longer living in the area after his flat got done over by a rival (wasn't me, I have to add).

Selling drugs wasn't a glamorous business. It involved a lot of standing around in the street, often in the pissing rain, sleet or even snow. My clients were heroin-riddled stick insects with blackened teeth, if they had any at all – grotty nitties, wannabe gangster cokeheads, people like that. A few were OK and, as I established more lines, I also grew a team of nitties, those I could trust to help me run the show. Frank, a crackhead I could actually have a conversation with, became my driver. He had Chelsea tattoos and a gold hoop earring and ran me around in his VW Golf that stank of crack and damp dogs. Other nitties would let me use their flats to bag up. Sometimes I'd stay overnight in those crackhouses. When the line's on, I was active, y'know? I had to be on it in the area. Man, that was the worst part though; I'd wake up on a nittie's floor – or sofa if I was lucky – with spots on my forehead, dog hairs everywhere, itching like fuck, with that Key House smell up my nose, on my skin, on my clothes. Disgusting. Man can only do that shit for so long, y'know.

Inspiration struck when Midnight introduced me to the Old Kent Road boys. That area of Southwark – also known as Brooklyn – was not one with which OC would normally associate. But recent beef between Brooklyn and Peckham meant we now had a common enemy. We met Kipper and Lazer at an address in the nearby borough of Greenwich. They had a hammer for sale that he was interested in and I went along as an extra pair of eyes.

I had been expecting to go to an estate and I was surprised when we rocked up at this pretty maisonette on a quiet, tree-lined street. It was dark and some of the houses didn't have curtains; I could see right inside their living rooms as we walked past. I spied a young couple cosying up on their sofa, an imitation log fire glowing as they watched telly together. They had framed photos on the mantelpiece and I remember thinking how beautiful but odd that couple's life seemed to me.

Kipper answered the door. He was older than I'd anticipated, possibly in his early forties. Black, he had a short, angular beard and firm handshake.

'We've got a business meeting going on but come through,' he said and led us into the living room where two black guys, also fortyish, were sitting on the sofa, staring at another guy who was reclining in a chair in the corner. His eyes were closed, his arms crossed over his chest, palms resting on his shoulders. He looked dead.

On a coffee table next to the sofa was an A3 sketch pad, open at a blank page, and a flowery, china mug holding pens and pencils.

One of the guys got up from the sofa, introduced himself as Lazer in a hushed voice. His mate on the sofa nodded at us but offered no name, while the guy in the other chair lay still and I stood there thinking, What kinda business meeting is this?

'Wanna see this ting then?' Kipper said.

Midnight rubbed his leather hands together. 'Yeah, man.'

Upstairs in a chilly bedroom, Lazer explained what was going on downstairs while Kipper showed Midnight the handgun, a boxy, black affair with a rubber handle.

'He's astral projecting,' Lazer said, referring to the guy in the chair.

'Oh, right, that's cool, man,' I said. I'd heard of people doing that crazy shit. 'That's like when you leave your body and that, innit?'

'Yeah,' said Lazer, 'He's shit hot at it. He can travel outside his body and go anywhere, into any home, whatever. He's like the invisible man.'

Metallic scrapes, clicks and springy sounds came from where Midnight stood at the dressing table. He was stripping the gun; it sounded as if he was playing with a heavy-duty stapler. Me, Kipper and Lazer gathered round to watch. Midnight was clearly a pro, removing first the magazine, followed by the slide, spring and lastly the barrel, studying and fiddling with each component in turn.

Kipper wanted two grand for the gun, including a few teet, but didn't seem bothered when Midnight, after testing the mechanics and reassembling it, turned round and said, 'Fuck that, you're gonna get me killed, Kip. Ting keeps jamming.'

'Shit, really? Ah, well, no worries, man,' went Kip.

I wasn't convinced. It looked like a lovely little gun to me. Without saying anything, I picked it up, leaned through the gap in the window and, aiming the gun skywards, banged it off. The window frame shuddered on my shoulder blades. My ears rang. A few lights went on in the row of houses at the end of the little garden below. I ducked back in the room, laughing my head off. Kipper was already fumbling to close the blinds.

'What the fuck are you doin', bro?' he demanded. 'Are you trying to get us nicked?'

I handed the gun to Midnight. 'Works fine, y'know,' I said, 'It just ... ' I couldn't go on for laughing. I couldn't stop, man.

Midnight and Lazer started laughing too. At last Kipper got the cord on the blinds to work and they rattled shut. He looked at me and Midnight, both rattling.

'Man, you two together,' he went, pinching the bridge of his nose. He was giggling a bit though. Once we'd calmed down, Midnight inspected the hammer again.

'Man can't take this ting. It's unreliable,' was his verdict.

Kipper and Lazer were fine with that; they were more peeved about the gun being iffy, y'know.

We went back into the living room to find the astral projection boy was back from his trip. He was on the edge of the sofa, leaning over the coffee table with his eyes closed as he drew on the pad what looked to be a floorplan of a building. The other guy was next to him, watching. I was intrigued. We stayed for another half hour or so, talked about the Peckham utes but, to be honest, at that point, I was more interested in what the astral guy on the sofa next to me was telling his mate as he marked circles and crosses and arrows on his picture. I was hearing snippets: 'As you go into this room, you wanna go into this cupboard here in the far left corner. Shiny stuff in a red velvet box in there ... brown is located behind this picture – it's that black-and-white one of the workmen sitting on a steel girder in the sky ... tea, coffee and sugar jars, red with black writing, are to the right of the microwave. Rocks inside those ... '

Those boys were planning a robbery from the comfort of their living room, swear-down. While astral projecting, the guy – apparently, a witch doctor or something – had sent his spiritual being into the home they were about to rob and seen where the drugs, money and other expensive belongings were hidden. From that he produced the blueprint. I later found out that his information had been bang-on.

The Old Kent Road lot impressed me, man. I sat in that living room, listening to their chat. And it wasn't just gang-related. I remember thinking, These guys ain't got no gang name. They ain't got no guys fearing them. These guys are making money. These guys are organised. Yeah, I made a decision that day: these guys are gonna be my friends.

We arrived back at HQ before 9 p.m. The night was young, especially for Midnight, who split to visit a jezzie he was doing the love thing with. I went to see who was on the block, still buzzing after witnessing the robbery being planned. I walked through the estate, checking every few seconds that my spinner was still in my waistband and bumped into Mikes, Shellz and Ratty chilling on Crawshay Court. We just stayed there, y'know, talking, smoking, not much happening. It all felt a bit boring compared to where I'd just come from. But I could always be sure, in those rare quiet moments, that was when madness would happen on the block.

From nowhere, a short, hooded figure crept out of the shadows to our left, at the corner of the alley and the slope. Ratty was the first to notice.

'Who the fuck's that?' he said, running towards the figure.

I ran after him. As he hit the corner, he came face-to-face with two boys, both in balaclavas, one aiming a sawn-off shotgun at Ratty. Everything happened on fast-forward from thereon. I pushed Ratty out of the way, lunged at the boy with the shotgun and reached for my spinner, but it got caught in my jeans; my fault for rushing. I heard Mikes and Shellz behind me. They both had machines on them.

My voice played in my head. *Cowards, how dare they come for man half-heartedly.*

The boy with the shotgun was on his back heel, pointing his gun up, aiming between Ratty and me. I lunged towards him again, ready to grab the gun or knock it out of his hands. *Get the shotgun, Boost. Kick 'em, punch 'em, smash 'em. Get the gun, get the gun, get the gun …*

First came the flash. A blinding, yellow light, flying towards my face like a firework. Next, the bang, though I didn't pay much attention to the noise. It was all about the bright light, and the heat, man. It was like that scene in *The Matrix* where Keanu Reeves dodges bullets. Kinda. I swung my head as if I was avoiding a slap and ducked, but something hit my face. My mouth was burning. My face had been torched. That's how it felt. In the shock of the moment I didn't realise, not fully anyway, that if I hadn't turned my head and dropped when I did, I would've taken a bullet full in the face. I'd cheated death by millimetres. I crouched on the slope, sounds of shouting, running footsteps and more gunshots blurring into one.

The boy with the shotgun and his mate had run. Shellz was beating after them. Ratty and Mikes were crouched next to me.

'Fuck, you're leaking everywhere, man,' Ratty said.

I touched my face. Yeah, blood was pouring, either from my mouth or my nose, possibly both. I could see the blood even in the darkness, flowing like black emulsion paint down the slope of Crawshay Court.

Pastor Mimi screamed when she saw me, flanked by her own son and by Ratty, who were propping me up on the doorstep. My blood marked the route we'd taken from Crawshay Court to her house. Still my face burned. Mimi hurried us in, calmer now.

'What's happened? Have you been stabbed, Terroll? Shall I call for an ambulance?' It must've felt like Groundhog Day for Mimi.

'Rah, get me to the toilet,' I said.

'I've got ya, bro,' went Ratty, rubbing my back as he guided me to the toilet. 'You're gonna be good. C'mon, man, I'll help you.' His voice was reassuring. I'll never forget that. He helped me wash my face while Mimi and and Mikes did the towel run. The water felt like acid, burning my top lip. My head was thumping. Had I been shot in my face? Or my head? Did I have a pellet in my head?

'Shall I call an ambulance?' Mimi asked again, passing me a clean towel.

'Nah, I'm good,' I said, blood all over her bathroom.

I wet the towel and wiped my face again and checked out the damage in the mirror, expecting to see half my face blown away. My features were still intact and the only sign I'd been shot was a long, deep graze above my top lip. It looked like somebody had drawn a moustache on me with a thick, red marker pen. The bullet must have skimmed my lip when I'd moved my head. It seemed like a lot of blood for a graze, y'know? Just then, Ratty's face appeared behind me in the mirror. His reflection looked at mine and he closed his eyes briefly, as though in prayer.

'No need for an ambulance, Mimi,' he added. 'T's good, y'know.'

17

BULLETS AIN'T GOT NAMES ON THEM

Behind the locked door of the downstairs bathroom, I sat on the carpeted toilet lid and finished loading my machine. I dropped the last, silky bullet into its chamber, wincing at the fiery pulse between my nose and top lip. It was a burning reminder that somebody had tried to shoot me in the head with a sawn-off shotgun the previous night.

If I shut my eyes for more than a second, I recalled the sensation of a firework flying towards me once more. *Fuck, Boost, how are you not on a slab right now?* I straightened my back and looked at the ceiling, taking a deep breath through my busted nose. It smelled bleachy in here. I clicked the cylinder into place. *Bullets ain't got names on them … or have they?* Ten minutes later, I was out of the front door, the fully-loaded spinner in my man bag, the March mid-morning sun beating my face. It felt weird seeing the trail of my own, dried blood on the ground as I made my way along the walkway of Treherne.

I was supposed to be in the shop right now, but I'd called in sick with a dodgy stomach. I wasn't going in there with a bullet graze and, besides, I had more pressing things to do today – like hunting down the boy with a sawn-off shotgun. I'd already made a few calls and trusted contacts were in turn making inquiries. In fact, I was on my way to meet one of my boys right now, but first words needed to be said to the Tinies, y'know.

The Tinies were at the OC meeting spot at the end of Treherne Court. Some were sitting on the wall smoking weed, others were sat under them on their pedal bikes and many more stood in and outside the stairwell that led to nowhere. Basically, the Tinies swarmed that whole area, from the wall to the first floor of the stairs. I spotted Adam and Baby Boost on the steps, pulled my bandana up from my neck to my nose and went over.

I heard shouts of, 'Yo, Boost, go shop for you, man?' as I weaved through the knots of boys in New Era caps and hoods and green bandanas.

'Yo,' I called out, 'We need to talk, brothers.'

I spudded Adam and Baby as I took the steps, clocked a group freestyling on the landing, spitting about 'head shots, not leg shots' while others filmed with their phones. Credit to them; their bars sounded great, but they hadn't bothered covering their faces. I'd seen so many of these videos posted on YouTube too. It infuriated me to see them putting their faces out there, man.

'Right, you lot. Downstairs, now,' I said, my voice bouncing in the hollow stairwell.

The cameramen shoved their phones in their pockets and jogged down the stairs, followed by the rappers, one of them recognisable as Younger Mikes. Within thirty seconds all the Tinies were semi-circled around me by the wall at the bottom of the stairs. I kept my mouth covered as I spoke. They would've heard about my being shot and I was trying to set an example.

'OK, listen up. Do you lot know where you're from?' Before they could answer, I went on, 'You're from Brixton. Baghdad. All shot up. And do you know what you are? You're untouchable. You lot are bad boys. You lot are dangerous. You lot are feared.' I drilled and drilled and drilled that spiel into them, man, every single time. And they stared at me in awe, y'know. 'But … ' I gazed around the crowd and picked out my special ones. Adam, arms folded over his chest, nodding slowly, black leather glove on his left hand, gun grip poking out his waistband. He was one white boy in the middle of thirty-odd black faces. Not a trace of fear in his eyes. Baby Boost and Little Boost, side by side next to Adam, their little ears sticking out beneath caps worn backwards. My boys.

'… You lot need to step up. *Don't* discredit the name of the ends. *Don't fuck* up the ends. *Don't* show your faces on music videos online. And make sure you've got your armour.'

To illustrate my point, I unzipped my bag, extracted my loaded spinner and placed it on the wall where everybody could see it.

'See this machine? It's no rebore. This is *live.* It could take off your head and I am showing you that this is *power* that you're stepping on. You need to be able to protect yourselves from the enemy; from the Other Side. They see you slipping, you could get yourselves killed. One of you could die today. Know what you're doing. Step up or step down.' I grabbed my gun. 'It's a battlefield out there, y'know.'

Sponge, filter. Sermon over, I got on my way.

My friend Steven picked me up on Cowley Road. I'd asked him to get me away from the area for a while. As I bundled into his BMW he took one look at my lip and sucked in his breath. 'Fuck, that could've gone different way, man,' he said and turned up the stereo. He had Uncle Murda's *Respect the Shooter* mixtape playing. Any other time I would've wheeled that up myself but, today, much as I'd given it the hard man act for the Tinies, I did feel shaken, y'know? A bit fragile, but I didn't give in to those thoughts or the firework image that once again kept exploding in my head. Today was about revenge. One hundred per cent. I flipped down the passenger sun-visor, angling the small mirror in it at my mouth. My wound was caked with dry blood and had started to go gunky and yellow in places.

'Yeah, fuckers need a lesson on head shots, y'know what I'm saying?' My words came with a laugh, but I meant every one of them.

As Steven pulled away I leaned over and dimmed Uncle Murda, thinking it ironic how the American rapper, real name Leonard Grant, had himself survived a bullet to his head after releasing that mixtape. 'Anyway,' I added, 'what d'ya know? Found anything out?' Steven shot me sly smile.

'Got a name for you, bro,' he said I felt myself go hot then cold. I looked at Steven.

'Seriously?' I said.

The story he told wasn't what I'd expected to hear. I'd assumed the shooter deliberately targeted our group. Could be he was going for Ratty, Mikes, Shellz or me. Or all of us. Mikes and I had ongoing beef with other drug dealers, for example. And, of course, OC had enemies all over. I didn't for one second believe Peckham was behind this one, as they tended to operate in numbers. But no, according to Steven, it wasn't any of the usual suspects, but just a young boy from Brixton who'd been sent in to do some dirty work on behalf of a group, rather than a gang, who had a problem with Myatts Field. Steven didn't know why they didn't like us, but he did confirm that the bullet didn't have my name on it. Apparently, when the two boys arrived back in their area last night, news filtered through that I'd been shot. 'They were like, "'Fuck, shit, we might've killed Boost"',' said Steven, 'so they're fucking shitting it now, y'know what I'm saying?'

'Yeah,' I said. The facts were on the table and I had no reason to disbelieve Steven. Although not a gang member, he had many associates and intel he'd passed on to me before had been right on it, y'know.

'As ever, Boost, do with that info how you like, but don't mention my name, man,' added Steven, 'though I know we're good.'

'Deffo, bro,' I said.

I didn't know what to do with what I'd heard. See, the name of my shooter – let's call him Matthew – was already known to me. His mum, a nice Irish woman, was a good friend of my nan's. Matthew was about two years younger than me. We'd played together a few times as kids.

'Listen, man, do us a favour and drop me back in Brixton, please?' I said. We'd reached Croydon, but I needed to be back home. Steven did a U-turn. I made a couple of calls, scribbled an address in the Vassall Road area on the back of my hand. Soon, there'd be a rat-a-tat-tat on the door of that address.

If Matthew's mum answered, I'd come up with an excuse, I decided. But I got lucky and I didn't even need to hit the door. I saw a boy of Matthew's age leaving the house. He didn't see me and I followed him. He had his hoodie up and a New Era cap on top, peak forwards and down. Must be him, I thought. He was walking in the direction of Stockwell, away from Myatts Field. I reached him at the lights at the junction of Vassall Road and Brixton Road.

I tapped him on the shoulder from behind and said, 'Yo Matthew.'

He spun round and, swear-down, I thought he was going to disappear. I imagined his body turning to water and flooding the pavement, leaving nothing but a soggy heap of clothes behind. He went see-through, man. He looked like Casper the Ghost in his black hoodie.

I said, 'You and I need to talk.'

Matthew stepped backwards, dead-ending himself between railings and me. 'Listen, I didn't mean … it was an accident … they said … I thought … I didn't know… ' I stared down at him, playing with the zip on my man bag.

'Listen,' I began, 'see, I'm not happy about what you did to me last night, Matthew. It's caused some uneasiness, some upset in my camp, y'know.' Matthew attempted a nod but his jaw was trembling. 'I could be dead right now and you'd be going to jail for life. 'Cos people are talking. People *know* it was you.'

'Look, I'm … '

'But, y'know what?' I went on. 'It's OK. Don't worry about it. I know who sent you – and I know you didn't mean to shoot me. It's cool, brother. I forgive you.'

'Really?' said Matthew, eyeing my man bag. I think he thought I was bluffing.

'Yeah, man. It's cool. I forgive you,' and now it was my turn to back off. 'Have a good day,' I said.

As I turned I heard a shaky voice say, 'Thanks, Boost.'

I walked back to Myatts Field feeling grateful that it had been Matthew who'd shot me. You don't mix family with gang shit. There was no way I could hurt the son of my nan's friend.

I could've gone after the boys who'd sent Matthew, but I decided to leave things there. Whoever they were warring with at Myatts Field would seek retribution, anyway. I'd had a minor setback. A shot is a cough in Myatts Field, right? Yeah, I walked home feeling peaceful that day. That feeling wouldn't last for long.

18

ROUGH JUSTICE

I stood behind the police tape with Lox, watching Ratty being wheeled to the ambulance, not knowing whether he was dead or alive.

You couldn't see his face as it was dark and there were too many figures in hi-vis jackets in the way, but word on the street confirmed Ratty was on that gurney.

'Rat's been shot. Doesn't look promising, man.'

The stretcher went in, the doors slammed and the ambulance howled away with our friend.

Blue lights flooded Fountain Place. There were police officers everywhere. More crime scene tape was going up, with residents told to go around the court to get to their homes. Walkie-talkies crackled with fragments of police talk that made no sense. People from all over the estate were gathering, anxious to know what was going on. Among them was Mikes' brother Peter. He appeared at my side. 'They're saying it's Ratty,' he said, his voice breaking. 'Is it true? Has Ratty been shot?'

I put my hand on his shoulder, unable to speak.

Lox dropped his forehead into his palm, inhaled with a shudder, 'Fuck. Fuck, no,' he exhaled.

A police officer on the other side of the tape came marching over. 'Sorry, guys, I'll need to ask you to move away from the scene, please,' he said.

Behind us, a man was sobbing.

Lox lifted his head, glared at the officer. 'He's our friend,' he went. 'He's our friend, man.' But we did what we were told and moved back a bit and, as we did so, somebody grabbed the arm of my jacket. It was the man I'd heard sobbing. A black guy, around mid-forties, his face slick with tears.

'Excuse me,' he choked, looking up at Lox and me, 'do you know him? Do you know our Nicholas?'

'Yeah, he's our friend,' I said, 'a very good friend.'

The man's eyes bulged with fresh tears. He blinked them, spilled them, filled them again. 'Do you know what Nicholas said? Before he … ' The guy swallowed as he wiped his eyes. 'He said, "Don't let my little brother be like me".'

Man, my throat closed-up, y'know. Lox was looking at the sky, trying to keep it together. But the guy wasn't seeking a reply. He said 'Thank you,' and walked away. He hadn't introduced himself but he was obviously related to Ratty. An uncle perhaps?

It was 14 March 2008. A Friday night, and just a few weeks after I had been shot at. I'd first heard that something had happened while Lox and I were at a house party at Cowley. We didn't know the specifics at that point, but we jogged it back and, by the time we reached the Hills, both our phones started going off. Everybody was calling each other at once, repeating the message, 'Rat's been shot.'

Rat had been taken away and it was just after 10 p.m. when we left Fountain Place. I met Nan and Granddad in the crowd of spectators and I returned home with them. I wasn't in the mood for doing much else, y'know. When we got in, Nan and Granddad said they were off to bed.

'Do you know that poor boy well?' Nan asked me before she went up.

I shrugged. 'I know him to say "hello" to but he's more a friend of a friend. We're all about the same age, innit.' I had to be careful what I said because Nan had overheard conversations in the street about the shooting being gang-related.

'Well, I'll say a prayer for him, Our Boy,' she said, 'What a terrible world we live in nowadays.'

I gave her a peck on the cheek. 'Thanks Nan,' I said.

I locked myself in the downstairs toilet and cried and cried and cried for ages.

My phone woke me just after 5.30 a.m. It was Lox, calling from Mikes' house. I knew just by the time of the call that it was bad news.

'He didn't make it, man. Rat died in the early hours,' he said.

The line went silent for a few seconds. Even Lox was processing his words. Another piece of us had gone. We'd lost yet another brother. First Tiny A, now Ratty?

'I'm on my way,' I said.

I spent the rest of the day at Pastor Mimi's with Mikes and Lox. Mimi was crying, having lost another of her 'babies'. We were all lost for words. Only a few days ago, Ratty, Mikes and me had been in this same house playing *Burnout Paradise*. No more than two weeks had passed since Ratty helped me in the bathroom of this very house after I'd been shot at. I could still hear his calming voice. *I've got ya, bro. C'mon, man, I'll help you.* Yeah, Ratty was a good boy. He was very bubbly and cared a lot for his family. He'd been studying to become a vet at South Thames College – a clever guy, y'know. He worked hard to get what he wanted. He was a go-getter, a hustler. Ratty died at King's College Hospital after being shot in the head. He was only nineteen.

Others popped into Mimi's, including Syikes, Troopz, Abz and a few Tinies. Shellz turned up later in the afternoon but left after ten minutes or so. He was heartbroken, man. He and Ratty were best mates. Many tears were shed but anger was brewing too. We wanted to find out who'd killed Ratty. Of course, there were rumours circulating, including a suggestion that Ratty was embroiled in beef with another gang. Another claimed Ratty had been armed and had fired at his killer first. Nobody dared to claim responsibility because they knew that they would have had their household destroyed. Deleted. Y'get me? Nobody wanted that energy on them, man. OC would go out in the aftermath, G-checking people and asking questions. Nothing. The sad truth was that being part of a gang like OC meant young people getting shot or stabbed to death was part of everyday life. We were heavily involved in the streets to the point that we were prepared to risk our own lives and defend our friends' lives, at all costs. Because this stuff was real. People were dying. Friends were going to jail, some of them for life.

In Mikes' bedroom on the day we heard about the death, we talked for hours about Ratty, recalling the good times, funny moments and conversations. We laughed and cried but no one dared to ask the question that grew in our minds like an undetected tumour: which one of us will be next?

Sometimes, when I was away from the noise and alone with my thoughts, I'd ask myself: 'Do I want life or do I want death?' And despite choosing life, I did nothing to change my lifestyle. Not at that point. Ratty dying only fuelled my anger. I wanted his killer to suffer the same fate, such was my mental state at that time. I wanted revenge, as did most of our OC family. That's what gang warfare does to you. It fucks with your head. Evil thoughts you never knew you were capable of creep into your mind. I'd be like, 'Rah, if somebody even attempts to hurt me or my families, both blood and gang, then I'll just shoot them.'

The demons overpowered the voice of reason that would say, 'Nah, you don't wanna hurt no one. You're not a violent person. You want peace, man.'

I would go out on the block and say to my Tinies, 'There's a time for peace and a time for war.' For me, at that time, there was no peace, only war.

Now I am pleased when I remember that, however, that amid the darkness, hope was on the horizon, at least for Mikes and Lox. Yeah, Ratty's death engendered a positive fighting spirit in those two, with help from Pastor Mimi.

In the days leading up to the Fountain Place shooting, a police officer visited Pastor Mimi. During that conversation, I believe the officer told Mimi that her son was a gang member. Now, I don't know the full ins and outs about how Mimi broached the subject with Mikes – to be fair, that was their business, not mine – but what I do know is this: Mimi opened her heart and her home to every one of us boys, determined to help us leave the world of hate and violence and sadness. She listened to us and advised, without being preachy. In time, Mimi would make many of us see that we were young men who *did* have potential, who *could* make futures away from the streets. About a week after Ratty died, Lox moved in to 13 Treherne Court and, soon after, he and Mikes started going church a lot.

But, even as their journey towards leaving the streets got underway, the route I had taken was leading me ever deeper into gangland.

I began spending more time with Midnight and the Old Kent Road boys, Kipper and Lazer. We'd sit down and have proper chats, united by our common enemy that was Peckham. One of the Brooklyn utes, a fifteen-year-old, had recently been stabbed to death by four boys from a gang in Thamesmead, one of Peckham's allied areas. We were beginning to think about how Brooklyn and Baghdad could come together as one unit, y' know?

Watching Kipper and Lazer plan robberies – with and without the help of a witchdoctor – made me realise I'd been going about this drug business the wrong way. I began to shift my focus to robbing the drug dealers down the road.

I started farming out the day-to-day dealing business to the Tinies. I put them on lines and gave them a cut of the earnings. They were doing for me what I had done for my Olders, leaving me free to concentrate on the bigger picture. I studied my rivals to work out where they operated from and then it was a case of me bursting in on them, sticking a gun to their heads and saying, 'Tell me where your food is.' I'd also target dealers in the street, anybody who was shining, y'know. I could spot them a mile off – watches by Jacob & Co, Santos, Cartier, Aqua Master or Rolex; bracelets and chains; big cars. They thought they were Mr Pimp. I'd pop their chains and, if they had a problem with that, I'd take out my nank or my gun.

About three weeks after Ratty died, I was in Jonnies Café, Loughborough Junction, waiting for my full English to arrive. I turned on my phone to receive about a dozen notifications of missed calls, all from Mum and Nan and Granddad. Scrolling through the list I began to panic, y'know. Mum rang again. She sounded stressed, hitting me with question after question.

'Where are you? Are you OK? What's going on? What's happening? What are you doing?' A waitress came over with my breakfast. I mouthed a thank-you and unwrapped my cutlery. I was starving, man. 'Fuck's sake, T,' Mum went on, 'The police have been here looking for you.'

I almost choked on my toast. 'What? What are you on about? What do they want?'

'They didn't say, but they were here at 4.30 this morning, with guns and lasers and all that. Came through the door. Woke me and the kids up. Scared the life out of Tyrell. Before coming here, they knocked on your Nan and Granddad's door, trying to find you.'

'They did what? What the fuck?' I was livid, man.

'Well, at least they didn't force their way in.' Mum started to say that I was to call a particular officer, but my mind was already elsewhere. First, how dare the jakes go to my grandparents' house and frighten them like that? Secondly, why were they even looking for me? Had they found out about a dealer I'd robbed? Surely not. Drug dealers don't go to the police and say, 'Boo-hoo, that dealer over there robbed all my crack and smack. Bang goes my new Rolex.' Yeah, there had to be some kind of mistake here. I called the officer who'd visited Mum.

'We want to discuss something with you,' he said, 'Could you come into the station?'

It sounded reasonable enough. I was, like, 'Yeah, sure, I can pop in sometime. When's good for you?

'Now would be amazing,' was the PC's response.

'Well,' I went, 'I'm eating my breakfast right now. I've got a full English in front of me, so I'll come when I've finished.'

'Right, whereabouts are you?'

Now he was really beginning to irritate me. 'Listen, bro,' I said firmly. 'Let me sort out my breakfast and I'll come this afternoon. Say two o'clock?'

'Fine,' he said. 'Two o'clock at Kennington station.'

That afternoon, after traipsing back to Myatts Field to ditch my nank and drugs, I found myself heading back to Kennington police station, a place I'd vowed never to set foot inside again after the CS gas palaver. There were two Operation Trident detectives – officers specialising in gang violence in black communities – waiting for me, both looking to be in their mid- to late-thirties, one with babyish blond hair like the Milky Bar Kid, the other balding and seeming tired. They took me into an interview room with moody walls the colour of mushroom soup and got stuck right in.

'Terroll Kersean Lewis, you are being arrested on suspicion of your involvement in a gangland shooting in which Nicholas Clarke was murdered,' went the blond, using Ratty's real name.

What the fuck?

They went on, 'You do not have to say anything. But it may harm your defence if you do not mention when questioned something which … '

I sat there with my hands on my thighs, shaking my head. Was this really happening? Like, were they joking or what?

'… anything you do say may be given in evidence.'

I stared at them, said nothing at first. I couldn't put what I was thinking into words, y'know what I mean?

'We want to speak to you about the death of Nicholas Clarke,' repeated the balding guy.

'You mean Ratty?' I said. 'Is this some kind of sick joke?'

'We've been told you were involved in a gang-related shootout in which Nicholas Clark was killed,' he said again.

The pair then pulled out laptops, one with a slide show of stills, the other showing some grainy CCTV videos. Both sets of images were of the same subject: fuzzy pictures showing a group of figures, all of them in dark balaclavas, one who was possibly brandishing a gun, though again, it was too blurry to say for sure.

The detectives kept pointing at a random figure in each picture, saying, 'That's you, isn't it?' I mean, seriously, I couldn't even work out where these pictures had been taken.

I sat back in my chair and folded my arms. I didn't have time for this. On and on they went.

'You're in a gang called Organised Crime, aren't you?'

'Your street name is Boost, isn't it?'

'Where were you on the night of March fourteenth?'

'This is you in this picture, isn't it?'

'Have you anything you'd like to say, Mr Lewis? Anything that will help us with our inquiries?'

They fell silent and, for a few seconds all you could hear was one of the laptops overheating, the fan whirring, accelerating. I'd answered some of their questions, but this was turning into a bullying session now. I leaned forward, slapped my hand on the desk.

'Yes,' I said, glaring at them, 'I have something I'd like to say.'

I could feel tears welling in my eyes, man, but there was no way I was going to let them see me cry. I inhaled sharply through my nose, exhaled slowly. Then I continued.

'Yeah, I'm a gang member. I'm Boost, but I wasn't involved in this madness. That boy was our friend. He was our *brother*. We're *grieving* right now. You don't know what … ' I took another breath. Those two were looking at me intently now, narrowing their eyes, heads on one side and all that bollocks. 'Listen,' I said, slapping my hand on the desk again. 'You lot don't live my life. You lot come here, do your job then go back to your homes on the outskirts. You go back to your nice houses. But it's us, the gang members, who live on the estate. *We* go through the trauma, not you.'

I pointed at the still on one of the laptops. 'So, is that all you've got? Because, if so, you need to do your homework, y'know. You will *never* understand. *Never*. But you're sitting there, passing judgement on *our* people. Death is all around us. We're *seeing* it, we're *feeling* it. And I'm getting arrested in connection with my friend's death? I don't know what psychological trick you guys are playing here, but this is not good, man. This is not good.' I sat back again, ran my hands over my face. I still couldn't believe I was even having this conversation.

The two detectives closed their laptops, looked at each other, then the fluffy-haired one blinked a couple of times before starting up again. 'So, what can you tell us about the murder of Nicholas Clarke?'

19

AMMUNITION

I spent the day Kennington police station being questioned, the jakes going round in circles, showing me the same shitty pictures while both pointing at one hooded figure, going, 'That's you, that *is* you,' like a pair of parrots.

'Go on, then,' I told them. 'If you're so sure, prove that that's me in that picture. *Prove* it.' At the end of the interrogation they told me I was getting bail 'pending further investigations.' No charges, no going court, I was free to go home 'once we've completed our paperwork'. As part of my bail conditions, I would need to show my face at the police station on a set date every month.

'What if I'm working?' I'd asked, 'or have football training or a match?' I was still doing days here and there at the shop on Oxford Street and playing for Tooting and Mitcham. Mattered shit to the jakes.

'If you break your conditions, you could find yourself being charged under the Bail Act and remanded in custody,' they'd told me.

It was evening by the time I left the building, feeling violated, man. Losing Ratty was painful enough, but to be accused of killing him? It seemed to me those Trident officers were targeting any bad boys they could find in the area, going through their list of gang members, hoping one might look at those murky pictures and go, 'Yeah, that's me there. The one in the balaclava who's pointing something that could be a gun,' y'know what I mean?

I wasn't the first – or last – person to be arrested over Ratty's death. Two guys had been pulled before me and, over time, a further five would be arrested. To this day, it remains untold who killed our friend Ratty.

I got a cab back to my area. I wasn't getting caught slipping; I didn't even have my nank on me, y'know. Man had enemies all over south London. I could be on Kennington Road and bump into the brother of a dealer I'd robbed or a dealer whose line I'd nicked. If man's not got his armour, man can't defend himself, especially if that pagan's fully loaded, y'know what I mean? No way was I walking home naked.

Fortunately, it had been Granddad who'd answered the door to the jakes that morning. Nan was in bed at the time, which was a blessing. She might have had a heart attack or something. The police could try anything they wanted on me. They could nick me for this, nick me for that, whatever, but I had one only message for them: hurt my family and I *will* commit a crime you can nick me for … beyond reasonable doubt. Y'know what I'm saying?

When I explained the situation to Nan and Granddad, they were obviously worried, but mostly, they were furious at the police for arresting me. They had been out in the court on the night Ratty was taken away in the ambulance. I'd gone home with them afterwards. They'd seen I was upset, even though I'd tried to hide my emotions.

'They're bullies so they are,' Granddad said of the police, 'wasting time on innocent young men when they should be out there finding who did do it. It disgusts me. It really does.'

While it came as a shock to be questioned over Ratty's murder, I was used to being harassed by police. Like, I'd be walking to Saji's shop and the undercovers would appear in one of their Mondeos and start crawling alongside me. Then one of the officers would wind down his window a bit and shout questions through the gap. A typical conversation between an undercover and me would go like this:

Undercover: Rah, did you hear about the shooting the other night?
Me: I'm going shop, bro. Leave me alone.
Undercover: I heard you were involved. Were you involved?
Me: I said, leave me alone.
Undercover: We heard it was to do with the Peckham Boys.
Me: Look, I'm tired, I'm not interested. Leave me alone.

I never understood how the undercovers got a kick out of this. Fire creates fire, y'know. Being on bail in relation to my boy Ratty's death made me even more hot-headed. Now, as a leader of OC, I was on a mission to make Baghdad completely impenetrable. No pagans should be able to get within an inch of its borders, let alone kill *our* boys on *our* soil. But the gang was undeniably weaker without Mikes and Lox, who were still trying to leave the streets for good and it was weird not having them by my side on the block. I respected their decision and their difficulties.

Leaving the streets was not an overnight process. Your enemies don't vanish the moment you decide to hang up your MAC-10, y'know what I mean? Mikes had even made enemies on our side. The Tinies talked about killing him – and they meant it, too. Mikes would bully the Tinies. I overheard a few conversations that started, 'Yo, we need to get rid of Mikes, man.'

I'd step in and mark their cards, pulling them aside and saying, 'Listen, all of you. Know what you're saying and doing, right? Because if anything happens to Mikes, all of you are going. Deleted.'

The Tinies needed a kick up the arse, I decided. At that time, hundreds of utes from PYG – Peckham Young Guns, the Peckham Boys' tinies – were roaming the streets of Brixton and there were lots of fights, man. It riled me when the OC Tinies came back from those battles, stabbed or beaten up, whinging because 'there were far more of them than us'.

Yet I knew that they did have a point. Fuck this, we need a bigger team, I thought. Obviously, this recruitment drive wasn't one for LinkedIn. I had a word with Kipper and Lazer and met the OBY (Original Brooklyn Youts) on an estate in their area around the Old Kent Road. Like our Tinies, they were all aged around thirteen to fourteen, but there were many more of them, all of them on pedal bikes, spitting stuff like 'fuck 'nam' and 'pussy boys don't slip'. They wore grey bandanas or ballies and rolled with knives hidden in the soles of their shoes and, wow, the speed at which they'd pull out those blades was crazy, man. I hadn't seen anything like that before. Yeah, this lot were a wild bunch of kids, man.

'Mm, they'll shake the Tinies' tree,' I said to Kipper and Lazer. 'Rah, let's get these utes together with ours.'

They were like, 'Yeah, great idea.'

That afternoon, I led the Brooklyn boys into the Fields, all of us on bikes, moving like a colony of giant army ants. Introductions were made and from thereon it was Baghdad and Brooklyn against Peckham. OC became stronger and more fearsome. The whole team would ride into Peckham, a sea of young boys in green and grey bandanas, armed with knives and balls of steel. I left them to do their thing, while I focused on earning money and investing my cash in more drugs and new weaponry.

The more dealers I robbed, the more enemies I made and, occasionally, people would come after me. I was shot at a number of times. Sometimes, I would even see my enemies off-duty, in Foot Locker, Brixton, and say, 'Hey, how's your day going?' knowing they might be shooting after me later, or vice versa. Exactly when those bullets would fly, I never knew. It could happen day or night, outside my house, at the bus stop or sitting in one of those church services that Mikes and Lox talked me into going to. But I wasn't looking for peace and salvation in a place of worship – my peace was my gun. That piece of metal was my security in the concrete jungle. I'd buy guns, I'd sell guns and I'd also chip in for machines for the block.

Calli, a friend of Midnight, knew some north London boys who had a sub-machine gun on sale for six grand. We were like, 'Rah, we could do with one of those for the block.' I went halves with Midnight. Calli knew his way around a machine and offered to view the weapon on our behalf, seeing as it was being offered by his own contacts. We would bung him a bit for doing us the favour. Midnight drove us all to the meeting in Wood Green, north London, in his Audi.

I remember it pissed it down that day and the windows kept steaming up, which wasn't a good thing when I was trying to keep watch for jakes. In the car was six thousand pounds, a grand of which was tucked in my boxers (a roll either side of my balls) and the remainder was hidden with Calli in the back seat.

Midnight's driving expressed his personality, y'know. Calli was sat forwards, his head between Midnight and me, distracting himself by talking non-stop about his girlfriend and about the imminent job. I just sat tight and gripped my seat.

'I think man can get 'em down to five,' Calli said. 'I'll go for five first but they might want five and a half, man. Y'know how it is?'

Midnight was like, 'Rah, do your ting, man.'

We parked a few streets away from the address and Calli jumped out with the five grand. If the gun was good he'd either buy it or be back for more cash. Ten minutes ticked by and Midnight started getting edgy.

'What the fuck's he doing? He's been gone ages. Let's call him, man,' he said, wiping condensation from his side window with the leather arm of his coat.

I laughed. 'C'mon, Midnight, it's only been a few minutes. These things take time. You know that.'

Midnight grunted, turned on the CD player and blasted out a random rap mixtape, some boy spitting about shooting a rival. It was completely out of place. We were in a quiet residential street in broad daylight, sitting in an Audi S3 with blacked-out windows, the front windows half wound-down, allowing us to keep an eye out for potential signs of trouble. We were waiting on our boy to return to the car with a sub-machine gun. I was in the passenger seat, on bail for a rime I didn't fucking commit. Know what I'm saying? I hit the dial fast. 'Fuck's sake, Midnight! You fucking mental or something?'

Yeah, I said it, right. Midnight just banged back his head, laughing.

'Yo, chill man, it's funny, innit.'

I laughed too, then. And that felt good because man hadn't done much laughing in a long time. We sat in that street for about fifteen minutes in total before I spotted Calli in the wing mirror on my side, bombing up the pavement like he was being chased by police or something. He dived in the back of the car, panting. 'Drive,' he gasped. 'We've gotta get outta here, man. Just drive.'

I turned around but Midnight slumped in his reclined seat. He said, 'Where's the machine, man?'

'Yeah, where's the machine?' I repeated.

Calli's breath accelerated as he wiped rain and sweat off his forehead. His hands were trembling. 'I got robbed, man,' he said, 'Them north London boys robbed me. Took the five grand, man. Sorry. They had knives and shit.'

Midnight sat up then. 'Where are they? Let's go lick 'em,' said Midnight.

'Fuck that,' I said, 'We're naked, y'know.' This was true. We'd left our machines and nanks behind in case we got pulled. And, if all had gone to plan, Calli would have got a cab back to the Fields – and taken the machine with him. But had Calli been robbed? I wasn't so sure, y'know.

Midnight started the car. 'That's that fucked, then,' he said as he pulled away.

I was laughing again. At the absurdity of it all. Something didn't add up.

'Yo, Calli,' I said, I didn't even bother to face him. I could see him in the rear-view mirror that Midnight hadn't bothered to adjust, much less use. 'If I find out that you've robbed us, I'm gonna lick you down.'

'I can't believe you'd say that, bro,' he said, head down, 'I'd never do that.'

Calli lived on the Cowley Estate. A week or so after our wasted journey north of the river, we found out via a mutual friend there that he hadn't been robbed by the north London boys. He had, as I'd suspected, robbed us. Stupidly, Calli had told this friend as much. I was boiling over when I heard. I got Calli's number and gave him a courtesy call.

'You robbed us,' I sneered. 'You're playing with your life. If you don't get mine and Midnight's money together, your girlfriend's gonna get deleted.'

We never did get our money back and Calli had to move out of the area. But we knew there would be other sub-machine guns.

20

LIGHTS AND SIRENS

After three months of investigation, Trident detectives were no closer to finding Ratty's killer. They still had me on bail and my pointless visits to Kennington police station continued. I couldn't plan anything because my whole life revolved around those bail dates down the nick. I was *sick* and *tired* of the place.

Every month, when I showed up to sign the bit of paper that proved I hadn't done a runner to Barbados or wherever, I'd be greeted by a different member of staff who could offer me no further updates on the case. And still, they had no evidence upon which to charge me. Tooting and Mitcham banned me from two matches when they found out about my arrest, telling me I was 'bringing the club into disrepute'. The whole tragic saga – and the stress of street life itself – were beginning to affect my mental health, man. Sitting on bail in connection with my friend's death – when I was still trying to recover from losing that person – I can't even begin to tell you how that feels. It was as if somebody was continuously smashing a sledgehammer into my chest, over my heart. That's the closest I can get to describing it.

By now, I was a full-time gangster, one hundred per cent. I'd kissed farewell to my shop job – the nine-to-five was getting in the way of my twenty-four-seven, y'know. Plus, I really feared I'd do something bad to Brian.

I was making a lot of money on the streets. I had rolls of the stuff stored in various locations: in jezzies' houses, in a shoebox under my bed and in the sofa in my living room. I'd made a hole in the underside and would stuff the notes up for safe-keeping. I used the money for more drugs which I sold on and then spent cash on guns, clothes and trainers for myself and flowers for my nan and Mum. I couldn't do anything like splash out on a good holiday somewhere sunny because of my bail conditions.

I'd built up a reputation. People feared me. Some hated me. Robbery followed robbery followed robbery. And woe betide any prick who tried to muscle in on my lines. My list of enemies grew and grew. This wasn't even postcode-based stuff, but mainly local drug dealers, although beef could also arise over silly things. If I'd slept with a girl and her older brother wasn't happy about it, for example, then that could result in a fight, stabbing or a shooting. It was crazy, man.

Paranoid thoughts occupied my mind. Walking down the street, I'd only have to see a car with tinted windows pass by and I'd be reaching for my machine. I'd take a different route every time I left the house, just as Zam – God rest him – had taught me years ago. Some nights I'd stay over at my mum's place in Angell Town, just to mix things up a bit. She had divorced Dwight and as she was still single she enjoyed having a man around the house.

I would have flashbacks of that bullet grazing my lip. Even when I was asleep it affected me, with nightmares in which bullets rained down on me like fireworks. In some dreams I wouldn't survive those bullets, y'know.

Did I want to change? Did I need all this violence? I'd downloaded violence subconsciously from when I was a young kid. But I couldn't find a route through it yet; I didn't know how to address it. Violence and gang life made up my world. I knew no different.

The excitement had gone. All that remained were evil thoughts – pain, death and bullets. Once, I spent an hour running around south London, machine on my waist, hunting one of my enemies. I looked everywhere but I couldn't find him, man. I staggered back to Myatts Field, hoodie soaked with sweat, conflicting voices raging in my head. I was furious that I hadn't done what I'd set out to do. Furious that I was even in this position, and thinking, 'You used to be a good person, you know, Boost'.

I reached the Hills and sat on the grass, holding my machine and I sobbed and sobbed. Across the path, at the end of Crawshay Court, I remember seeing a group of kids, aged around eight or nine, kicking a football around. And that upset me too. *You went from being a kid playing football and street games to being a gangster with a machine on his waist, holding down the block. There were no in-between stages. None.*

Yeah, that's where I was at. I didn't know how to change. It was around that same time that I wrote some verse that started out as a poem about the kids' playground on the estate, but kind of went off course.

Woke up with a gun in my hand
No one understands because they don't live the life I live
Grab the bally and the gloves, see how much bullets are in the clip
You see, if I don't carry this burner it's gonna be the end of me
Thinking about the enemy from the Other Side that wanna put ten
in me
You don't live my life, you don't know how I feel
To be honest, I'm not a bad person
I can ring off my burner, eight or nine times
Then I'll go help my grandma with the curtains
It's just a lifestyle I live
The life of pain, struggle and gang warfare
Again, you don't live my life

I'm from a place where you can't bring your kids to a park
In case an argument breaks out and someone starts to squeeze off
You don't live my life
I could be walking down the street and a tinted car pulls up next to me
That could be my enemy, or it could be my friend, but I ain't taking
no chances so I squeeze off that ting
You don't live my life

I was searching for peace but didn't know where, or how, to find it. I had a name, recognition, money and drugs, but I wasn't happy.

Mikes and Lox, meanwhile, had found peace, it seemed. They were still adjusting to life away from the streets but appeared to be doing well. I would still go to Mimi's most days. Sometimes I'd laugh, man. There would be Lox's XXL, long-armed and long-legged clothes swamping the clothes horse (all washed by Mimi) and he and Mikes would be sitting there working on their CVs and shit. Lox would often be writing poetry. We'd still play computer games in Mikes' bedroom and, when he and Lox weren't looking, I'd slip my MAC-10 under the bed – and leave it there for safe-keeping.

Now regulars at the Word of Grace ministry, Mimi's evangelical church, they'd be like, 'You should come along, Boost. It's comforting, y'know.'

And I'd go, 'Rah, I get that you get all this "Jesus" stuff, man. But I don't think it's for me, y'know. Jesus ain't gonna make me money.'

Midnight introduced me to some of his black magic, voodoo shit. He took me to see a shaman who performed protection prayers that would supposedly keep me safe on the streets. I had to wear a particular T-shirt for three days to get my sweat on it before it was sent to Algeria where a high priestess character in the mountains sniffed it and said prayers for me. I also bathed in what I was told were ground gorilla bones, which came in the form of a poly bag filled with brownish powder that didn't smell of anything. This all sounds like bullshit but back then believing I was spiritually protected made me feel untouchable. 'If a bullet hits me, that's OK 'cos I've sent my T-shirt to Algeria,' I told myself. Midnight was heavily into this stuff and that was why he moved so loosely; he believed he was protected by a spiritual realm that gave him immunity from death or a jail sentence. Maybe there was indeed something in it – he never did go to jail and he's still out there, somewhere.

But how could I find peace when I was so consumed with anger? I wasn't ready to leave the streets. I couldn't *walk* the streets if I didn't have my machine on me. OC needed me. Troopz, Shellz, Abz, Syikes, Midnight, the Tinies, even those Olders who remained active, they all needed me, didn't they? I couldn't give up the fight. Not yet. I would have to drop into the abyss riding that rollercoaster before I could begin to climb out. There would be a few more events yet – and it scares the shit out of me when I remember the extreme lengths to which I would go.

I was in Streatham one Sunday afternoon, walking down the high road to the bus stop at the station where I'd catch the 133 back to Brixton. My mood was chilled after spending the night with Gabriella, a pretty Latino girl I'd met in a West End club a few weeks ago. Yeah, I was feeling good – until I spied these four south London boys who I had a problem with. All of them in their late teens, this team from Tooting had been late jumping on the streets. They'd come into a bit of money, bought a few guns and suddenly they'd got their little batteries on their backs, know what I mean? One of them had just got out of jail. They were flexing, acting the hard gangsters in their low-slung jeans. They'd known each other for a while.

They saw Boost, on his own, wearing a Jacob & Co watch with a diamond bezel and obviously thought, 'He'll be easy to rob'.

As they approached, I backed into the doorway of a dry cleaner so that they couldn't take me from the sides. If they tried to give me a cracking, at least it would be head-on. I'd see it coming. They crowded me in the doorway of the shop, four smirking faces.

'Yo, Boost,' said the one who fancied himself as the ringleader, I'll call him Marcus. He had a wiry build and looked familiar. Like I'd met him somewhere other than the streets before, y'know. I stood there with my arms folded, smiling down at him.

Marcus pointed at my wrist. 'Rah, that's a nice watch you've got there,' he said and, as the other three mumbled assent, he came close enough for me to smell his weedy breath, and went to claw my Jacob off my wrist. I flung his hand off me as soon as his fingers touched my watch. Now I was in demolition mode, but continued smiling all the same. An evil smile. And as I looked each one of them in the eye, I could see they weren't sure of themselves, y'know. Their attempt to intimidate me had failed. You see, where I'm from, we don't get intimidated. We Myatts Field people are comfortable if we're uncomfortable, y'know what I mean?

I slowed my voice. 'Remember this day,' I said. 'Remember that everything that you do is gonna make a reaction – and you will all suffer as a consequence of that reaction.'

Marcus stepped back onto the pavement, his cronies moving with him. He attempted a laugh. 'Was only admiring your watch, man,' he went.

I stepped out of the doorway. 'You lot are gonna remember this day,' I said.

One of the boys, a big fake diamond stud in his ear, gave Marcus's arm a tug. 'Let's go, bro.'

I stood and watched as they walked away, imagining what I could do to them within seconds. That would have to wait though. There were too many people around, including kids.

And besides, I was naked, y'know? I walked to the bus stop, fuming inside. On the way home I made a few calls.

When I got back to our area, I told Midnight what had happened with the boys in Streatham. 'Right, let's go for 'em now,' he said. A contact gave us the exact whereabouts of Marcus and his little friends at that very moment: a youth club in Streatham. We got one of the boys on the block to drive us to the area but only made it as far as Tulse Hill when my snitch called again.

'Don't touch it, it's hot,' he said. There had been an incident at the youth club and the police were there. I was really pissed off. I'd got myself all fired-up, y'know.

Opportunity to lick over those boys struck again the following Saturday night. I got the call around 9 p.m. from the same contact. This time, things sounded more promising. They'd been spotted outside a nightclub. 'They're drunk, chatting up girls and stuff,' said my guy. 'They went back inside the club, so they might well be there until it closes at three.'

I pulled on my grubbiest jeans and grabbed my machine. I was on it, man.

Tonight is the night one of those boys gets touched, was the mantra playing in my head as I walked to the club, *Tonight is the night.* I had a spring in my step to the rhythm of it. But how would I get close to them pricks? I couldn't risk going inside the club with a firearm.

A long queue stretched back from the doors guarded by two bouncers in jackets so large they could upholster a vast armchair. I did a walk-by on the opposite side of the road (I couldn't risk being seen at this stage) but Marcus and his crew were nowhere to be seen. I assumed – I hoped – they were still inside the club. Conceding this was now a waiting game, I looked for a suitable hiding place.

I spotted a bench across the road from the club in a small, community garden area set back from the pavement. It was perfect – I'd still be able to keep eye on the doors while not being too conspicuous. I scooped some mud from a flower bed, rubbed some onto my jeans and a bit on my face and lay on the bench as though I were a homeless man. A homeless man with a gun in his waistband. Four hours dragged by, with no sign of those boys. At 3 a.m. I got up to wait next to the bench, barely blinking as I scoured the clubbers exiting, in a trickle at first, then in a tsunami of bodies and now I couldn't see the doors for the tangle of people outside the club. I heard a bottle smash, laughter, chanting, shouting. Then, a little agitation at the far right of the crowd. A group of boys emerged from the mass. Their features were hard to make out from where I was standing, but I was ninety per cent certain one of them was Marcus. He had on a lime-green shirt that looked slimy and had the same build as the boy who'd touched my watch.

My heart walloped. *That's him. That's gotta be him. He touched my watch. How fucking* dare *he? I'm sure that's him.* Now he was at the kerb, looking right then left as though he was about to cross to my side of the road. In one action, I lifted my coat and pulled out my gun and ran over the grass, my target bouncing up and down in my vision. Was I playing one of those virtual reality games? As I hit the pavement, Marcus and his mates were just stepping into the road. I stopped, pressing my machine against my thigh. Now, with about twelve metres between Marcus and me, I got a better look at his face and …

… *Fuck it. It ain't him. I strangle the grip with my fingers. The nose pummels my thigh. Blood thumps and thrashes through me. I stay where I am. The boy who's not Marcus doesn't cross the road, as two police vans, lights and sirens blazing, pull up. Jakes get out. I stay where I am, gun by my side. There's noise. Shouting. More lights and sirens. It ain't him. I can't believe it ain't him. I'm hearing snippets of the police issue a caution.*

OK, so that wasn't Marcus, but I was going to find him or his mates that night, no matter what. I was certain he was somewhere in that crowd and I didn't care that the police were there. In that moment I thought, I'm gonna lick over one of these boys even in front of the police. The jakes were bundling a group of lads into the back of the vans. I hadn't been paying attention to the fight that had started outside the club. My eyes had been on my target, y'know. I put my gun away and walked back to the bench, where I stayed, my eyes trained on that club.

The police vans drove away. Clubbers dispersed in different directions. I didn't spot Marcus. I sat on the bench and stared at the building, lifeless now. I watched the street lights go out, the sun come up and a newsagent filling the stand outside his shop with Sunday papers. My Jacob & Co watch confirmed it had just gone six-thirty. Time to call it a night. I walked back to Myatts Field, my eyes burning with tears. Only now was I beginning to question my actions. I felt as though a hypnotist had just gone, 'Three, two, one, wake-up,' and clicked his fingers in my face, y'know. Again, I sat down in the Hills, crying and thinking. Right now, I couldn't face Nan and Granddad or my mum. Mikes and Lox wouldn't be up yet. I sat there in the Hills. This morning it was quiet, but for a few older residents walking their muzzled dogs. I drew my legs to my chest, rested my chin on my knees and closed my eyes. I was tired, man.

Later that week, I had a dream. Mikes was in it. We were on the block, sitting on the wall at the end of Treherne Court, chilling. No other gang members were there. There were no lights in the windows, and the estate was eerily quiet. Abandoned. As we sat there, I turned to Mikes and said, 'I ain't on the block no more. I'm coming off the streets, man.'

And Mikes said, 'Yeah? Shut up, man.'

But I was adamant. 'Nah, I mean it,' I said, 'I want a life. I want a family. I want the dinner round the table and fresh orange juice, bro. I ain't on the block no more.' And then I woke up, realised it wasn't true and this dull, dragging sensation shot through my chest.

Having that dream made me question my life and what I was doing with it. I know it sounds clichéd, but I began to wake up, y'know.

I remember being in Brockwell Park one time, machine on my waist, watching all these happy couples go by, playing with their kids and pushing buggies about the place. And, just as I'd said in my dream, I thought, I want that. I want to be holding hands with a wife. I want kids. I want the dinner round the table with the family and fresh orange juice. I didn't have any of that when I was a small kid. I never had that mum-kissing-you-on-the-forehead-before-school shit. Then I started to think about how I could make all these 'wants' a reality, which I wouldn't be able to do if I ended up dead or in jail. I thought some more. *Yeah, I don't want this life no more. I want out, man. I'm getting out.*

I give thanks to whoever was watching over me the night I went after Marcus. If the boy I'd seen crossing the road had turned out to be him, I would have fired at him. It wasn't bad luck but very good fortune that I hadn't seen him – not only for him, but for me too.

I later found out Marcus was my blood cousin. Only then did I remember where I knew him from. I'd seen him at Pups' house one time, years ago. I never ran into Marcus again after that day in Streatham. He's now serving life in jail for murder.

21

DILUTION

Leaving the streets is hard. Just as it takes time to become a gang member, it's impossible to break free of that world and lifestyle overnight. Especially as I was still living in that gang's area, surrounded by my brothers and enemies in crime. Making the transition from gangster to 'normal' person is challenging on so many levels. Those bullets don't stop flying, y'know. And I had to be bold to make the move.

By the time I turned nineteen, I was beginning to make some progress, thanks to the love and support I received from Pastor Mimi, Mikes and Lox and other friends, old and new. My grandparents, as far as I knew at that time, had no idea I'd been a member of OC. I'm not sure they knew OC existed. Either way, I didn't want to hurt or worry them by saying, 'Hey, guess what? I've been a gang member for the past five years. I've been running around banging guns and robbing drug dealers, but I'm giving all that shit up now. Please help me.' That wouldn't be cool, man.

Mimi, as I've mentioned many times throughout this book, was our angel. Never did she make us feel bad about all the terrible shit we'd done. Nah, Mimi was – and still is – all about positive energy and elevation. She listened to us. She made us feel worthy. Mimi's house at that time was like a youth centre. She moved all her furniture out of the living room to make way for a snooker table and a big telly and that space became a safe haven for any boy or young man whether they were trying, like me, to leave the streets, were still on the streets and wanted to get away from the noise or maybe just fancied a bowl of Mimi's jollof rice. Sometimes, Mimi would take us to the cinema or go-Karting and generally get us involved in activities away from the estate, y'know. Mimi would ask me what I wanted from life. And she instilled in me the belief that I could be a decent human being with potential. That I could love and also *be* loved. Mimi helped me find peace within myself. This all took time.

There are stages we all go through when voluntarily leaving the streets. I call this process 'dilution'. Emotions hit me: guilt, anger, realisation. As far as OC was concerned, the Tinies had, by now, joined forces with the Y28s, a gang formed by younger members of the the fragmented Pell Dem Crew (PDC) that ruled Angell Town. Together, they became GAS gang, which would go on to become one of the most dangerous outfits in London. Sadly, I couldn't undo the damage I'd done when I recruited those Tinies myself and there was a part of me that now thought, 'Fuck, did I groom those boys to become gang members?' Previously, I hadn't thought of it as grooming. I was doing what I knew, what I'd learned from my Olders. I genuinely cared for those boys. I would play football with them, just as my Olders had done with me and encourage them in the sport.

As I distanced myself from OC, I spent a lot of time in my head, y'know. There had been a point when that gang was my world. I'd risked my life out there and now I wondered what it had all been for. To fight for an estate where my grandparents didn't even own their own property? Fighting for Baghdad? OC was nothing like the Italian mafia. We were kids in tracksuits with guns and knives, rapping about shooting pagans and shit like that. *OC*, Organised Crime. One Chance to live. Twice we'd paid a devastating price for the sake of that name. Tiny A, gone. Ratty, gone. Two young boys, killed in gang warfare. One with a blade, the other with a gun.

In April 2009, still in the early stages of exiting gang life, I finally received the news I'd been longing to hear. After attending those futile bail appointments for a year, Trident detectives informed me that no further action would be taken against me over Ratty's death. I was relieved, of course, but I was not happy at the news. First, because nothing could bring Ratty back and secondly, because I didn't know why I had been arrested for my friend's murder in the first place. I had been forced to live with that stigma for a whole year, during which time the police had been unable to find any evidence whatsoever to support their accusations, other than a few grainy shots of random figures wearing balaclavas. Still, at least my name had been cleared.

One of my biggest challenges was learning how to control my anger. Until now, I'd settled most disputes by fighting. Any sign of trouble, I could pull out my gun or knife. How would I protect myself now? Saying 'bye-bye' to the streets didn't rid me of my enemies. They weren't going to shake my hand and say, 'Good fight, man'. If anything, once word got around that I'd left the road, my enemies would see me as an easy target. They were gonna come out of the woodwork. Payback time, innit.

My family were still at risk too, even now I no longer considered myself to be active. One group of boys, who had been drug-related opponents, fired a shotgun through my mum's window, man. One of the guys had been seeing a girl from Angell Town who apparently pointed out 16 Peckford Place as they drove past, saying, 'That's where that Boost lives,' so my sources say. Luckily, nobody was home when it happened. Mum, Jazz, Tyrell and I were on a train when the police called, on our way to Butlins, Skegness. I was fucking raging. Any one of my family could've been killed. My natural instinct was to grab a MAC-10, hunt down the gunman's family and put one or ten through their living room window. But the new me wasn't supposed to retaliate, right? Reluctantly, I let the jakes take care of matters but man, my mind was plagued by 'What if?' after that day.

I did still carry a machine, at least to begin with. I had no choice in the early days. That's what I mean by diluting the gang life. Initially, that machine was still my safety net. As the weeks went by, I started going to church more often, but I'd sit through services thinking, 'Somebody's gonna shoot at me as soon as I step outside.' So, yeah, I'd have my gun on me in church. I wasn't going out like that, man.

Fast forward a few months, though, and my confidence was slowly increasing. Nobody had tried to shoot me in a while so, y'know, maybe now it was time to ditch the machine and just carry a knife. That was how it worked for me, anyway. Then, further down the line, I told myself, 'Yo, y'know what? You don't need that nank to go go-Karting with, you can just take a screwdriver this time.' And eventually, man didn't need no weapons no more. Although now and then I might stumble across a stray rock in a drawer or under the bed.

Things were looking up for me, man. Church became my sanctuary. Mimi's services were uplifting. She made all the Jesus stuff accessible, y'know. I mean, she would work that room like she was on stage at Knebworth, strutting among the congregation, always in a sparkly or big-patterned dress, marking her words with big gestures, her voice over the mic more powerful than gunfire. And I'd sit there thinking, 'Wow, this is passionate. Why didn't I come here years ago?' Mimi would stress that we weren't there to 'do religion'.

'This is a teaching ministry,' she'd boom. 'This ministry teaches you that you are empowered, when you're out there, to do the works of God.' Through that empowerment, we would learn how to pray, Mimi explained. We would learn how to face, deal and overcome troubles by worshipping a 'powerful God'. Mimi would start her sermons by saying, 'Don't come here thinking, "Oh, it's another Sunday, I must go church." This is *not* another Sunday. This is another revelation time. We're here to worship a God who is *active*.' Yeah, Mimi was speaking my language, man.

I started going to church classes too. On Mondays I'd go to boys' club, which provided a safe place for us to talk about our problems. We'd also discuss the scriptures and how we could learn from them to uplift ourselves. Bible study classes were held on Wednesday evenings. Those nights were popular, man. Young people from all the estates in the area would come together in one room. And there was good energy, there was a vibe in the place, y'know. I also liked the social aspect. These people were so kind and loving. They got along with another. I began to fall in love with people and kindness and this gave me spiritual growth, y'know what I mean?

In some ways, my life hadn't changed. I was still living on the estate and playing football. After Tooting and Mitcham banned me, I went for a trial at Whyteleafe FC in Surrey and they signed me on the spot. At home, Mikes and Lox were still my closest friends. If anything, we were probably closer now. Just as we'd walked the same path to get to OC, we were on the same road leaving it, man. Lox continued to make rap videos, only now he was known as Mr C'mon and did conscious rap – basically, rap with a positive outlook. I wrote a CV and got another shop job, this time in Next on Oxford Street. It wasn't my dream job, but it was a start, right?

There were sceptics out there though. Undercover officers didn't give up pestering me in the street, for instance. They would test my patience to the brink, man. It was the same record every time.

'Hey Boost, what do you know about that shooting last night in Peckham?', or 'What do you know about the Brooklyn boys?', or 'What are you up to, where are you going?' They would never get out of the car.

I turned round to the guy once and said, 'Listen, I ain't on the streets no more. Go bother somebody else.' He smirked at me, zipped up his window and drove off. Yeah, that kinda shit fucked with my head. I knew I was trying to change. My friends knew it, but far as the police and pagans were concerned, I was still Boost, feared OC gang member.

One Saturday, days before I was due to start my new job, Lox and me went shopping on Oxford Street. As usual, we took the 159 from Vassall Road, got off at Oxford Circus and hit Nike Town. We had a browse, tried on some trainers, checked out the swag and thought about buying some stuff but it was too busy. The queue for the till went on forever and we were starving. We were like, 'Rah, fuck this, let's go McDonald's.' It never crossed my mind that somebody might be following us.

All I was thinking about was a McChicken sandwich, y'know. We came out of Nike Town and crossed Regent Street with a sea of slow-moving shoppers and tourists. When we reached the H&M side I felt a tap on my right shoulder. I turned, slow off the blocks, too late to dodge the leather-gloved fist that cracked into the side of my face.

I stumbled backwards as my attacker, this huge African guy, stood there, nodding. I saw a smug smile on a face I recognised from a Peckham Boys' rap video on YouTube. Behind him, dotted among pedestrians, were about thirty other black guys in balaclavas. *Where the fuck had they come out from?*

'Fuck you,' I yelled and pulled off my hoodie, ready to fight. A dull, warm pain pulsed around my cheekbone but I'd had far worse.

Lox, moving like a basketball player, pushed past H&M sales shoppers to the shop entrance, grabbed a metal barrier and lifted it above his head. 'Come inside, then,' he yelled, swinging the barrier.

I couldn't remember the last time I'd seen Lox lose it. He'd become this poetry-writing, peaceful guy, getting involved in community projects and shit like that. Now he'd gone all Incredible Hulk on me. A group of women who were coming out of the shop started screaming and ran back inside. And in those few seconds, I instinctively touched my waist, going for my gun. It wasn't there. I'd no weapon on me, did I? Not even a small screwdriver. Other shoppers caught up in the commotion hurried off, making room for the boys in the balaclavas to get behind the one who'd banged me in the face, who was looking as though he was about to crack me again.

Boom, I took off on my back foot like a hare out of its trap, running down Oxford Street, hoodie bunched in my hand, dodging, weaving, ducking through the crowds, gasping air that tasted of hot caramel nuts and exhaust fumes.

The Peckham boys were behind me, shouting, 'Get him, get him.'

I tanked it past John Lewis, almost mowing down a mob of Hara Krishna chanters, past Debenhams and the Disney Store pumping out sickly music about Mickey Mouse and shit. Just before Selfridges I cut a right down a side street. I kept on sprinting, even though I guessed I'd probably lost the Peckham lot amid the masses on Oxford Street. By the time I'd reached Marylebone, I knew I was safe, walked to Baker Street and jumped on the tube. I wasn't risking going anywhere near Oxford Circus or the number 12 bus.

Yeah, the story doesn't end the day you leave the streets, y'know.

I'd like to say I whistled all the way home from Baker Street, but I had too many thoughts fucking with my head, man. That madness on Oxford Street could have set me back big time. Had it happened two months ago, I would've had my machine with me. Would I have pointed it? Or banged it? There was still so much to go through, so much to learn, but my latest encounter with the Peckham Boys made me realise was this: 'Rah, all this gang warfare business is a self-hate thing.' All those times I was hunting the enemy I was looking for somebody just like me. We looked, dressed and talked the same, give or take. We came from similar cultural backgrounds and struggles, listened to the same music. In a nutshell, I was looking for somebody just like me before deciding, 'Rah, y'know what? That person needs to get stabbed right now.' It's so fucked up. And why hadn't I thought of this years ago?

A few days later, I had a conversation with one of the Peckham Boys. I got a number for one of their guys via a football contact. This guy had appeared in many of the gang's music videos, and, when I was on the streets, there had always been a kind of mutual respect between us. I wouldn't have said as much back in the day, but I did take a liking to him.

I said, 'Yo, I know it was your lot who came for me on Oxford Street at the weekend but, y'know what? It's OK. I'm gonna let this one slide.'

He denied any involvement at first. 'Yo, dunno what you mean. Nothing to do with us y'know,' he said.

'Really, it's OK,' I said, again. But listen, I've left the streets, man. I'm trying to move on, to better myself. Have a future and all that y'know? I'm not trying to be a dickhead.'

He admitted he had heard about the Oxford Street chase. 'I wasn't there, though,' he added.

I said, 'Listen, it's fine. This is all part of my transition. Right now, this is burning, but I'm letting you know, I'm not coming over there. OK, you've got one up on me but, rah, you don't need to hide on your block. No one's coming round your area. I forgive you.'

There was a few seconds' silence, then he said, 'Yo, I respect that.'

I came off the phone feeling good about myself. I had some peaceful vibes going on, y'know what I mean? I like peace.

22

THIS IS YOUR DAY

I was watching a sermon about the rapture on the God TV channel when armed police burst in and arrested me for murder.

I remember the programme was *This is Your Day*, hosted by Israeli pastor Benny Hinn. It was getting on for four in the morning. I could've gone to bed three hours ago, when I'd got back from Mikes', but this was my vibe of late: chilling on the sofa in the early hours, watching the God channel. This time, somewhere between night and day, was my 'me time', y'know what I mean?

Tonight, or this morning, Benny was in Jerusalem, speaking about the rapture of the church and the second coming, over fuzzy organ music, his congregation clapping and crying and stuff. It was moving, man and his soothing voice, combined with the boiled sweet glow from the Christmas tree lights, was making my eyelids go heavy. Ironically, Benny was talking about God 'not allowing judgement to fall' when movement at the window made me sit up. I'd opened the curtains for Nan when I'd got in so she could get her 'natural light' in the morning. Now I was seeing red laser beams and human-sized beetles shuffling in the garden. I shot from the sofa and jumped when I heard the front door going upstairs. It was no normal knock. Nah, this shook the house, man. *Boom, boom, boom.* One of Nan's dollies fell off the dresser. I was like, *What the fuck is going on?* I went over to the window. Now I could see them. A whole army of officers in helmets, armed with machine guns, in our back garden.

Next, rumbling upstairs. Nan's voice. 'What's happening? What do you want?' Then Granddad's lower tones, dissolving in the thunder of boots down the stairs. A red beam blinds me. I turn and blink and more of those helmeted jakes come into view. They pour into the room. Nan, in her nightie, comes running in after them, Granddad behind her in his stripy pyjamas. Benny's still preaching. An officer steps forward, swipes his handcuffs from his belt. 'Terroll Kersean Lewis,' he begins ...

The handcuffs iced my wrists. What was this, some weird nightmare? Had I fallen asleep on the sofa? My nan cupped her mouth and started crying as the officer continued reading my rights and I wanted to go and hug her, tell her everything would be fine, y'know. But I couldn't move for the cuffs and the room full of men with machine guns and the words spewing from the officer's mouth.

'We are arresting you on suspicion of the murder of Ryan Bravo. You do not have to say anything.'

Who? *What's happening? What the fuck is going on?*

The officer finished his spiel and I closed my eyes for a second or two, gained some composure. Then I looked at Nan and Granddad. 'It's OK,' I said, 'Everything's gonna be good. This is a misunderstanding. It will all be sorted.'

'Yeah, get ready,' went the same officer. 'Grab your trainers and your tracksuit. I doubt you'll be coming back here today.'

'What's that supposed to mean?' I snapped, but I continued to try and be strong for my grandparents. 'Everything's gonna be good, y'know.' I told them again as the jakes marched me out to the van. The house was surrounded by armed officers. All the neighbours had come out to watch, too. 'Somebody call Pastor Mimi,' I called out and she came running down.

'What's going on, Terroll?' she went and, bless that woman, she walked alongside me in her slippers, all the way to the van. 'Keep strong. Keep your faith. We'll pray for you,' she said.

'Blessings,' I replied.

Slam went the doors.

It was still dark when we pulled into Kennington police station. God, I still hated that place. They fast tracked me straight to the cells, where I had to take off all my clothes and put on a flimsy pair of overalls that looked like a forensic suit. At this point I was beginning to worry. I hadn't murdered anyone. I knew that, but the police seemed convinced that I had. Negative thoughts tiptoed up there, y'know. *Innocent people go to jail.* I stepped into the suit as a police officer bunged my clothes in a see-through bin bag.

'Yo,' I said, 'hurry up and get me in the interview room so I can go home.'

'Yeah, your solicitor's on his way,' he said, 'Your interview is scheduled but I doubt you'll be going home today. You'll probably be going to court in the morning.'

'Court? What d'ya mean I'm going court?' I said. I was confused, innit.

The officer was already on his way out. 'We'll let you know when your solicitor arrives,' he said. Another door slammed, and I was left alone in that freezing cell. I was sitting on a single bed bolted to the floor, overhead lights flickering, fucking with my head. Stencilled on the ceiling was that familiar message: 'Are you sick and tired of feeling sick and tired?'

My solicitor arrived within the hour. In the interview room the detectives started the tape and told me why I'd been arrested. They'd pulled me for the murder of eighteen-year-old Ryan Bravo, who had been shot in the doorway of a Costcutter store, Walworth, in August 2008. He'd gone into the shop to buy milk when he inadvertently got caught in the middle of a gangland clash between OC and the Peckham Boys, police claimed. Trident detectives said five OC gang members on mopeds opened fire at the rival gang members inside the store. Tragically, Ryan, who was not linked to gangs, was shot dead. I'd heard about the shooting. A guy called

Ashley Bucknor, who police said was a member of OC, had been jailed for thirty-two years for the crime in September 2009. I knew Ashley through friends in the area, but he wasn't an OC member I had encountered. He appealed his sentence and won a retrial. I'd been hauled in because the police believed I was one of those moped guys.

It was just like the time I had been arrested over my supposed involvement in Ratty's death. I was shown grainy pictures of guys with their faces covered. This time the figures were on mopeds and wearing helmets instead of balaclavas and my interrogators pointed at random figures, going, 'That's you, isn't it?' I was also asked about three other guys, Nathaniel Bailey, Nathaniel Grant and Anthony McKenzie. They were from my area and around my age, give or take a year either side. After I'd confirmed that I knew them, I was told that they too had been arrested in connection with Ryan's murder.

The questions went on and on, identical subjects asked different ways, y'know. Where had I been on the day of the shooting? I honestly couldn't remember. I mean, how was I supposed to recall my movements from one random day sixteen months ago? I wasn't the type to keep a diary, y'know what I mean?

'You're Boost. You're a member of the Organised Crime gang, aren't you?' they kept saying.

'You've got the wrong person,' I said repeatedly. 'Yes, I was a gang member, but I've been off the streets for a long while now. I've changed my life. I want a future.'

At the end of the interview, they charged me with murder. I felt like I'd just stepped off a dizzying fairground ride, man.

'I'm innocent,' I said, for what it was worth, 'When can I go home?'

Murder. Such a serious charge, yet everything was processed so quickly. Like they were handing me a speeding ticket or something.

The next morning, I was in the dock at Camberwell Green magistrates' court, alongside my co-defendants. Man, I was on the ceiling looking down, drifting in and out of consciousness or something, y'know what I mean?

The magistrate called my name, told me to stand. I'd been charged with murder, he said. He alleged I was a danger to potential witnesses of this crime – this crime I hadn't committed. I'd be held on remand until my trial date. Same applied to the others. By early afternoon, I was being strip-searched and getting my mugshot taken at HMP High Down, Sutton.

How had this happened? Less than two days ago, I'd been too busy enjoying my life to pay much attention to the outside world. Today, however, as my co-defendants and I were taken to the introduction wing, I knew full well that it was Wednesday 9 December 2009. The day I was charged and jailed for a murder I didn't commit. My twentieth birthday was in four days' time. *Innocent people go to jail.*

On the introduction wing, we were given cheese and lettuce sandwiches and I was, like, 'Rah, wicked, something to eat.' I didn't realise how hungry I was until I lifted that sandwich to my mouth. I bit hungrily into it and, as I did so, bang, crunch, I thought a few teeth had come out, man. I spat the lot into a paper towel and gagged at the result: a mess of mushy cheese, slithers of browning lettuce and fucking gravel. I peeled the sandwich apart and lifted the lettuce; more stones lay embedded in the cheese topped with a few dark hairs. I wanted to kick off, y'know, but sense told me this wasn't the time or place. If I'd been a seasoned con, I would've known not to touch that sandwich. I would have known that life was only going to get worse.

I made my one permitted phone call to Nan and Granddad. Granddad answered. I told him what had happened at court, how I'd been refused bail then shipped out. 'I'm innocent, Dad,' I finished. 'I don't know why I'm here. It doesn't make sense.'

Granddad was calm as ever. 'I know, son,' he went. 'Just you keep your head up. Keep your wits about you in there. Keep strong, Our Boy.'

Man, I could feel tears welling. I fought them. 'How's Nan?' I said.

'Well, she's a bit shaken, so she is but, you know your Nan,' he laughed a bit. 'She's tough. But listen, we're behind you every step of the way. Everything will work out.'

'Blessings, Dad, blessings,' I said, then hung up. I was choking, man.

The guards marched us along to our cell and all the inmates who were out on the landing turned to stare. 'Who's that?' I heard a few say as we shuffled past with our see-through bin bags stuffed with clothes and a few possessions.

From somewhere behind us on that hollow landing, one guy shouted, '*OC*,' and, swear-down, the whole wing fell silent.

The guard unbolted the steel door to our cell, a gun-metal grey room that smelled of unflushed shit and stale sweat. Against its side walls were two skinny bunk beds. One corner housed a toilet and sink. In the back wall was a small barred window. We stepped inside. There was piss and grime all over the floor. Another door slammed.

Once the guard left we scraped our toothbrushes against the metal window frame, fashioning them into homemade knives. This was prison, we needed protection. There I was, a guy who had put so much effort into changing his life around, one who'd turned his back on guns and knives, slipping straight back into my old ways – just because I was now in 'the system'.

On my third full day in High Down, Mikes and Lox visited. Man, it was good to see them. They were supportive, boosting me up and shit, telling me I'd be 'out of here soon', in between fishing for jail gossip. 'So, who's in with you, anyone we know?' Mikes kept asking. Which made me laugh. I would have asked the same question if our situations were reversed. The hour flew by too fast and, when the time came for us to go our separate ways, I felt like my heart was being ripped out of my chest. They were going home. Why couldn't I go home with them? Yeah, I couldn't get my head around that. Only when I returned to that shithole cell did it finally hit me: *I'm in prison. I'm in fucking prison.* The next morning, the authorities sprung a surprise on me that would further cement my new reality.

One of the guards, a mean-looking white guy with a shaved head packed with lots of wriggly bones, dragged me out of the cell before breakfast. 'C'mon, Lewis,' he said, 'You need to pack your stuff. They're moving you.'

'You what?' I said. I was confused, then hopeful for a second or two. *Maybe they have realised their mistake and they're sending me home? Giving me bail?*

'Yeah, there's been a mix-up. You're in the wrong prison,' he said. As he spoke, I could see all those bones moving beneath his skin. Looked like he had crabs living in his head, y'know.

I pulled an exaggerated, double-take expression. 'I don't get it.'

'There's been a mix-up,' he repeated. 'You're in a B-cat jail but you're an A-cat prisoner. So, you're being moved to Belmarsh.'

'Belmarsh? What kind of games are you guys playing with me?' I said. I was shocked, y'know. An A-category prisoner was high-risk, deemed a danger to the public, police and national security and shit.

'Get a shift on,' went the guard.

23

BELMARSH

On the eve of my twentieth birthday, I was bundled into a van and driven to high-security Belmarsh, the jail reserved for serial killers, terrorists and sicko nonces. I was like, 'Rah, how bad is this getting?'

Cuffed and stuffed inside a cell so tiny I could barely move in it, I watched the Kent countryside bump along outside the window, wishing I could smash my way out of that fucking box and go hug one of those skeletal trees. At least, I thought, I get to wear a green-and-yellow boiler suit. It was a regulation travelling suit for A-cat prisoners in case they escaped during transit. I thought that suit was cool. I liked the colours.

Man, the second they drove me through those gates, I thought, 'Where the hell are you bringing me?' I mean, there was some hard-core security stuff going on here. All around me were steel walls, razor fences and cameras. It was like a metal jungle. Inside was no different. They took my mugshot and strip-searched me to ensure I had no drugs or anything hidden up my arse. I was taken through corridors and rooms that were locked and locked again. Every time we passed through a door it would get locked behind us, then the door ahead would be unlocked. At last we reached my cell in house block 3.

Being an A-cat, high-risk inmate did have one advantage – I got a cell to myself. And compared with the one I'd shared in

High Down, my Belmarsh accommodation was not bad. It was small but clean, with a bed, toilet, sink, kettle and TV. Through the obligatory barred window I was able to watch the ongoing construction of HMP Isis.

It took me ages to fall asleep that first night, my mind racing, going over the previous days' events, trying – and failing – to make sense of it all. It was freezing and I had just a thin scratchy blanket on the bed. I missed my family. They knew I was in here – I'd been told the prison admin had informed them. I dropped off, aged nineteen and thinking about my grandparents. I woke up at 6 a.m., aged twenty, thinking about my grandparents.

I kept my head down. The wing they'd put me on was also the methadone dispersal block that housed all the junkies. And I wasn't in the mood for chit-chatting with any nitties, y'know. I'd done enough of that shit in my twenty years, thanks. I spent my birthday going through more doors that locked behind and before me, attending induction sessions where I was told about all the services on offer inside Belmarsh. Apparently, there were experts I could reach out to regarding my mental health and well-being, or any drugs issues I might be facing. Or perhaps I'd like to learn how to manage difficult emotions? I wasn't sure whether that last one was a joke, y'know. More useful was the information on education and work opportunities. There were lots of good classes I could attend and, by getting a job, say in the laundry or kitchen, I could earn some money.

Visiting procedures for A-cat prisoners were a strict affair, I was told. Anyone wishing to visit me would need to submit a request to the prison in advance. I would be strip-searched before and after each visit, which would take place in a secure room with a screen separating me from my guest. Who the fuck did they think I was, Hannibal Lecter?

The gym sounded good, with lots of weights and machines and stuff. Being an A-cat guy, I would need to fill out an application to use the facilities, which would need to be approved. They were fucking with my head, man.

During social time that evening I called Nan and Granddad, but they didn't pick up. I rang Mum instead. I just needed to hear a familiar voice. After all, it's not every day you spend your birthday in HMP Belmarsh. Part of me wished I'd never made that call, though. After she'd wished me 'happy birthday' and all that, I started talking about the visiting arrangements – and Mum dropped something that fucking broke my heart, man. 'You know your granddad went to visit you today?' she said.

'What? I'm not allowed no visitors yet.'

'Yeah, he got all the way there and they sent him packing,' said Mum.

Poor Granddad had to catch a number of buses and trains to get to Belmarsh. He'd told the people at reception that he'd come to 'see my son'.

'It's his birthday,' he'd explained. 'I'd like to visit my son on his birthday.'

Bless him. Granddad thought he could just turn up and they'd stick him on the visitors' list. He had no idea he would have to apply in advance. I went back to my cell, sat on the rock-hard bed and cried my eyes out. Picturing my granddad – my *dad* – coming all that way, just to see me in prison on my birthday, only to be told to go home … yeah, that killed me. Big time.

Belmarsh birthday was followed by Belmarsh Christmas and New Year's Eve in fucking Belmarsh. The festive season was grim. I pretended it wasn't Christmas, y'know, which didn't take much effort, given my surroundings. They did lay on a dinner with stuffing and shit, but I didn't eat it. It looked disgusting, man.

Back in my cell, I turned to the books of Proverbs and Psalms that Mimi had posted to me. Those books were keeping me going. I would read one psalm and one proverb a day. Today,

I read Psalms 23:1, 'The Lord is my Shepherd', which was my favourite. Its theme was that God always protects and provides. Reading it gave me some comfort but, still, I was scared. I was lonely. I felt so trapped. I didn't know my future. There had been no further news about my trial.

I knew that even when the moment did come to fight my case, I would have no control over the jury's decision. What if they didn't like the way I looked? What if they judged me on my gangland past? What if the judge decided Belmarsh should be my home for the next thirty years? *Innocent people go to jail.*

On New Year's Eve, as I sat on my bed watching the countdown to 2010 playing on the television, I had a breakdown. On the screen came footage of fireworks exploding over Big Ben, Tower Bridge and the London Eye, interspersed with shots of happy people in bobble hats and gloves, counting, 'Ten, nine, eight, seven ... ' I heard fireworks banging nearby too, beyond the steel walls and razor fences. 'Six, five, four, three ... ' Tears flooded my eyes. *Innocent people go to jail.* I shivered, wrapped the scratchy blanket around my shoulders. 'Two, one ... ' More fireworks, the big display now. 2010 glittering before fizzling in the sky. 'Auld Lang Syne' played and all that crazy stuff. It was too much, man.

My chest heaving, I dropped to my knees on the cold floor and, hands together, like I was arm-wrestling myself, allowed hot tears to stream down my face, as I said, 'Listen, God. I'll leave it in your hands. Only you can prove my innocence.'

Yeah, that was heavy shit, man, but things did pick up a little in the new year. I landed a job as a cleaner. The money wasn't much – about twelve quid a day, paid directly into my canteen allowance – but it soon mounted up. And besides, I didn't need much money in prison. Cash, bank cards, cheques, postal orders ... none of them are legal tender for prisoners. People on the outside could give us money but we didn't see the cash itself.

I didn't mind that job, y'know. It gave me something to focus on other than stressing about my case. In a weird way the job was a bit like doing meditation. Plus, I had the cleanest cell on the block. I had my own mop, bucket, brush and little packets of disinfectant and I'd scrub my cell every day – sometimes twice a day.

It was as I'd finished mopping my cell one morning during social time (this was a good time to clean as I could leave the door open), I spotted this guy in the hall outside who looked familiar. I couldn't quite place him, though. Mixed race, fiftyish and bald but for brown-grey tufts above his ears, he was talking to some junkie boy with drumsticks for arms. I watched for a few seconds, trying not to look obvious. For all I knew they could both be psychos, right? After a while, the junkie handed his newspaper to the mixed-race guy, whose face broke into a massive smile, displaying a big gap between his front teeth and, bang, I've got it. It's only Mo from Key House, ain't it? He and Mandy were the kind couple who'd lived in the flat above my mum's when I was little.

The junkie shambled off and I strode over.

'Mo,' I said. 'How're you doing, bro?' Mo looked a bit confused. He didn't recognise the six-foot guy I was today. Last time he'd seen me was thirteen years ago. 'It's me, Terroll,' I said. 'Remember? From Key House.' Mo looked lost for a moment. He squinted at me, tapping the rolled newspaper against his temple, then he started laughing.

'Fuck – Terroll!' he said and gave my arm a playful punch, 'What the hell are you doing in here, man?'

Wow, talk about a blast from the past. We chatted in the hall for a while. Mo was one of the methadone lot, in for 'drugs stuff'. I told him about my predicament and he assured me, as everybody else in my circle of friends and family had done, that I'd be 'out of here soon'. I wasn't so sure, but at least I now had a friend in this godforsaken place.

My application to join the prison gym would take a month to be approved and in the meantime walking round and round the exercise yard was the only form of physical activity on offer. This frustrated me, man. On the outside I had been training several times a week. Determined to keep up my fitness, I started working out in my cell – and discovered I had some good equipment in the form of the regular cell furniture. Press-ups could be done with my legs elevated, feet resting on the sink. I used my television as a weight while doing squats and did tricep dips on the edge of the toilet. Soon, I had my own mini-gym thing going on.

In mid-January, a solicitor called Anan an Asian guy from my legal team, told me that my co-defendants had been sent to HMP Feltham, a young offenders' institution. This seemed weird to me. Why had I been slung in a high-security nick? Surely, I should've been sent to Feltham too? Anan said he'd lodged a bail application on my behalf and a court date had been set for the following week.

I was duly ferried out of Belmarsh, wearing my green-and-yellow jumpsuit, to my hearing. I was excited, y'know, thinking about seeing my friends and family again once I got bail. At least I would have my support network close to me as I prepared my fight for justice. If I were still to be on remand in Belmarsh when the trial started, I would have to sit in the dock in my high-risk jumpsuit, looking like some fucking death-row nutter. How would that look to the jury?

My optimism turned out to be misplaced. There would be no reunion with my friends on the outside. The judge refused my bail application and I was back in Belmarsh by dinner time, another major head-fuck accomplished.

Over the next few months, I had further bail applications refused, each knockback chipping away at my mental health. But I did my best to remain positive and retain my sanity. Mopping helped, as did prison church services and enrolling in education classes, including poetry. They proved to be a great conduit for the raging emotions I was battling. There were also visits to look forward to, even though they were like some crazy US *Prison Break* set-up. Picture it: me, in my jumpsuit, talking through the glass partition over a speaker. When Mum first came to see me, we both sat there in tears.

Mum also sent money to my canteen account. She pawned a few of my chains, although she didn't get nearly the amount I'd paid for them. But at least her efforts meant I didn't have to go without, y'know. My cell was stocked like a supermarket with mackerel, tuna, noodles, pasta, bread, mash potato packet mixes and bottled sauces. I learned how to cook meals in my kettle – a hack passed on to me by another prisoner – which meant I could dine alone in my cell.

My favourite recipe was mackerel stew. I'd boil the mackerel in stock, throw in a few glugs of Worcestershire sauce, add a dash of jerk sauce, then tip some rice or noodles into the kettle. To make dumplings, I'd soak bits of bread and oats in a bowl of water before moulding the mixture into individual balls that I'd cook in boiling water before adding them to the stew near the end. I had to be careful though. Cooking in the cell was a punishable act – if the screws got a whiff of my prison cuisine I'd be placed on basic regime: no gym or classes and limited visits. They might even take my television away. I always made sure I stuffed a towel along the bottom of my cell door before I started cooking.

Although I mainly kept myself to myself, I did make some friends in Belmarsh alongside Mo. Kane and David were also on remand for murder and I had some good chats with those guys over games of dominoes, man. They were good brothers who would later be acquitted.

I was amazed at how humble some of the cons were. I'd speak to fellow prisoners while working out in the gym every day, including this Asian guy, Ishmael who was also my cell neighbour. He was forty-two and, at six-foot-four, had the body of a twenty-something ripped athlete. He was the humblest guy on the wing. You'd see him walking around, Quran under his arm. I liked the way he carried himself. He had this 'Don't-fuck-with-me-and-I-won't-fuck-with-you' vibe going on. Me and Ishmael got each other, y'know. He understood I wasn't one of those young boys on the wing making noises to the governor. Yeah, he recognised I was just a cool brother who wanted to go to the gym and better myself.

I remember our first conversation took place during a weight-lifting session. I told Ishmael 'I spent five years on the streets, then turned my life around and got arrested for murder.'

'Keep your head down, stay focused and loyal to yourself and you'll come through this. You will get out of here,' he said. Ishmael himself was on dispersal from another jail as part of his rehabilitation programme. He'd already done ten years for jewellery robbery and was soon to be released. 'I never meant to hurt anybody,' he said. 'I just wanted to feed my family, keep a roof over their heads. Keep them safe.' Ishmael was cool.

I still had my dark moments. Being locked up in Belmarsh was tough, man, one hundred per cent, although going to the gym, working out in my cell, cleaning, praying and having some friends to talk to kept me going. I used to sit in my cell and stare through those bars, watching the construction workers on the Isis site put down their tools at the end of each day and I'd think to myself, Wow, those guys are going *home*. I would hear planes flying overhead and think, 'Shit, people are going on holidays out there, man. That's nuts.'

My trial date was eventually set for 18 November and the months dragged by. By mid-October I had resigned myself to the fact I'd have to wear that jumpsuit to court when, on a day like all the others, a screw called Lennon came to fetch me. I was in my cell, getting my cleaning gear together ahead of starting work. Lennon was a decent guy who had helped push my gym application through.

'Right, Lewis, pack your stuff,' he said.

I thought, 'Shit, these guys are shipping me to another prison'. I propped my mop against the wall. 'Why, where are you taking me?' I had a sweat on, y'know.

Lennon jangled his keys and rocked back and forth in his shiny shoes, a little smile on his face. 'Nowhere,' he said, 'You're going home. Your latest bail application has been granted.'

Man, my whole body went limp at that moment.

'Is this a wind-up?' I asked.

'No, Lewis, it's not a wind-up. Get packed.'

I grabbed my see-through bin bag.

24

BACK ON THE BLOCK

Granddad was waiting for me at the gates when I walked out of Belmarsh at lunchtime. As soon as he saw me he smiled and spread his arms, and swear-down, I felt like the luckiest man alive. I bounded over, 101 kilograms of solid muscle filling my tracksuit, yet I felt light as a paper cutout.

'Yo, Dad,' I said, dropping my bag and throwing my arms around him. We hugged in the autumn sunlight for a whole minute, neither of us saying a word. I took a few deep breaths. The world smelled good, man, a mix of leaves and fresh air and Nan's washing powder on Granddad's scarf. He patted my back.

'Good to see you, son,' he said, 'let's get you home.'

You'd think I'd want to tank it away from that prison, but instead I walked over to the nearest tree and gave that a tight hug too. After ten months inside, I'd missed nature and I felt blessed to be a part of it again. Granddad understood.

'Take all the time you need, son,' he said. When he could see I was done with the tree, he pulled a twenty-pound note out of his back pocket. 'Here, take this,' he went.

I didn't want his money, man. 'Nah, I'm good, Dad,' I told him, but he was already stuffing the cash into my hand, insisting that I keep it. The note looked and felt alien. Weird, I used to have shoeboxes full of the things. I thanked him and shoved the note in my pocket. 'Let's get outta here,' I said.

I'd been released on tag with a daily curfew and I wasn't allowed to stay in the area where the crime was committed. I ended up at my mum's friend Bobby's place in Tunbridge Wells, Kent, and I was grateful to her. I'd known Bobby since I was a kid and she'd always been Aunty Bobby to me, y'know. She welcomed me into her home, gave me a bedroom and cooked for me.

But I felt cut off, out there in Kent, man. Life wasn't easy. I had to report to the police station at 8 a.m. every morning and I didn't know anyone in the area besides Bobby and her kids. I couldn't go to football training. I didn't have the money for a gym pass and I missed my church services and bible classes too. Under curfew I had stay in the house between 7 p.m. and 7 a.m. If I got home a minute late, or strayed into a banned area, the signal box installed in Bobby's house would send an alert to the monitoring centre. Crazy though it sounds, after a couple of weeks I was beginning to wish I was back in Belmarsh. At least in there I could go to the gym every day.

A week before the trial was due to start at the Old Bailey, my bail conditions were adjusted to allow me to move back to Myatts Field and that meant I'd be closer to the court. The curfew and 8 a.m. sign-ins would've made it impossible to get to the Old Bailey on time each day if I had been travelling from Kent. At least now I would have my family around me during the trial. I started helping out at the youth church too, doing fitness activities with the kids and stuff. And because most of those activities took place in the evenings, my curfew got extended to 10 p.m. after Pastor Mimi wrote a letter to the authorities. It still wasn't very straightforward to work my day – I had to bus it over to Streatham police station every morning to sign in, which proved to be another headache because I couldn't leave the house until 7 a.m. If the bus was late or I got held up for whatever reason, I was screwed. Once when I was fourteen minutes late they threatened to arrest me for breach of bail.

I barely ate in the days leading up to the trial. This was mostly down to my nerves but I also wanted to lose weight. I was wary that if the jury saw a bulky guy flexing his muscles in the dock, they'd find me intimidating and thuggish, and that wasn't the look I was going for.

I was clueless going in to the first day of the trial. I sat in the dock at the Old Bailey, alongside my co-defendants and Ashley Bucknor, shivering in my suit. Two other men were in the dock too – brothers Raymond and Nathan Miller, both accused of possession of a pistol and ammunition with intent to endanger life. There was a presence in that old building, man. I felt it. A cold sensation, heavy on my shoulders. The air was damp and loaded with tension. People in wigs were forever telling us to stand up, sit down, stand up again and muttering legal jargon I didn't understand. Twelve unknown faces spread along two wooden benches, there to decide my future. Thoughts merry-go-rounded, y'know. *What if they don't like the look of me? What if they judge me on my past? What if they don't like the colour of my skin? They could put me in jail for life. Innocent people go to jail.* Yeah, even getting shot in the face didn't come close to the fear I felt in the icy confines of court room three.

Fighting my corner was Michael Wood QC, a tall white guy with hawkish eyes who talked really slowly, every word considered before it left his mouth. Anan the solicitor who visited me in Belmarsh, was there too. I couldn't believe how composed they were during the prosecution's opening speech. They both sat there making notes as Neil Atkinson QC, prosecuting, marched up and down in front of the jury, basically telling them to find me – and my co-ds – guilty from the get-go.

I can't remember Atkinson's exact words, but he described Ryan Bravo as a 'respectable young man' who had got caught up in 'gangland crossfire'. It saddened me to hear how Ryan died, man. Atkinson said Ryan was walking home with his cousin when they stopped to buy milk at a Costcutter store in Walworth on August 6, 2008. They had chosen to shop at the supermarket chain to save 20 p, he added. As the pair entered the shop, 'two youths barged past them' as they allegedly fled 'rival gang members on mopeds'. Atkinson went on to describe how two of the pillion drivers 'opened fire'. Ryan died at the scene after one bullet hit him in the back.

I wanted to stand up and shout, 'I didn't do it. I'm innocent.' I resisted. Every so often I'd look up and catch the eye of Nan, Granddad and Mum, all there supporting me in the public gallery and they'd give me a reassuring nod or a smile. I can't begin to tell you the love I felt for my family in those moments. Just them being there meant the world to me, man.

Atkinson continued his speech, detailing how police had allegedly spotted Ashley walking close to the scene of the shooting, carrying two crash helmets. A handgun was discovered, Atkinson said. He further claimed officers raided the Miller brothers' home and found 36 bullets.

One day in court bled into another, the proceedings slow and littered with adjournments. Often, the judge would boot out the jury to allow the men in wigs to discuss undefined 'legal matters'. The prosecution's evidence didn't seem to go anywhere. They cross-examined the detectives who'd interviewed me and got them to repeat various things that I'd said. The jury was also shown the CCTV stills that captured helmeted men on mopeds. Then they started pulling all this social media shit out of the bag – showing grabs of my Facebook page that had a green background, that 'represented OC'. Because they had no concrete evidence to prove that I was at the scene, they were playing the 'He's a gang member' card, and that was pissing me off, man. When would the jury get to hear that I was no longer a gang member? When would they be told that I'd changed my life around?

Michael Wood told me, in his measured manner, to sit tight until the prosecution's case had been presented. He planned to submit a half-time submission of 'No case to answer' to prove my innocence. My co-ds' legal teams would be doing the same, he said. I was like, *Cool, I've no idea what that 'half-time' business means, but do your thing, brother.*

The prosecution closed its case on day thirteen and, as promised, Michael submitted his legal argument to the judge while my stomach felt like it was on a spin cycle, man. Lots of legal chat followed, back and forth between Michael and the judge. Precedent was quoted at length, stuff like that.

I occupied myself by looking down and picking at the skin around my thumbnails, too scared to listen closely in case I heard something bad. Snapshots of Belmarsh haunted my mind, y'know? I could smell the disinfectant in my mop bucket. And, fuck, I missed something because, when I looked up, Michael Wood had turned round and nodded at me. Then the judge told me and my co-ds to rise.

As I stood the room kinda shook a bit and I can't remember the judge's exact words, but I do recall hearing, 'unfair to continue' and 'no case to answer' and, finally, 'Terroll Kersean Lewis, you are free to leave the courtroom,' and I was like, *Did he really say just say that?*

In my peripheral vision I sensed a movement in the public gallery and, as I turned my head, there was Granddad, on the edge of his seat, pulling the same face he pulled whenever Man U scored: chin jutted, ecstatic smile, followed by a mouthed, 'Yes!' I smiled back. *Rah, I take it that's a 'Yes', then.*

Walking out of the Old Bailey with my family, into a heavy snowstorm, was the best feeling ever. I'd proved my innocence and now I could get on with my life. I could be a good man and make a future for myself, away from all the noise and violence – and without the nuisance of that tag. My co-ds were also released on no case to answer submissions. Ashley Bucknor's trial continued and he was subsequently found guilty and sentenced to twenty-four years. Nathan Miller was convicted of possessing ammunition without authority and with intent to endanger life. He was jailed for five-and-a-half years. His brother Raymond was cleared of all charges. Later I received a thousand pounds in compensation for wrongful arrest and false imprisonment. Which was nothing compared to the year that I lost in jail. But y'know what? It wasn't about the money for me. It was about justice.

Adjusting to the outside world after being locked away for so long was difficult. But there was a lot of positive stuff to come out of my spell in jail. I realised, for example, how much I loved working out in the gym. I wanted to continue that routine and one morning, a few days after my trial ended, I took myself along to a nearby branch of Fitness First. Yeah, I was all good to go, man. Strode into the reception in my tracksuit and told the woman, 'Rah, I wanna join the gym.' She was all smiles, handing me a form.

'What do I need this for?' I asked.

'We just need a few details. Your fitness goals, what type of membership you'd like, and your bank details for your direct debit.' I had no idea what a direct debit was. Didn't even have a bank account, y'know. I told her I'd just take a day pass instead.

'Sorry, sir,' she went, all singsong, 'we don't do day passes.'

'Rah, I'll leave it then,' I said, and walked out. One of the best moves I've ever made in my life. Who needs a gym when you've got parks, right? And I knew just the place.

On the edge of the Myatts Field Estate, sandwiched between Fountain Place and Akerman Road, and just along from the Camberwell Submarine – the nautical-looking chimney stacks of an underground boiler room – stood a dilapidated kids' playground known as Red Park. I remember Mikes having a crazy fight with some ute there years ago. No kids went as most of the equipment was broken. The place was deserted.

Looking at the frame that once held swings, the remaining monkey bars and steps leading up to what used to be a mini-rope bridge, I saw potential, man. In prison I had created a personal gym in my cell, proving that I didn't need fancy machines to get fit. Any object can become a weight, including my own body, as the great Mighty Wanderer had taught me years ago in school. 'Rah, yeah, Red Park could be my new gym,' I thought. I put my headphones in, got some 50 Cent playing on my Blackberry, slipped on my leather gloves and got stuck in, using the swing frame as a pull-up bar and building heat in my muscles through sets of ten reps. It was cold and I liked seeing my breath turn to fog clouds in the air. It had been a while, y'know.

I moved over to the steps to do sets of tricep dips, followed by press-ups, using the step to elevate my legs and, wow, I had some proper energy going on, man. As I built up a sweat, I started to think about these exercises I was doing. The idea had come to me while locked inside a prison block. Now I was back on the block. 'Rah, this is my Block Workout,' I thought. 'Maybe I'm on to something here?'

Back to the swing frame and on to the monkey bars for lateral moving pull-ups. 50 Cent was giving it attitude, but I had lateral thoughts going on at the same tempo, right? I was back on the block and I was not hearing gunfire; I was back on the block and I didn't need no machine. Boost was back, but he was a good man now. Boost had got a future.

I swing off the monkey bars and drop to the road, plant my hands in the frosty grass, tuck my head in and bunny-hop my legs off the ground. I find my balance then push my feet towards the sky. I'm doing a handstand and it feels amazing. I have this chant going on in my head: OC, One Chance, OC, One Chance. *I have been given a chance. One Chance to live. Rah, I'm taking it. One hundred per cent.*

25

PAYBACK

Yeah, Red Park, Baghdad. That's where my Block Workout began, man. The playground got bulldozed in the Myatts Field-to-Oval-Quarter revamp, but the old estate will remain in my head and heart for ever. I fought and banged and put my life on the line for Baghdad, for the sake of OC. As an OC Younger, I terrorised and intimidated outsiders who dared enter our area. Later, I used my 'Older' authority to recruit and manipulate another generation of violent youngsters. I'm deeply ashamed of this now. I'll take those thoughts to my grave, y'know. But man must also give thanks to the Myatts Field estate, where through the chaos and carnage, I would eventually turn my negative past into a positive future, not only for me but for the whole community.

After my initial workout in Red Park, I couldn't keep away. I loved the open-air gym vibe and the idea that street furniture could be used instead of exercise machines. I thought, *Who needs direct debits and expensive Lycra when you have parks with broken swings?* I would go to the playground every morning, armed with my music, water bottle and black leather gloves – once a gangland accessory, now super handy when gripping the monkey bars. I mixed things up, had some fun with my workouts. Like, some days I'd do sprints interspersed with burpees, dips and pull-ups. Other times I would spend an hour or so doing only handstands, or planks, or bear crawls.

I thought a lot about my OC past as I exercised. A past I cannot erase; it's inked on my neck, 'One Chance to live', innit. Guns, knives, dodging bullets, chasing pagans, pretending to be homeless as I planned to shoot a guy who'd touched my watch... I mean, what the fuck? Remembering this incident alone scares the shit out of me now; I could, inadvertently, have killed my cousin, or another man, that night. Sad and shocking as this sounds now, such was my reality back then. I would never return to that heinous life, *never*.

My road to redemption stretched ahead. More than two years had passed since I left the streets. Almost half this time I'd spent in jail for a crime I did not commit. I'd been a good boy in prison, but it was here, on the outside, where I could truly begin to make amends. I wanted to heal my relationship with my family, which I had neglected in favour of the OC. Y'see, being in a gang I had to pretend I didn't know who my relatives were at times. Whenever I saw Mum in the street in Brixton, I would cross over or duck into a shop. There would be no, 'Hey Mum, how're you doing,' or 'Let's grab a coffee.' Nah, that would be too risky, man. If a pagan spotted me chatting to her, they might follow Mum home, then she would become a victim because of my actions, y'get me? I had practically disowned my family to protect them.

Two people I most wanted to make amends with were Nan and Granddad. I had let them down, big time. Granddad, bless him, remained measured and magnanimous from the moment I was arrested for the murder of Ryan Bravo until the second I was acquitted of the crime, despite learning about my gangland past in the courtroom. Massive respect to Granddad. 'You've got to live your life, son. You need to make your own choices. This is a fresh start for you,' he said as we walked away from the Old Bailey. Then, giving me a playful nudge, added, 'Oh, and don't be lazy. Learn how to do the housework, always do the washing-up, don't argue with your mum, and let me know if you want to come to mass on Sunday.'

I was like, 'Thanks for everything, Dad. I'm gonna do good things from now on, y'know. I'm gonna transform. I want to give back, deffo.'

Nan wasn't so forgiving. Hearing about my OC involvement destroyed her, man. She never said as much, but her mannerisms spoke volumes. After the trial, she became subdued. She didn't want to look at me. She *couldn't* look at me. Obviously, Nan knew I was no angel, but in her mind I was her little Terroll, innit? I was that vulnerable boy who sobbed over his toy car as he spoke about his mother's drug abuse. Little Terroll, her bingo companion. I was 'Our Boy', right? Nan didn't need to speak. I saw in her eyes what she was thinking: *My little Terroll ... a gang member, involved with guns and drugs and violence? What do you mean? How? Why? Why did you do this to us, Our Boy? Why?* Yeah, I was heartbroken to know I'd hurt her so badly, and this made me more determined than ever to regain her trust and make her proud of me.

But my good intentions would not make it all daffodils and roses out there, y'know. There would be struggles and repercussions. Same for Mikes, Lox, Dread and many others who had departed the OC. Gangs were still active in the area. I might have turned my back on guns, but the enemies I made along the way were still out there, ready to fire their machines. Likewise, the utes were still engaging in random acts of violence.

Not long after I left Belmarsh, I was on the Cowley Estate with Mikes and Lox and a younger boy from the estate. I'd started to write conscious rap as Mr Garshh (you can check my work out on YouTube) and we were filming a video near the football cage when two guys on mopeds pulled up. One of them, some ute in a helmet, dropped his bike like it was a BMX, stepped over it and pulled his gun from his waist.

Mikes flipped, charged at the guy and gave it, 'Go on, bust your ting, do your worst,' and, *boom*, the guy started shooting after us, y'know.

We ran and the ute got on his bike and left, but our younger friend got hit in the gunfire. A bullet skimmed his leg and he had to go to hospital, man. Fortunately, he was OK, but any one of us could've been killed that day. We never found out who the ute on the bike was, but watching him pull and fire his gun with such alarming alacrity? Yeah, that was an uncomfortable flashback. A stark reminder of my trigger-happy days and the destruction I caused. It pained me that so many young kids were still active. Worse, I previously *encouraged* this violence. I had fucked up a lot of young people's minds, man. Now I wanted to help these people. Ideas formed. I thought: *Wouldn't it be good to get youngsters interested in my Block Workout? Maybe I can start a boot camp.*

I began working out with an old school friend called Yinks, who also lived on the Myatts Field estate. One day, he shot a video of me training on the block and we posted it on YouTube and social media, telling people to come join us in working out on the block. And the whole thing went crazy, man. The video got around five thousand hits. People started to join in. We took the Block Workout to Angell Town and Kennington Park and posted information and videos on social media. I started running Saturday morning sessions in Brockwell Park.

Man, I remember that first session. Our equipment consisted of parallel bars and pull-up bars that were already in the park, plus cones and ladders I bought from Argos. I was expecting around thirty people to turn up, y'know, but crowds were coming into the park from all sides. Soon, there were at least 150 people warming up on the grass. People of all ages and from all over London. There were people I recognised from the streets, including former Peckham Boys who had turned their lives around. Youths from Lewisham, Tulse Hill and Hackney came along. People were doing sprints, ladder runs, press-ups, pull-ups, crawls, crunches and squats and the energy was immense. The sun was shining, too. It was a beautiful scene.

ONE CHANCE

Religion, class, skin colour, age, gender, postcodes ... none of
that mattered to anybody in that park. They were all there to
enjoy the workout and enrich their lives.

Those Brockwell Park sessions became hugely popular, but
they did attract some police attention at first. Picture it: former
gang leader, in a public park with 150 youths in tracksuits,
hoodies and leather gloves? Some sporting gang tattoos. Yeah,
they probably thought there was some kind of *Fight Club* shit
going on. But, after weeks spent watching our sessions from
their car, they finally plucked up the courage to approach us.
And they were cool, man. One time, I even got a couple of
police officers to join in. I had them doing dips and pull-ups
on the bars and they loved it. I was like, *camera, action* with my
phone. I took shots of the officers' attempts and posted them on
Twitter. Community spirit, innit.

Block Workout gathered momentum, attracted a wider
audience. A year on from its humble beginnings in Red Park, I
knew it had potential to become a community enterprise. I began
to think about branding, and my friend Jojo kindly designed a
logo featuring a silhouette of a muscular man on a pull-up bar
beneath an arch of black text saying "Block Workout". It was
perfect. We got the logo printed on T-shirts, which I gave to
people attending the sessions. Yinks shot videos in Brockwell
Park and, over time, my YouTube channel would attract 45,000
subscribers. I uploaded news and pictures on social media, and
Block Workout's audience grew and grew. (Today, I have 191,000
followers on Instagram and 22,000 on Twitter.) But man must
be humble, y'know. This was not about me or how many 'likes'
or followers my posts generated. Social media was – and still is –
a vehicle to make Block Workout accessible.

I attended classes myself and gained a personal trainer
qualification. In 2013, a producer from Sky hit me up with an
offer I couldn't refuse: Did I want to travel to Brazil and South
Africa to be in a television series called *Star Block Workout*, which

would see me devise workouts for local celebrities? I was, like, 'I'll get my passport.' Signed. *Star Block Workout* aired on the global entertainment channel Trace Sports Stars and it was an amazing gig. They flew me first-class to all the filming locations. My seat on the plane turned into a bed, man. That was too cool, y'know. And I got paid a thousand pounds a day.

It was back in London, at one of the Brockwell Park sessions, where I met my now business partner, Ben Wachenje, or Bro Ben, as I call him. Ben's son had been coming to Block for a while and had gone home raving about it. Bro Ben had wanted to lose some weight at the time and joined in. He told me that he specialised in videography and offered to shoot some videos and testimonials for Block Workout. From there, Bro Ben came on board. We bought extra equipment – skipping ropes, weights, new cones and ladders – as more people flocked to the workouts. Every Saturday, at 10.30 a.m., Brockwell Park became a hive of positive activity. These youngsters were becoming addicted to Block; no matter the weather, numbers never waned. It could be lashing rain, snowing or hailing golf balls, yet still we kept on going, doing press-ups and burpees and sprints in the deep, sloppy mud. Soon, Lambeth Council started to make some noise, y'know. Various committee chiefs said our workouts had wrecked the grass in Brockwell Park. Other complaints branded our sessions 'intimidating'. 'Why are all these youths gathering in Brockwell Park?' I was asked at one meeting with councillors.

So I told them: 'It's like this y'know: Some of these "youths" can't afford a meal, let alone a gym membership. Many of these kids come from the blocks, man, where gang activity is rife. Would you rather they were out on the blocks getting involved in crime, or training in the park. Doing something positive?'

Our conversations with the council continued, while behind the scenes, Bro Ben and me came up with a business plan. We now had two qualified personal trainers in our team, Diesel and Phil. Diesel's twin brother Munch was also a regular at Brockwell Park. We completed necessary health and safety risk assessments and secured insurance certificates. Positive feedback from our Block followers proved there was a high demand for outdoor exercise in the community. We had a banging dossier, man, which Bro Ben and me presented at a meeting with the suits from the council. And y'know what? We smashed it. The Brixton Street Gym – the first outdoor street gym in the UK – was coming to the blocks, man.

In 2014 Lambeth Council offered Ben and me a space at 6 Somerleyton Road, as part of the Brixton Green community project, dedicated to the redevelopment of the Somerleyton Road area. The site was a former lorry-loading bay, a one-level reclaimed warehouse with two small adjoining office spaces. It was a mess. Like a massive ramshackle bus shelter, with bits of metal holding up a broken corrugated roof. But it worked for us. We had faith in our vision: to create an affordable and safe place for people to get fit. With the help of the community, we worked tirelessly to make our dream a reality. We fixed the roof and installed pull-up bars, climbing frames and punch bags. We used tyres and hammers for weights. Local artists painted a rainbow-coloured street-art style mural on the back wall. The Block Workout logo was spray-painted on old road signs. In April 2014, we were ready to open to the public.

From day one it was clear Brixton Street Gym had a unique energy about it, a certain edge. People worked out to the thrum of blaring hip-hop music. There would be Diesel teaching youngsters gymnastic moves on the bars. Sometimes those kids would fall, but they fought and tried again. Seeing this determination and transformation warmed my heart, man. This was the environment we had set out to achieve. We wanted to support our members. Keep an eye on those who are depressed or facing struggles. This business was not just about taking people's membership fees, y'know. Our gym was free, with members donating one or two pounds when they could.

Diesel is super talented and went on to create a new style of calisthenics called Flow with Wayne, who was also in our park training team. Today, Wayne runs workout sessions at Brixton Street Gym and his younger brother Fred is now a manager. Together, we're one big family.

Our members came from all walks of life. City bankers would travel to Brixton to work out with us. But we also worked closely with youths on the fringes of crime. There were – and still are – many young people, not only in Brixton but all over the UK, who are active on the streets. Likewise, there are those who are desperately trying to leave the hood but don't know how to. Some fear for their lives. These are real people, man, and I understand their difficulties because I've been there. I've been through the barbed wire and survived. So whenever these youngsters come to me for guidance, I listen. I have conversations with them.

One afternoon a young boy, I'll call him Hoops, came into my office. 'Hey, T, I need to speak to you,' he said. His voice wobbled as he shuffled into the room. Hoops, no older than eighteen at the time, had used the gym a few times. Brown-skinned and powerfully built, his thing was boxing and martial arts. He sat on a pile of tyres, hugging his rucksack to his chest. He said nothing at first. Water dripped from the ceiling and plopped into the bucket below. Man, we were always getting leaks here.

I gave it a minute, then said, 'Hey bro. What's up?' I knew from previous conversations with Hoops that he was affiliated with people on the streets. Kinda dabbling in criminality, maybe dealing drugs but not a fully-fledged gang member, if y'know what I mean? He lived on an estate in Brixton with his mum and younger brother.

Hoops tightened his grip around his bag, fiddled with its zip. 'Listen T,' he went, 'I don't know where to go, who to talk to. I'm confused, man. See … I'm scared for my life. There's madness on my block. I don't feel safe there without a weapon.' He paused, looked at the ceiling. I followed his gaze. There was something hypnotising about that steady drip.

'I hear you, man,' I went.

'Thing is, I'm thinking about buying a gun,' said Hoops. 'To protect myself, y'know. In case somebody tries to shoot me. So many utes on the block have machines, right?' Wow, this was my younger self talking to me. I could relate so much to everything Hoops had told me, but what could I do, what could I say? Had he already bought a gun? If so, was that machine inside his rucksack? I wouldn't ask him that question.

'Listen, I know where you're coming from, man,' I said. 'But what comes of the energy of holding a machine? Right now, your thoughts are dangerous. You need to control those thoughts. There's anger, but there's controlled anger, y'know what I mean?' Hoops nodded. I hoped what I was saying made sense. I didn't want to be preachy. 'Man, I lived that life for years,' I went on, 'Playing hide 'n' seek with my family. Being half good boy, half bad boy. That game bottles up inside you until you burst. And that explosion could lead you to a prison cell or six-foot under. I can't tell you not to buy a gun. What I can offer is a safe space, here at the gym. This is a safe space for you to train. Away from the noise. I'm here for you, man.'

I'll never forget that conversation. Hoops became a regular at the gym, landed a job in recruitment, and he continues to thrive today. I'm proud of that boy, man.

Meanwhile, a friend helped Bro Ben and I to submit a bid for the gym to become a Community Interest Company. We had to jump over hurdles and through hoops to achieve this, but we did. The result of our efforts is the Block Workout Foundation, which is kinda half charity, half business, but means we're eligible for funding for specific projects.

Brixton Street Gym flourished, attracting not only a cult following but attention from the world's media. At one point, a day wouldn't pass without a camera crew being on site. The papers and television stations went crazy for my gang-member-turns-good-boy story. I didn't deserve so much attention, but the exposure for Brixton Street Gym was amazing. Nan and Granddad were overjoyed at all the publicity; their faces lit up whenever they saw me on the telly. 'You've done yourself proud, Our Boy,' Granddad would say. The twinkle had returned to Nan's eyes too, y'know. She kept every newspaper article on me and told all her mates at bingo how proud she was of her grandson.

I'm so grateful Nan and Granddad got to share my success in those infant days of Block Workout. Sadly, they wouldn't follow my journey further than 2016, when they both passed away. Granddad lost a battle against stomach cancer. His death destroyed me, man. At Granddad's funeral they played 'Too-Ra-Loo-Ra-Loo-Ral (That's an Irish Lullaby)', which he sang to me every night when I was a kid. And it took all my strength to keep it together in the church. I forced back tears, telling myself, *Be brave. Don't cry. Granddad wouldn't want you to cry. Granddad wants you to be strong today.* Inside, I was broken. Five months later, we would grieve again after Nan died suddenly. Her death certificate states she suffered a fatal stroke, though I believe she died of a broken heart. One hundred per cent.

My grandparents were the beating heart of our family. They kept us going through all our trials and tribulations, and losing them in such a short space of time was hard on the whole family. I lost my way for a while, y'know. Nothing made sense to me without Nan and Granddad around. However, I knew my being successful would make them happy, so I pushed on with things. Yeah, Mick and Rose deserve some happiness up there.

Three years later, we were offered a bigger space for Brixton Street Gym, this time in an industrial unit at 10 Somerleyton Road. When we viewed the space, I was like, *Wow, this is luxury, man.* There was a kitchen and enough room to create indoor studios, plus an outdoor gym. We snapped up the place and, in August 2019, the new Brixton Street Gym flung open its doors as a thriving community project. We had a new addition to our team, too: Boyd Hill, who runs Book Stop Brixton, an initiative providing free books to people in the community. He started the project from a self-made stand in Somerleyton Road, which he still runs today, alongside his library inside the gym, where people can donate and borrow titles. Boyd, also a part-time art teacher, is a Jack of all trades, man. Not only does he run the library, he's also our janitor and gardener and deals with most community issues affecting the gym.

As the gym grew in popularity and our membership swelled, we were able to create jobs. Today, we have twelve members of staff, including our trainers, receptionists and a bid writer. We run classes and events and continue to support our community. This is more than a gym; it's a hub, a hospital, a place where people heal and grow. It's a safe space.

In early 2020, a surprise visitor turned up at Brixton Street Gym. It was Ishmael, the guy I had met in Belmarsh. Wow – it was good to meet him in a positive environment. He had read about the gym in a newspaper article.

'I just had to come along and see it for myself,' he said. Then, shaking my hand, he added, 'You've come such a long way. I'm so proud of you, Terroll.' He wanted to reconnect with his two sons, who had moved to Scotland with their mum after Ishmael went to jail. 'They follow you on Instagram,' he explained, 'But their mother painted a bad picture of me and now they won't speak to me. If you could reach out to them, tell them I'm here for them, I'd be so grateful.' Man, I was touched.

'Yo, of course,' I said, 'I'll send them a video message.'

That night, long after the gym had closed, I sat in my office and recorded my message to Ishmael's sons. I said, 'Yo, wagwan, hope you're all good. Me and your dad were in jail together. Your dad mentored me. He's a good person. He's a checkpoint in my life that got me here today. Your dad's reaching out to you, man. Just remember that we all have our own struggles and stories. Your dad's got his story, I've got mine. Just hear him out.'

After I sent my video, I got up and went for a stroll around the building. It was almost midnight and the place was deadly quiet compared to the grunts and laughter and pumping music that filled it by day. In the main studio, I sat on the floor and looked around. The punch bags were still swaying a little. Skipping ropes snaked over gym mats. The air smelled of sweat and leather, and the geometric artwork on the walls screamed, 'We are strong'. I thought to myself, *Yeah, owning a gym is pretty cool.* And just then, a tear came down my eye. I was overcome by this strange yet beautiful warmth that came from deep within me. More tears welled. I felt proud, man. Really proud.

EPILOGUE

The Brixton Street Gym is my saviour. One hundred per cent. Once upon a time, I got my kicks from being a ruthless gang member. Today, giving back to the community via the Block Workout gives me an adrenaline rush.

Our gym provides a neutral ground; there's no room for negativity at 10 Somerleyton Road. Nah, this is a positive environment. One of love and healing and progression. It's a place that *I* need, for my own physical and mental wellbeing. Every day I give thanks for this opportunity. We're a family here at Brixton Street Gym.

The gym continues to prosper, even in challenging times. I started writing this book in March 2020, as COVID-19 gripped the country and life as we knew it changed beyond all recognition. When Boris Johnson announced full lockdown of the UK on March 23, we had to temporarily shut Brixton Street Gym. I felt bad that my family could no longer come together in this space, one that's a lifeline for so many. But as a team we pulled together and adapted. Our main priorities were to continue to engage with our members. To keep roofs over heads and food on the table for all. We ran remote Zoom classes, people made online donations to the gym and, fortunately, all twelve staff members kept their jobs. The gym has since reopened on a part-time basis, and there are some exciting projects in the pipeline.

A recent addition to our class timetable is seated circuit training sessions for wheelchair users. Currently there is no wheelchair access to the gym (a bid to fund this work has been submitted), but we have constructed a makeshift ramp so the classes can continue in the meantime.

I'm also excited to announce the addition of a recording studio, which is being built as we speak. It's gonna be cool, man; people will be able to record music and podcasts or do live broadcasts. We also plan to fix-up the kitchen soon, and maybe apply for a licence that will enable young chefs to run food businesses from the gym. Our aim is to create more jobs within the community. This is how we grow. This is how we win. Results don't lie, y'know what I mean?

Sometimes I wonder which direction my life would have taken had I not grown-up on the Myatts Field Estate. Would I have become a premiership footballer? Or gone down that nine-to-five road? Truth is, I'm glad things turned out the way they did. I'm not proud of my violent past, but I have learned life-changing lessons because of it. The estate, for all its problems, taught me the importance of community. When I left the streets I realised how much love existed within those bullet-ridden walls of Baghdad. I was fortunate to be surrounded by kind people such as Nan, Granddad, my mum, and Pastor Mimi, who all played huge roles in helping me to find peace and become a better person. Mimi, particularly, is a cornerstone in my life. She inspired and encouraged me to look to God for spiritual guidance, which helped me through my days in Belmarsh Prison and beyond. She would laugh and smile through the hardest of times. She opened her home – and her heart – to us boys. Mimi, without manipulation or preaching, made me realise that I did have a future. That I could progress from that life of guns and drugs and fighting. Thank you, Mimi. You're an incredible lady – and your jollof rice is banging, man!

ONE CHANCE

In 2014 Nan and Granddad were rehoused to a council flat in Kennington, their home in Treherne Court soon to be demolished to make way for the Oval Quarter development. They were gutted, as too were many other residents who were forced to move. Despite the troubles that plagued Myatts Field, my grandparents loved living there. It marked the end of an era when the bulldozers rolled in and flattened decades of memories.

Watching the estate being torn down, court by court, tugged at my heartstrings too y'know. Some of my happiest childhood memories are of playing Bulldog and run-outs and football with my friends in the square.

I bear physical and psychological scars from the battleground. My moustache hides the evidence of that bullet skimming my top lip. I have nightmares in which I'm back in the hood, bullets flying towards me, friends being killed. I don't think this fear will ever leave me. Not completely.

In 2018, my mental health took a battering, to the point where I thought I was going to do something stupid, y'know. I think my depression was brought on by an accumulation of factors: the death of my grandparents, violent flashbacks from my days on the streets, and guilt. Yeah, I was in a dark place for a while. Luckily, exercise helped me cope with my problems, but I knew, particularly from conversations I'd had with gym members, that depression is prevalent among young men. Later, I had a similar conversation with my friend Leon Lewis, who was designing some fitness flyers for the gym. He said, 'Hey, Terroll, I want to create a safe space – just like your gym – where men can come together and talk about anxiety and depression or money worries. A platform to raise awareness surrounding mental health issues.'

I was like, 'Rah, that's a great idea. Let's do it.' In early 2019 we launched The Man Talk, a forum for uplifting and elevating men through conversation. For our first event we hired out the

251

biggest auditorium at the Ritzy cinema in Brixton and filled it with 500 men. We had a panel of speakers, including social media influencers, myself and Leon, and we touched on some real conversations, man. Now, we broadcast podcasts, run Zoom sessions and post daily motivational quotes on social media. We will continue to host bigger events once COVID-19 restrictions (hopefully) ease.

Talking of big events... Something else amazing happened in 2019. I became a dad. My beautiful baby girl, Milani, was born in May and, swear down, that was the happiest day of my life. Her mother and I are no longer together, but we remain on good terms and I get to spend lots of time with Milani. Man, you should see her. She's sixteen months old now and beginning to walk and talk and stuff. I'm determined to be a good father. We have fun together, hang out and play games. I love singing 'Too-Ra-Loo-Ra-Loo-Ral (That's an Irish Lullaby)' to her as she sleeps in my arms. When she's older, I want to climb Mount Kilimanjaro with Milani. Maybe we'll do a skydive together too (if she gets into that crazy stuff). Milani is my world, and I hope she'll grow-up to be proud of her dad.

This book would not be complete without a word or two about my former OC brothers. I cannot account for all members. Some have not escaped gangland, but it's not my place to comment or pass judgement on them. They have their own stories to tell, their own struggles, and man prays those boys find their way in life, away from the streets. To all of you still on the battlefield who are looking for way out, I'm here for you, man. One hundred per cent.

So, what became of some of my other boys?

Mad Mikes is a suited and booted city slicker nowadays, working as a financial advisor to businesses. I can just picture him in that job – he's always been good with the chat. A great negotiator on the streets. Transferrable skills, innit. Mikes lives in London and, like me, is grateful for his 'One Chance' to live.

You may have read about our boy Lox (Karl Lokko) in the press. He's a man of many talents: a rapper, poet and anti-knife crime campaigner. He volunteers with the Youth in Action charity and has played a pivotal role in reforming gang culture. You'll catch him at TED Talks events; he's a captivating and inspiring speaker. Lox also made headlines when he was a guest at Prince Harry and Meghan Markle's wedding at Windsor Castle in May 2018. 'Royal wedding guests to include London gang leader,' gushed the *Sun*. Yeah, Lox and Harry are mates, but it's not something my friend brags about, y'get me? Both Lox and Mikes are humble brothers who have done well for themselves. I'm so proud of them.

Abz, Stinks and Dread (Aaron Simpson) were among those who also turned their backs on gang life. Stinks is busy making conscious rap music while also working on a documentary about gang life. Dread left the streets around the same time as me and is now a dad-of-three, his days spent 'doing the school-run' while trying to launch a career in modelling and acting.

I squandered my teenage years when I became embroiled in drug dealing and gang warfare, but I don't blame my Olders for this. I had a choice, and I decided to become that villain with a gun on his hip. For all the violence the OC inflicted upon its rivals, the Olders did care about us younger boys. Recently, I spoke to Dread about how the OC originated.

This is what he said about his generation and how the gang formed: 'We were a group of kids who grew up together on the Myatts Field estate. Many of us, myself included, came from broken or violent homes. We were lost, but we boys had each other. We were brothers. We played football and knock down ginger. Then we became teenagers and crazy stuff started happening. The area was violent. There were shootings and stabbings. Beef within the estate, but also with the Peckham Boys.

'We never set out to become one of the most feared gangs in London. Our brotherhood grew in numbers as we protected our estate. It became a clash of egos and postcodes. The Peckham Boys were the hardest boys in south east London. We became their equivalent in south west London. I don't even know who came up with the OC name, but that's what we became. It evolved.

'We watched you younger boys grow up on the estate and we wanted to protect you. We wanted you to be able to protect yourselves, too. We considered you all to be our little brothers. I would have given my life to save any one of you boys on the streets. I regret that we passed on our violent ways. Unfortunately, that was all that we knew back then.'

Dread's words resonated with me. Looking back, I didn't intend to become a gang member either. I was lured by money and warped excitement, but I was lucky to escape when I did.

Unfortunately, gangs still operate in south London. The streets are brutal, the consequences of senseless gang warfare tragic. People die, some go to prison for a very long time. For every death on the road, mums will cry; the mother of the victim will mourn her lost son, and the killer's mum will lose her boy to a prison sentence. But there is hope; while I'm not proud of my violent past, I did survive gangland, and my experience has shaped me into the man I am today. A grateful man who appreciates life and work and family. A man who is lucky to be alive. I must give thanks for my journey.

Blessings, man, blessings. Thank you for listening to my story, and please keep safe out there.

ACKNOWLEDGEMENTS

Writing this book has been a form of therapy for me. I smiled and laughed at some of the happy memories contained in these pages. I also cried a lot. Tears of *guilt*, tears of *shame*, tears of *grief.*

This is not a story to glamorise gang warfare, but one to show the trauma, hardships, pain and suffering I endured before I joined OC, during my time in the gang, and after I left the streets.

Tattooed on my left arm are these words: 'Cry now smile later.' I lived it and came out the other side. Now I smile - because we only have One Chance to live. But y'know what, those tears were worth it, man, because I am so grateful for this chance to tell my story – and I must give blessings those who have made this adventure a reality.

Thanks to my mum. Without your help I would not have been able to piece together the early chapters in this book. You had your struggles, but you overcome them and turned your life around. You're my inspiration, Mum.

To my amazing publicist and agent Diana Young for her unwavering support and advice throughout the writing of this book. Blessings to you, Diana.

ACKNOWLEDGEMENTS

Special thanks to my co-writer Nicola Stow who helped me bring my memories to the page. I enjoyed our long phone conversations during lockdown.

My literary agent Oscar Janson-Smith who first suggested this book. Thanks Oscar – that was a banging idea!

And lastly, but by no means least, many heartfelt thanks to the talented team at Ad Lib Publishers. Without their passion and vision for my story, *One Chance* would not exist.

Blessings and thanks to you all.

Terroll Lewis